Scribe Publications
RUDD'S WAY

Nicholas Stuart joined the ABC in 1985, worked in Radio News, ABC Radio Current Affairs, and ABC TV, and was the ABC's Indochina correspondent before returning to Australia after a severe car accident. He is a regular columnist for the *Canberra Times* and has written two critically acclaimed books analysing Labor and politics: *Kevin Rudd: an unauthorised political biography* and *What Goes Up … behind the 2007 election,* (both published by Scribe). He is married to Catherine McGrath, the political editor of *Australia Network.* They live in Canberra and have three children: Anastasia, Eugenia, and Maximilian.

Rudd's Way
NOVEMBER 2007–JUNE 2010

Nicholas Stuart

SCRIBE
Melbourne

Scribe Publications Pty Ltd
PO Box 523
Carlton North, Victoria, Australia 3054
Email: info@scribepub.com.au

First published by Scribe 2010

Copyright © Nicholas Stuart 2010

All rights reserved. Without limiting the rights under copyright reserved above, no part of this publication may be reproduced, stored in or introduced into a retrieval system, or transmitted, in any form or by any means (electronic, mechanical, photocopying, recording or otherwise) without the prior written permission of the publishers of this book.

Typeset in 11.5/16 pt Minion Pro by the publishers

Printed and bound in Australia by Griffin Press. Only wood grown from sustainable regrowth forests is used in the manufacture of paper found in this book.

National Library of Australia

Cataloguing-in-Publication data

Stuart, Nicholas

Rudd's Way: November 2007–June 2010

9781921640575 (pbk.)

1. Rudd, Kevin, 1957- 2. Australian Labor Party. 3. Political leadership–Australia. 4. Australia–Politics and government–2001-

324.29407

www.scribepublications.com.au

Contents

Preface — vii

Chapter One: 2020 Vision — 1
   Interlude: The Beginning — 15

Chapter Two: Sorry — 27
   Interlude: Brendan — 47

Chapter Three: The Great Escape — 57
   Interlude: Peter — 79

Chapter Four: The Great Moral Challenge — 89
   Interlude: Malcolm — 121

Chapter Five: The World's My Oyster — 129
   Interlude: Julie and Joe — 155

Chapter Six: The Program — 163
   Interlude: Tony — 193

Chapter Seven: A Big Country — 205
   Interlude: Election 2010 — 223

Chapter Eight: 'Co-operative' Federalism — 237
   Interlude: Leadership — 249

Chapter Nine: The Fall — 267

Epilogue: The Verdict — 281

Acknowledgements — 293

'By their fruits ye shall know them.'
St Mathew (7:16), The Bible, King James Version

Preface

'He survives because he has been on the right side of every argument for the last two years and is a much better politician than anyone imagined. And they say when he falls — probably a very long time from now — it will be with blinding speed as his own party rushes to tear down his statue.'

ABC journalist Chris Uhlmann, 7 November 2009

The story behind the publication of this 90,000-word book about what is now known as the Rudd era — appearing so soon after the sudden replacement of prime minister Kevin Rudd by Julia Gillard — is remarkable. I believe it deserves a special explanation.

About a year after the 2007 election, I asked my publisher, Henry Rosenbloom, what he thought of an idea I'd had about writing a book on the Rudd government. Henry was interested — he had previously published my unauthorised biography of Kevin Rudd, as well as a subsequent book that looked at the causes of Labor's electoral success — but the idea of producing a third book on the Rudd project turned out to be premature. Although the government had been busy articulating its goals and aspirations, it proved far more difficult than I'd realised to assess what was being accomplished. The book would have to wait.

Less than a year later, the situation had changed dramatically. Although it was still riding high in the polls, the government was clearly having significant difficulties in achieving its objectives. A number of off-the-record conversations I had with ministers and senior public servants fingered the central cause of the problem: it was the prime minister himself.

Rudd appeared unable to delegate. His office was nicknamed the 'black hole', because briefs would vanish and nothing would emerge. The government's agenda appeared to swing suddenly and wildly. One moment there would be frenzied progress on an issue until, if it seemed intractable, it would simply be left in limbo.

Henry and I spoke again, and I went to work.

By early 2010, new faultlines had been established across the political landscape. These were not subjects on which there was a simple left-right divide; they represented serious problems for which the nation desperately needed answers — from reconciliation ('Sorry') through to health ('Co-operative Federalism'). But then Rudd's decision to abandon the government's emissions trading scheme was exposed in the media, and what I'd been seeing as the hollowness at the centre of the Rudd project was revealed to the public for the first time. He began to lose control of the agenda, and to plunge in the polls.

I submitted my first draft in late April. Henry edited it as quickly as he could, but urged me to wait and to keep the story current. Events began moving even faster. It had become obvious that the last parliamentary sitting before the long winter break would prove a decisive test for Rudd. On 3 June, I submitted a second draft; a mere six days later, Henry returned his edited version of what was already an 80,000-word manuscript.

With the exception of a few crucial paragraphs, I emailed the corrected second draft to my publisher a little before five o'clock on 23 June 2010. Two hours later, the ABC broke the news that Julia Gillard was meeting Rudd to inform him that she was challenging him for the leadership of the Labor Party. The moment I'd anticipated had finally arrived. Within 15 hours the country had a new prime minister.

The prescience of and confidential information provided by others had allowed me the critical ability to examine the Rudd government at the necessary distance. The only surprise was the speed with which the terrible, swift sword fell; the logic of the coup's actions had already been revealed by the analyses contained in the manuscript. The extent of the absence of support for Rudd within the parliamentary party was demonstrated by the fact there was no need for a caucus ballot to decide the leadership. Kevin Rudd had become the only first-term prime minister to be overthrown by his own party, after one of the shortest periods in office since Labor's James Scullin was defeated in the Great Depression. The party despatched Rudd, fearing that he was leading them to similar electoral oblivion.

More explanatory details, and a new ending and epilogue to the narrative were now required, but the analysis in the main body of the manuscript remained unchanged. My Rudd project — and the country's — was over. Eight days after Julia Gillard took over as Australia's prime minister, this book was sent to the printers.

CHAPTER ONE

2020 Vision

'I don't want to have to explain to my kids, and perhaps their kids, too, that we failed to act; that we avoided the tough decisions; that we failed to prepare Australia for its future challenges. We can either take command of the future or we can sit back and allow the future to take command of us.'

Kevin Rudd at the 2020 Summit in Canberra, 20 April 2008

Kevin Rudd weaved like a glowing firefly between the different groups dotted around Parliament House. He spoke encouragingly as he passed. Occasionally he'd pause and listen; sometimes he'd even join one of the clusters engaged in earnest debate on an issue. When there was an opening (and there always is, when you're prime minister) he'd contribute, pushing and challenging the intense participants to consider other issues. Sometimes he'd simply listen. Before long, his spirit appeared to have taken on an almost physical presence, floating through the chambers like some kind of giant balloon above the 1002 solemn delegates who'd come together to chart Australia's course for the future. No one could be certain where the PM would spring up next.

On his first Australia Day as prime minister, just a couple of months after the election, Rudd announced that his government wouldn't just be about accepting the future—he intended to shape it. This huge creative effort was scheduled to begin on 19 April 2008, when a special two-day summit would bring together some of the 'best and brightest brains from across the country to tackle the long-term challenges confronting Australia's future'.

Canberra was still bathed in early-autumn sunshine as the normally bleak and empty corridors of Parliament House rang with chatter and excitement. Rooms normally closed off to the public were flung open for the meetings. Finally (and for the first time in 107 years), it seemed that Australia was not just trying to imagine the reality of the challenges ahead, but was also prepared to conjure up solutions to the problems. Soon the phrases and words on the paper would be transformed into reality. The promise was enormous.

Earlier that morning, Rudd had welcomed everyone to the conference. Speaking under a huge banner proclaiming 'Australia 2020—Thinking Big', the prime minister insisted that, most of all, he wanted to encourage debate: 'Let's shake some trees and see what falls out.' It was the most radical agenda of all; absolutely nothing was pre-determined. The thousand who'd come to contribute broke up into ten streams of a hundred people each, and bubbled with enthusiasm.

Ten critical areas had been singled out for particular examination. Some (such as 'the economy', 'productivity' and 'governance') were contentious, having been fought over for years with little result; others (for example, 'rural industry and communities', 'supporting families', and 'the creative arts') appeared too broad-brush for any new or easy answers to be provided. Three other forums dealt with focused topics ('health', 'indigenous Australia', and 'international security') while the remaining one ('population, sustainability, climate change and water') seeming to list under a single category all of the greatest issues that the country would need to confront in the future. But, this time, no one was prepared to admit that the subjects might prove intractable; the meeting was about finding new ways to bypass the obstacles that were preventing the country from moving forward. Despite the fact that only two days had been allocated to solve the problems of the future, the delegates remained full of hope and expectation. Surely the government had a plan to implement the ideas that came out of the talks — otherwise why would Rudd have bothered to invite them?

As the summit broke down into its subgroups, Foreign Minister Stephen Smith continued the welcome for delegates considering 'Australia's future security and prosperity in a rapidly changing region and world'. The Members Dining Room rang with the famous words of Chairman Mao. 'Let a thousand policy flowers bloom', said Smith as he urged the delegates to speak out. This was, perhaps, an unfortunate choice of metaphor. Mao's actual words ('Letting a hundred flowers blossom and a hundred schools of thought contend') were followed a few months later with a ruthless crackdown on any dissident who'd dared open his mouth and express criticism of the Chinese regime. Smith obviously didn't intend this to be his message, and so he quickly added, 'all gratuitous advice will be gratefully accepted'.

Chunky sheets of butcher's paper were rolled out, joining others that had been Blu-tacked to the walls and windows. Thick black textas were issued by the 'facilitators', well-dressed and enthusiastic people with shiny MBA degrees, who moved in rapidly to smooth the progress of discussions. The talking began.

Of course, the cynics would assert that 1000 prominent Australians meeting together over one weekend could never manage to produce anything other than enough hot air to warm the globe. The only balloons that would supposedly stay aloft in this crowded marketplace of ideas would be the real ones floating across the Canberra skies in the autumn sunshine. More specific critics found fault with the participants. They noted that Cate Blanchett had been the only woman originally named as a part of the 11-member steering committee (although as soon as this was pointed out, Rudd hastily added another two).

The people summoned to appear treated the summit as a fantastic opportunity to shape the future in their own image. Their excitement was palpable. How could it be otherwise, when people are given the opportunity to grapple with the vital questions that will decide the country's future?

Anyone knocking the forum looked petty. After all, wasn't this a brilliant opportunity to begin interrogating the future; to start working out how to seize good ideas and transform them into working propositions? The very idea of a summit threshing out the issues facing the country was so obviously good that the flaws within the process itself were naturally ignored. Criticism of the make-up of the panels was easily dismissed as the mutterings of those who'd been passed over. It was obvious there wasn't room for everyone to be invited, but at least the government had made a start. The worthiness of the ideal had been allowed to crowd out a plethora of problems associated with the meeting. But the warm mood of goodwill flowing along the corridors of Parliament House didn't spread far beyond the front doors.

The first issue concerned the invitees. Early on the Saturday morning the conference had begun, I was buying groceries at my local Canberra shopping centre when I met the Australian National University's Paul Dibb. Some 20 years earlier, he'd been commissioned by the then defence minister, a young Kim Beazley, to prepare a seminal White Paper that would completely rewrite the strategic basis of Australian defence. The document called for a radical re-imagining of the comfortable assumptions previously governing defence strategy, thereby dragging military planning back to the realities of the region in which we live. For the first time, geographical and economic constraints were used to determine what types of forces Australia required, as opposed to allowing the military's structure to continue bloating formlessly, like a miniature version of American or British forces.

As we reached over, choosing our respective breads, I asked if Dibb was going to the talkfest. Seemingly caught offguard, he paused for a second, adjusted his glasses, and focused intently on the task of choosing the right loaf. Then he stood up, pulling his shoulders back, and looked me directly in the eye. 'I don't really find these sorts of conferences achieve a great deal,' he declaimed. 'Besides,' he added, 'I haven't been invited.'

Until that moment, I'd not spent much time considering who was part of the new 'in' group and who had been consigned to the outer extremities of the political debate; but, no matter what you thought of Dibb's strategic ideas, it seemed inconceivable that he didn't even have a seat at the table. As I returned to my desk, a new question began forming: exactly who had been invited to this summit and why had they been chosen? I was certain that everyone attending would prove to be worthy participants, but now I was looking for something more elusive — the gaps. Who wasn't asked who should have been? Which voices had been silenced, and why?

I realised at once that another professor, again from the ANU, had inexplicably been left off the list. Hugh White had written the most recent (2000) White Paper, but had also worked with Beazley. I knew that before Rudd had become a Labor leader he'd been keen to seek White's advice; why was he now discarded? Not everyone could have been invited, but why did Victorian police commissioner Christine Nixon, Jason Yat-Sen Lee, and retired general Peter Cosgrove make the cut when others failed? Of course, outside input was needed, but was it really necessary to have two ABC journalists (Leigh Sales and Geraldine Doogue) on the panel? Was Rudd simply overawed by celebrity?

Glancing further down the list, I could see there were a couple of very good people taking part, but the holes kept expanding as I looked further and further, searching for the others who should have been there. Instead of creating a genuine 'conversation', it suddenly began to appear as if one group of insiders, those who had dominated policy formulation under Howard, had simply been replaced with another group of similarly hand-picked individuals. They were capable, but many also appeared to have been picked (like Cosgrove and Blanchett) for their high media-profiles as much as their ability to generate new ways of thinking. These people weren't going to challenge the status quo, yet their participation effectively co-opted them to become part of the 'Rudd project'.

A decision had apparently been taken to keep controversy well away from the summit, and with that the chance for genuine inquiry had been lost.

Another issue was the structure of the conference. The opportunity for anyone to contribute a worthwhile idea was severely limited — if only because there was no time available to assess or examine the thousands of proposals. The idea of attempting to formulate an 'action plan for Australia's future' in a weekend was patently ridiculous. Surely it was necessary to follow up, refine, and further develop all the ideas, thoughts, and dreams that would be generated from the proceedings? But without any continuing secretariat capable of pushing ideas after the summit closed, it seemed obvious that any recommendations would slowly slip beneath the surface before disappearing off the bottom of the government's agenda. In fact, the whole exercise began to look increasingly futile, rather like some kind of very big PR stunt. It suddenly appeared as if the talk-fest wasn't really about 'Australia's future' at all — it was about something else entirely.

Many ideas were thrown up and debated at the meeting. Some of them were very good, or received a lot of support anyway, which may not have been quite the same thing. Later, such concepts became agenda items for subgroups that were duly noted by bureaucrats until slowly, inevitably, all vibrancy and life had been sucked out of them. The meeting turned into a huge English class as individual words were fought over and meanings debated, as if they really mattered. Quite soon, the platitudes and business-speak of 'objectives' replaced the older and better Anglo-Saxon verbs, or doing words. Fierce arguments erupted, until finally, right at the end of the weekend, everyone reunited in a satisfied, congratulatory spirit to admire the 'outcomes' of the different groups. Each of the 10 groups had generated three 'big ideas'. It seems doubtful if anyone — even the participants — could remember today what many of them were.

It appeared impossible that the summit could singularly fail to produce any worthwhile ideas, and yet this is very nearly what happened. It was only later that Treasurer Wayne Swan managed to rescue a project close to his heart, orchestrating a complete review of the taxation system. Nevertheless he did this, essentially, on his own. This had been a recommendation emerging from the summit, and that provided suitable justification for the assessment, but it was certainly not required before such a review could take place.

Naturally, the summit endorsed the concepts that had made it all the way through the culling process. These were 'excellent'. They were also achievable. All that was required was the addition of a (very slight) bit of political willpower to follow through and turn them into reality.

The session dealing with international-security issues, for example, had taken a broad-enough approach to their topic to recognise the importance of the wider acquisition of foreign-language skills in the Australian community. A mere 400 university students and fewer than 1080 school students around Australia studied Bahasa Indonesia — the language of our closest, strategically significant neighbour. Maintaining friendly relations with this archipelago of 230 million people will be critical in the future, and the participants at the summit didn't take long to isolate ordinary Australians' ignorance of anything beyond the nightlife of Kuta and the beaches of Bali as inexcusable. To counter it, they proposed a worthy (and simple) recommendation to address it: increase the emphasis placed on Bahasa-language teaching at schools and universities.

This simple idea could have been the government's point of departure for new measures and programs aimed at significantly strengthening language-training. Yet nothing was done by the government over subsequent days, weeks, or months to turn this noble objective into reality. Two months later, when he was visiting Jakarta, Rudd did announce a $60 million investment in general Asian-language instruction, but that was a program for all languages, aimed merely at staunching the loss of what few skills the country still possesses. The government has singularly failed to make even a token effort to promote knowledge about the country to our north. By 2010 it had become obvious that the numbers studying the language had fallen in every year of Rudd's prime ministership.

Throughout the Rudd government's period in office, Foreign Affairs — Smith's own department — bizarrely insisted on maintaining an official travel advisory that warned citizens not to travel to Indonesia. This was despite the fact that no significant terrorist attack had occurred since 2005. Every year the warning was ignored by more than 300,000 ordinary citizens, yet it still managed to achieve curious effects. The government's own 'in-country' Bahasa training programs, for example, had to be conducted in Darwin because studying in Indonesia was supposedly too dangerous. By 2010 this had become a farcical dance of utter stupidity. At the same time, universities across the country were busy either abolishing or scaling back language-teaching, even though Indonesia is Australia's 11th-largest trading partner.

Back at the summit there were plenty of ideas being debated intensely by the participants, who still laboured under the misapprehension that they were engaged in a worthwhile activity. One group wanted to work towards establishing an Australian republic. Another considered the extension of loans for students, and helping volunteers work in the community, in Australia or overseas. The urgent need to standardise transport and agricultural regulations across different states was put forward as a practical problem that could easily be solved with a bit of drive. There were also a number of bigger subjects to consider, such as the possibility of enacting an Australian Bill of Rights. Some ideas were controversial, but the government never even hinted that any were unwelcome.

The groups may as well have been working towards a project to land an Australian on the moon.

Exhausted after two days of intense haggling and debating, the contributors returned to their homes. More than a year later, the government finally generated its 'response to ideas' that had been spawned at the summit. By then, these had become little more than empty words left hanging limply in the air. The simple fact that very few people have ever called for a repeat of the summit suggests that most are well aware it was a disappointing failure.

The 2020 summit provided a paradigm for much of the activity in Rudd's term of office. The PM articulated many people's needs and ideas with crystalline specificity. He conjured up future possibilities, and fired people with excitement as they realised the opportunities that lay ahead, the options for change, and the ways in which threats and dangers in the future could be tamed and brought under control. His rhetoric inspired and enthused voters. And yet … and yet … nothing happened.

Rarely had an Australian prime minister come to office promising to engage with the future as enthusiastically as Rudd did. He demanded to be judged not simply as a manager, but as someone who could inspire and stir the country from its torpor. Yet every exciting vision appeared to end in bureaucratic lassitude or political deadlock. Rudd's government seemed to have a problem with implementation.

Years earlier, when Rudd was the senior public servant working for Queensland premier Wayne Goss, he'd been compared to a spider because of his ability to catch ideas he disapproved of in a sticky bureaucratic web. Until he was convinced of something, nothing would happen. That pattern continued in the Rudd government. The prime minister had few friends among his colleagues, who were keen to have their own input into government policy, because everything—everything—had to be channelled through him. Anything he didn't approve of simply didn't get done.

Rudd worked night and day, but insiders came to doubt the effectiveness of this *modus operandi*. 'We were summoned to the Lodge one weekend,' one senior public servant told me, 'yet, when we got there, all we did was sit round and listen to Kevin going through things that had already been decided ... and not even the important things. He simply seemed to want us around; as if we were the courtiers that the King had summoned because he could, and to show that he was important.' I asked if this comment was more a reflection of his own anger at having been disturbed on a Sunday. 'No', came the response, 'it's nothing to do with that. My point is simply that the man's output is negligible. He gets wound up around the detail, and loses the plot. You'd be concerned if a dep sec [deputy secretary] was working like this, but because he's PM, he can get away with it.' There was a pause for a second. 'He's not actually that clever, you know,' the senior executive sniffed, 'although he certainly thinks he is.'

Rudd appeared unable to delegate decision-making and, as a result, his time was always overstretched. Public servants became frustrated and confused. There appeared to be little connection between the ambitions that Rudd articulated so precisely and their implementation.

'I'd give him a distinction for vision, and a fail for execution,' my source continued, 'and, unfortunately, nothing counts in the real world apart from the end result. Perhaps politics is different.'

It wasn't difficult to find Labor politicians who were equally scathing about the PM, although only in private. The majority of caucus members grew increasingly impatient with Rudd's ways as time went on, but that didn't mean there was any agreement about getting rid of him. Until mid-2010, there was an overwhelming consensus that nothing would happen until the election was out of the way, although many in Labor were keen to go back to implementing policy rather than simply talking about it.

In Australia, the practice of politics revolves around finding a way to navigate between different sectional interests to achieve results. Measured like this, a gaping emptiness had opened up at the very centre of the Rudd project. The prime minister would state his ideals fluently and eloquently, but he proved consistently unable to translate these statements into concrete policies for action. There was no relationship linking the announcements to policy. 'The PM's office seem to believe a year is made up of nothing more than 365 24-hour news cycles all piled up on top of each another,' declared a Labor insider. 'But there's much more to government than simply coming top of each particular day's news agenda.'

It's to be expected that governments will have to compromise, or otherwise fail to implement their agenda. Quite naturally, this feeds suspicions that politicians are little more than 'hollowmen', the title of the television programme that was, ironically enough, commissioned by the ABC the week after the 2020 summit was held.

Filmed as if it were a 'fly on the wall' documentary, the series was almost too scathingly accurate to be considered a comedy. Watching each episode became almost compulsory viewing amongst the inhabitants of the big building in Canberra, one of whom describes the programme as 'similar to watching a car crash about to happen. You know exactly what's going to occur, but you can't drag your eyes away. It takes on a ghoulish fascination. The general gist of the stories was sometimes uncannily correct, even if the nuance was wrong.'

The episodes show the prime minister's staff, shorn of any idealism or principle, shamelessly manipulating their way through daily events focused on one simple objective: 'winning' the week. Their aim is simply to trump the opposition. Nothing exists for a moment longer than the current polling cycle. Only lip service is given to party values; principles are completely displaced by the desire to retain power. Being in government has become an end in itself. The apparatchiks understand they may be unable to achieve anything positive, but nevertheless justify their desire to stay in government on the grounds that they are better than the opposition. They've managed to convince themselves completely that their own self-serving desires are for the good of the country.

The title of the programme echoes the 1925 poem by T. S. Eliot. His verse is crowded with people ('the hollow men … the stuffed men, leaning together, headpiece filled with straw') who exist in a limbo world of nothingness; people who have failed to seize the opportunity to act, and are consigned to an ethereal existence in the shadow-lands. Their lot is simply to exist, without morals or values, whispering dry, meaningless words to one another. The poem ends in emptiness, 'not with a bang but a whimper'.

After nearly a full term in office, Rudd's government was in danger of finishing up in a similar way. The 2020 summit showed that he was prepared to ask the big questions and search for the answers. The auguries were good; the omens, propitious. Yet, despite all the sound and fury, nothing happened in many different areas where the PM had promised action.

Before he entered into office, Rudd had not outlined a clear, measurable program for getting things done; nevertheless, the polls demonstrated that Australians had no doubt that he would take action and make a serious attempt at tackling the problems facing the country. He began his prime ministership with a flurry of reports and investigations to determine the best policies. As the months went by after the election, his popularity increased to record levels. People invested so much faith in his method that, somehow, he briefly became the most popular leader since polling began. He seemed to find just the right words to articulate the desires of the electorate, and people felt confident that the country was in good hands.

The bubble lasted two glorious years. Then, in 2010, everything began falling apart. No longer was Rudd the Teflon man; the stains began to stick. The people he'd once inspired became angry as they waited for action. As his pet schemes disintegrated, many voters became disenchanted with him. The dramatic fall in his satisfaction rating (which had plunged on a sudden, downward trajectory) demonstrated that something very significant had changed in the relationship between the electorate and their prime minister.

Although the electorate was uninspired by the coalition, a growing anger and frustration directed at Rudd was fuelling a significant anti-government backlash. People began talking about this possibly being the first single-term government since 1931, when Scullin's Labor government had been thrown out after a massive swing swept it from office. The optimism conjured up by the 2020 summit had long vanished. Memories of the event itself had been trashed and discarded as people's vivid hopes for the future disintegrated into ashes. How had it all gone so wrong?

INTERLUDE

The Beginning

'Back when we were in opposition, it was like we were the Taliban,' the minister says, as we snack on canapés and sip champagne at a function in the Mural Hall of Parliament. He becomes enthusiastic as he talks about those easy days, long before the cares and worries of government. 'I knew where the other side was going. I knew where the danger spots were and where I could place the bombs.'

He looks up wistfully. 'Then we got into government, and suddenly everything changed. Now we're the ones trying to get the convoy through without any stuff-ups. So far, we've been lucky, but sometimes I think that's just because they're still trying to figure out how to make the bombs work.' He clenches one fist and waves it around, demonstrating how he's still managing to drive through the weak opposition. Then there's a pause. 'The real question is; when's it all going to change?'

At the time, no one had quite realised how much the answer to that question would depend on the convoy commander.

A few months after the election, 62 per cent of people were telling pollsters they were happy with the government. Immediately after he'd made the apology to the Stolen Generations, Rudd began breaking records for the highest satisfaction rating since the Newspoll series had begun 25 years previously. An amazing 71 per cent of Australians said they were happy with the way he was running the country.

Two years later, the situation was reversed. Labor had sunk back to its December 2006 lows, just before Kim Beazley had been deposed as Labor's leader. Support for Rudd had collapsed, with the March 2010 Newspoll showing him plumbing the depths below a 50 per cent approval-rating for the first time. This dramatic plunge was to continue over the following months until May when, over a three-week period, he shed a massive 14 per cent of his personal support. More people now disapproved of him than felt positively about his performance. Nearly 40 per cent of the electorate believed he was 'untrustworthy'.

There was only one person to blame: Rudd himself. He had relentlessly centralised power within the prime minister's office to such an extent that even Labor members complained of feeling angry and impotent. This was his government.

When Rudd usurped Kim Beazley and moved into the top job, he insisted he'd be doing things in his own way. He kept that promise. Labor had never previously invested so much power in a leader. In return, Rudd swept the party back into office after more than a decade in the wilderness. That was the deal. What many members hadn't realised was that Rudd meant to continue running his government with such a tight grip.

Before Labor had been in government long, another minister privately complained to me that the PM was 'a bloody perfectionist micro-manager' who, more seriously, 'couldn't give a rat's about what the party's policy actually is'. Then he paused for a minute. 'Thank goodness he's so good at it; otherwise we'd really be up the creek'. But the length of that pause was significant, and it's important to note that this comment preceded the party's decline in the polls. A number of Labor members chafed at the intense control that Rudd exerted over the party, but they were unable to do anything about it.

Understanding Rudd's prime ministership requires a grasp of

both individual ambition and the numbers in caucus. In 2006, his route to power had been inexorably blocked by his own faction. They'd seen him, close-up and personal, and they'd decided that he wasn't leadership material. But Julia Gillard had also been locked out because Beazley needed (or thought he needed) Jenny Macklin's support, and so she was promised the deputy leadership. He spurned an overture from Gillard's backers that might have healed the divisions in the party, gambled that Gillard and Rudd would never see eye-to-eye, and began rebuilding.

Eventually, Gillard decided to throw her numbers behind Rudd. The new leadership reinvigorated Labor, and the party was swept to power in November 2007. After more than a decade of Liberal government, a majority of Australians finally decided to switch their political allegiances. Rudd had made the case for change, and voters liked what they heard. His government, it seemed, would keep the good things of the past and yet would also be able to chart a new way into the increasingly challenging future. Perhaps most importantly, the electorate decided it trusted the new man leading Labor, even though they knew so little about him. If voters knew what members of his own party knew about his style, they might have had reason to pause. Yet, at the time, there was euphoria amongst Labor supporters. The coalition had been defeated, and they were triumphant. Now things could get done.

Looking back, it's easy to come up with reasons for the coalition's loss at the 2007 election, although it didn't seem so at the time. There's general agreement, for example, that no single factor was responsible for Howard's end. The causes of the downfall were, we can now realise, legion: the introduction of Work Choices; increasing recognition of the reality of climate change; and, finally, the party's simple longevity in government with a PM who refused to depart. People had got tired of the Liberals, and Rudd appeared to be someone who could be trusted to lead the country.

This desire for a new prime minister proved to be a critical factor in Labor's successful campaign strategy. The party offered Australia a fresh leader — someone still on the young side of 60, instead of an increasingly out-of-touch older man who seemed unwilling to consider any sort of succession plan that involved him departing from the little, faux-gothic mansion poised above Sydney Harbour at Kirribilli. Australians decided they wanted Rudd in the Lodge instead.

Voters don't get to cast a ballot for the prime minister — indeed, the job's not even mentioned in the constitution — but the personality of the leader has increasingly come to dominate Australian politics. Rudd told voters he sought power so he could act, because there was so much that needed to be done in so many areas.

Late on the evening of Saturday 24 November 2007, amid the detritus of streamers and the embraces of the party faithful, Kevin Rudd promised 'to plan for the future, to prepare for the future, to embrace the future and together as Australians to unite and write a new page in our nation's history.' This is the story of what happened next.

***

Once in office, anyone who doubted that Rudd was the new messiah was quickly silenced by the polls. Parliamentarians kept any misgivings they may have had to themselves. Rudd was invested with enormous power by caucus. For a moment, he even thought that he could pick whoever he wanted to be in the ministry. That wasn't the case, and he was forced to nip and tuck his dream list to accommodate factional reality. But Rudd had already begun the slow process of distancing himself from his colleagues and isolating himself. He continued to insist that *he* was the one who best knew what to do.

He also encouraged Gillard not to attend meetings of her own left faction as, supposedly, some kind of strange sign that the leadership wouldn't be beholden to factional imperatives. This meant that they quickly became distanced from views that did not accord with their own interpretations of the world. There is an inevitable tendency for anyone in power to gradually lose touch with reality. The process was exacerbated and hastened by Rudd, a man driven by work who had few, if any, genuine friends.

The second issue that soon complicated Rudd's incumbency was the manner in which he ran the government.

When Rudd came to office in late 2007, Labor had been in the wilderness for 13 years. Along the way, much of the corporate memory about the way government should work had been lost. Boosted by his phenomenal personal popularity, Rudd stepped into this vacuum and remade the workings of government around himself. The country had never before had a leader with such a need to dominate everything that happened in Canberra, from conception to execution. This was very much Rudd's government; he ran it his way.

Until 2007 there had only been five changes of government since World War II, an average incumbency of more than a decade for each administration. That was partly why, back in 1996, during the election that had swept Howard into power, Paul Keating had claimed that 'when you change the government, you change the country'. What he really meant, of course, was that he couldn't imagine his own grand visions being replaced by what he described as the 'myopia' of that 'suburban solicitor', John Howard. But voters wanted change. Howard would go on to become the second-longest-serving prime minister the country's ever had, and once again it appeared as if the Liberals were the natural party of government.

In the fading days of *his* leadership, confronted now by a resurgent Labor under Rudd, Howard repeated Keating's claim. 'You *do* change the direction of the country', he asserted. He was right. Rudd's accession to the prime ministership brought exactly this transformation — in the country's mood, anyway. Yet, in so many instances, the promise of change was not fulfilled.

After moving to the government benches, there was no shortage of major policy issues that Rudd identified and sought to address. As he campaigned for office in 2007, the then opposition leader didn't claim to have all the answers — he simply insisted that there had to be a better way. Labor's key undertaking or, if you like, its basic electoral strategy, was to keep things (more or less) the way they were, while investigating everything to see if there were better ways of achieving the desired outcomes.

This book specifically investigates the major areas where the government set itself serious targets that it wanted to achieve in its first term in office. Separate chapters are devoted to Aboriginal reconciliation, climate change, and international engagement. All these issues were specifically highlighted during both the election campaign and the first days of government. Rudd insisted that changing the previous government's policy in these areas was vital for the future health of the nation. In all of these critical arenas, Rudd was portrayed as a player, whereas John Howard was seen as having been content to remain on the sidelines.

Speed of judgement is often inimical to the drawing of sensible conclusions, and the effect of changed policy can often take years to become apparent. Nevertheless, it is already possible to make considered judgements about the effectiveness of government actions in the areas it nominated. The broader settings of government policy were indeed changed, and it's not necessary to extrapolate very far in order to measure results — or, perhaps more importantly, the lack of them — in these fields.

No account of the Rudd government would be complete without a consideration of three other significant events that seized the agenda, wresting it away from the politicians. One chapter is devoted to the most important of these: the global financial crisis. This rocked the government almost as soon as it came into office, and shaped its response to virtually everything that subsequently occurred. Another chapter considers the way a plethora of government programs were implemented in areas that had not fallen, for one reason or another, under the direct focus of the prime minister's controlling gaze — everything from 'the education revolution' to 'evidence-based action' in other areas of policy. And a third considers both immigration and the asylum-seekers who increasingly showed up in boats heading for the coast of Western Australia. In all these areas, the government's comforting rhetoric was thrown offcourse by events.

Any analysis must also take into account the political environment. Although Rudd regularly attempted to assure us that electoral considerations played no part in the formulation and implementation of policy, the reality was otherwise. As the government developed its agenda, these issues were increasingly at the forefront of its consciousness. The Liberals cast round for both a leader and policy framework that would successfully challenge Rudd's dominance, and yet these were little more than codas to the dominant theme set by Labor. That's why, interwoven through the chapters dealing with Rudd's policy challenges, are interludes that consider the rapidly changing situation on the other side of the dispatch box, as the opposition attempted to grapple with the emptiness of bitter defeat.

The next two chapters deal with 2010 when, suddenly, everything began to fall apart. It began with a resurgent opposition under Tony Abbott, but this alone was not enough to explain the collapse in support for Rudd. The PM had nominated health as a vital concern, and noisily hammered out an agreement on this issue with the Labor states, but this was not enough to stop the continuing erosion of the government's primary vote. Another vital factor was at work, eating away at Rudd's electoral dominance. The penultimate chapter considers the cause of this negative downwards spiral, together with Labor's desperate attempt to resurrect its chances before the 2010 election. And then, suddenly, came the fall, as Labor's leaders realised the party was facing oblivion and that the leader had to be despatched. **In** his final moments as prime minister, late at night and alone, he finally came to the realisation that he didn't have enough support to contest the caucus ballot without being humiliated. Rudd had once jocularly insisted that he'd either 'crash through or crash', never imagining that he would be left, discarded and broken, by the side of the road.

The Rudd project was over.

A key difference setting the new Labor government apart from its predecessor had been its preparedness to imagine and shape the future. Rudd seemed to promise us much more than just a government that would hop from issue to issue, or problem to crisis. He claimed he'd be tackling the fundamental core of the problem rather the superficial effects. This book considers how successful the Rudd project was in meeting the needs of Australia.

Rudd's message always remained simple. Perhaps surprisingly, it was based on trust. It required us to accept that he could identify the vital national objectives, as well as the correct means of achieving them. Where errors developed, he promised he'd work to put things right and that, because of his personal ability, the problems would be rectified and the locomotive quickly restored to chugging along on the right track. Where he failed to achieve anything, Rudd asked the electorate to understand that it wasn't his fault, but rather the fault of others who had stood in his way and prevented him from achieving his plans.

Rudd paid attention to the power bases that were already extant within the party — he never picked a fight he couldn't win — but, within these generous limits, the prime minister controlled everything. No public announcement — let alone shift in policy — occurred without his imprimatur. Rudd stamped his personality and style of management right across the country.

But ambitions and desires must be measured against results, and this simply provokes further questions. At times, the government, stretched rhetoric to its limits as it portrayed a better future, full of hope. Measured against the reality of accomplishment, these words fell short.

When Rudd came to power, Australia was uniquely placed to tackle the problems of the new century. The previous government had left the coffers overflowing. The country was deeply divided over important issues of national identity and the sort of nation it wanted to become, and Rudd appeared to offer an answer to these questions. He'd convincingly claimed that he'd be the author of a process that would take Australia forward. Somehow the country would become not merely a sustainable economy, but one that was also capable of developing its human capital until it evolved into a decent and humane society, in which everyone could be proud.

And so it went. As the months wore on, an unprecedented number of electors continued telling opinion pollsters they were not just happy with the new government; they were ecstatic about it. Something quite distinct appeared to have occurred in the national political consciousness, and it was intimately related to the new prime minister. This gave him remarkable power within the party, and he was determined to use it.

As soon as Labor took office, reports were commissioned and investigations commenced. Then, quite suddenly, the economic foundations of prosperity were thrown into chaos by the global financial crisis — or, as Rudd would soon come to popularise it (with his penchant for arcane abbreviations), the GFC. It was a nickname that stuck and, rather like Roald Dahl's book about the big friendly giant (the BFG), it soon appeared that Labor had, alone in the world, been able to tame this ferocious beast.

No matter that much of this was the work of Wayne Swan, the treasurer, built on a solid base bequeathed by the previous government; it was all credited to the PM. His power increased. Whatever Labor MPs thought of Rudd personally, they learned to keep it to themselves. His breathtaking approval-ratings acted like a conveyor-belt hauling more and more decision-making power directly to his office — and he knew how to exercise command. Soon, no one bothered muttering about their discontent; there was no point. Rudd was dominant.

The government carefully and successfully navigated its way through the shoals of financial catastrophe, but progress on other issues appeared to stall. As time went on, there were a plethora of plans and papers, but Labor appeared unable to implement further change successfully. It was almost as if evading the GFC had so exhausted the mariners piloting the course that they then gave up, leaving the wheel to spin, and letting the ship drift where it would. The government's agenda became consumed with explanations about why problems had occurred, and why some other objectives had been discarded.

Gradually, it became obvious that many issues hadn't been dealt with at all. The government's rhetoric was becoming overblown and detached from reality. The prime minister's overwhelming early popularity suddenly began to appear fragile. Some two years after Rudd was swept into office, Tony Abbott began to eat away at Labor's massive lead.

By early 2010, something quite radical was happening to Labor's polling figures. The public's view of the government's competence was undergoing serious revision. As a result, Rudd embarked on a remarkable succession of interviews, accepting that he'd made errors and promising to reform the government. Then he suddenly unveiled a massive, new initiative to reform the health system, and the mood swung again, despite the plan being remarkably devoid of detail. The momentum had shifted back; discontent within Labor's ranks was stilled, and Rudd's world began to turn on its normal axis again.

But then came further policy retreats, and the prime minister's support collapsed again as doubts about him personally began to crystallise. The opposition were galvanised — for the first time, some of them thought that government might be within their reach.

Yet the government was still demonstrating a remarkable discipline, even if it wasn't managing to achieve very much on the policy front. Personality clashes weren't allowed to seep out into the media. Labor still presented Rudd as the only person who could lead Australia to the Promised Land.

Until 2010 (and much to the surprise of some of his colleagues) the prime minister's appeal throughout the community remained immense. Many people remained eager to trust him, although those who knew him well couldn't figure out why. Some Australians remained prepared to turn to him as if he was a great leader, the helmsman who would lead the nation into the future. He, in turn, seemed to feed off this public affection. Rudd had convinced most voters that he didn't just have new and better objectives; he had a new way of travelling to a fairer society with shared humanitarian values.

However, reconciling this with the reality of his government was not always easy. It was as if the apparatus of government itself had been infected by a virus of bureaucracy, emanating from the very top. Instead of communication, politicians used what could only be described as rhetorical artifices delivering messages to a public that was no longer included in any genuine conversation. Feedback only occurred when focus-group organisers reported their findings back to the political machine. For the most part, the respondents' cares were massaged away with soothing words. People had become reduced to citizens who got their only chance to have an input into government processes once every three years — by voting.

Rudd made his conception of the administration of the country voluble when he said, 'Well, in our system of government, I am responsible for the lot of it. In terms of the accountability of that to the Australian people, they will make that plain when we next go to the election. I accept that. That is as it should be.' He seemed to be saying that we either accepted the package in its entirety, or left it. No negotiations would be entered into.

Then, as the election approached, many voters began having second thoughts. Doubts began to creep into the Rudd project, and they came to be increasingly focused on the personality and character of the prime minister himself. The party had to act.

CHAPTER TWO

Sorry

'For the pain, suffering and hurt of these stolen generations, their descendants and for their families left behind, we say sorry.'

Kevin Rudd, speech to parliament, 12 February 2008

The details of the federal budget are contained in four thick, dark-blue books consisting of more than 1,000 detailed pages of numbers, graphs, and tables. Every year the government adds a few additional statements of its own; smaller light-blue books of around 70 pages each, detailing particular areas where it's proud to highlight the money that's been spent. With sub-titles like 'building a stronger and fairer Australia' and 'a good international citizen', it rapidly becomes obvious that these documents are simply jazzed-up press releases made to look particularly weighty and significant.

Attached to the 2010–11 budget was a slim 38-page booklet promising to reveal how the government was 'closing the gap between indigenous and non-indigenous Australians'. It began with a repetition of noble sentiments, detailing the government's aspiration for every child in Australia to have the same opportunities and expectations. Then came the numbers: $1.6 billion (over four years) to tackle chronic disease; $5.5 billion (over 10 years) to address overcrowding and homelessness; $564.6 million (over six years) to support early-childhood development; and $228.9 million (over five years) to be spent on an employment program.

It wasn't until page 27 that, in the middle of dense information detailing further targets, aspirations, and hopes, a shocking detail slipped out. Because of 'a number of challenges arising from the implementation of a remote housing programme', only seven out of the year's promised 320 houses for the Northern Territory had been completed by the end of April. All the effort, fury, and noise of the government had barely brought forth a whimper.

The strategy of 'closing the gap' had always been driven by statistics. The plans and programs had been developed as a series of one-size-fits-all policy measures, handed down from on high, rather than animated by a desire to empower individuals and groups working in these regions. Gradually, as the intervention into Aboriginal lives had been rolled out over the previous three years, the hopes held out for it had shrunk. It had become increasingly obvious that nothing was being done to address the root causes of the problems bedevilling indigenous affairs, but the government had ploughed on, refusing to heed any warnings. Now it had finally become obvious that, even measured by its own rubric, the intervention was failing. It had turned into a disaster of its own.

Exactly a decade earlier, hundreds of thousands of Australians had marched for reconciliation in cities and towns across the country. Those walking had shared a tentative, inchoate desire to somehow fix things. Everyone was broadly aware of the depth of the crisis that had indigenous Australia gripped in a stranglehold, yet for years nothing had been done to tackle the problems that had shamed the country. Nothing had changed by 2010.

***

To achieve success in a televisual society, the modern political leader requires the ability to articulate the innermost desires of voters, to create a nexus between ordinary people's aspirations and their own party's policies. Once this connection has been achieved, subsequent policy failures can always be explained away: the aim, the objective, was right, but somehow immovable obstacles have come between to prevent those goals ever being achieved. By harnessing hope, the politician has already enlisted the public and become identified with the aspirations of a noble cause.

This act engenders a remarkable resilience in the relationship between politicians and the electorate. Both are engaged in a voyage together. If the ship is later to drift off course, the passengers are usually willing to try to understand how this might have happened, instead of simply rising up and storming the bridge. After all, the captain of the ship is in command; we invest our trust and faith in him to lead us to port.

By 2006 — as Howard notched up a decade as prime minister — it was apparent that indigenous Australians had been left behind. The very idea of reconciliation appeared to lie far ahead in some distant future. There were no concrete proposals to turn the concept into reality. Then, quite suddenly, John Howard grasped the urgent need to do something for Aboriginal people.

It wasn't the first time he'd tried to engage in this area, of course, but almost every previous interaction had been marked by hostility and suspicion. For most of the previous decade of Liberal government, there had been no common language capable of bridging the deepening gulf over Aboriginal issues. Communication between the first peoples and Howard's government had stopped. Despite the myriad problems and difficulties that were erupting everywhere across the portfolio, the split focused on a single word: 'Sorry.'

The nation's indigenous people and the conservative government had been driven apart by differing visions of the future, and the path that was needed so desperately to get there. But there remained one important issue to be resolved, long before a step could be taken down that long and tortuous road.

In the dying days of the Keating government, the PM had commissioned a former high court judge, Sir Ronald Wilson, to investigate the 'stolen generations'. He was to report on the government policy (which operated until 1970) of forcibly removing Aboriginal children from their families. Wilson had himself been sent away to a hospice at an early age, after his mother had died and his father had a stroke. He'd left school and became a court messenger at the age of 14; it was only after becoming a Spitfire pilot during World War II that he eventually studied law.

He said later that the evidence he'd heard during the inquiry was 'a life-changing experience'. Together with indigenous leader Mick Dodson (another law graduate), he travelled across the outback and through the cities, collecting testimony from 1,035 people and taking nearly 18 months to put together a remarkable account detailing what had happened. As well as recommending a compensation fund, the report called for an official apology. This would become highly controversial.

The duration of the investigation meant that the government had changed by the time the report was submitted. It's hard to remember now, but Howard was swept into Canberra by a flood of voters desperate to flush Keating's government away. Wilson's sudden emergence with his expressions of remorse didn't match the new spirit that was abroad in the land.

Conservative commentators quickly seized on alleged inconsistencies in the report. The claim of 'genocide', in particular, was fraught with possibilities of repudiation. Anthropologists such as Ron Brunton labelled these assertions as nothing more than 'embellishment'. Importantly, Howard insisted that there would be no apology, instead stating his 'regret' at what had occurred. The word 'sorry' stuck in his craw.

This divide became irrevocably fixed in the nation's consciousness a year after Howard's election, during the ironically named 'Reconciliation Convention' in Melbourne. Dodson attacked

Howard's expression of regret, insisting this was 'simply not enough'. As Howard began speaking, delegates began booing, hooting, and shouting.

A disconnect between the audience inside the theatre and 'mainstream' Australians (who'd voted for Howard in such numbers) was revealed to observers: they just saw people turning their backs on the PM. It's difficult not to suspect that at that moment a great divide slipped into place in Howard's mind. Meaningful dialogue with indigenous leaders effectively stopped. To use a term like 'stolen generations' became a political act completely divorced from factual content.

And a decade passed. The years were punctuated by the wilful ignoring of reports, like the one by Dr Paul Memmott investigating violence in indigenous communities. Completed in 1999, it wasn't released until 2001, and the idea of taking action to deal with these issues was dealt with in a similarly relaxed way.

By now, however, Howard had come to feel secure in his occupancy of the Lodge. Even when hundreds of thousands of people walked for reconciliation through every city in Australia; even when they streamed across the Sydney Harbour bridge and walked past Kirribilli House (which the PM had made his home); and even when his treasurer, Peter Costello, joined the marchers and was hailed for doing so, Howard simply closed his eyes.

The forgetfulness about Aboriginal issues was completely bipartisan. In 2007, at the end of April, Claire Martin's Labor government in the Northern Territory received a concise, explosive, and harrowing 316-page report into indigenous child abuse and sexual violence. And there it sat. One of the authors insisted that little in the report was 'actually new'. It wasn't released until mid-June, and it referred to a crisis that had existed for years.

Perhaps the truth was that everyone knew about the calamity, but no one had an answer.

Then, on the last day before the federal parliament adjourned for the winter recess in 2007, Howard announced that he would be sending in a mixed force of soldiers and police to 'deal with what we can only describe as a national emergency in relation to the abuse of indigenous children'. Some ten years after Wilson had handed in his report, Aboriginal issues had apparently worked their way to the top of the agenda again.

The issues involved in a long-running crisis are often complex, intractable, and detailed. The political agenda, however, is simple and short-term, demanding straightforward answers. So Howard sent in the troops, harnessing patriotism and closing off debate.

Those who ascribed more Machiavellian political motivations to Howard's inspiration saw this as a classic example of wedge politics. As opposition leader, Rudd needed, very quickly, to decide between two alternatives: either he backed the intervention (which would have the advantage for Howard of making the government look strong and effective because it had come up with the solution for the problem), or else he lambasted the move as cynical politics (which would have placed Labor in the position of being the party defending child abuse, paedophilia, domestic violence, and drug pushing).

Rudd decided to throw Labor's support fully behind the government. He wasn't given time to consider any alternative, and his immediate reaction was to embrace the intervention. Not a skerrick of light emerged between his position on Aboriginal child abuse and that of the prime minister. If Howard was horrified at what was going on in the shanties and settlements of the outback, so was Rudd. If Howard wanted to send in the troops, so too did Rudd. As the chief bureaucrat for Wayne Goss in Queensland, he had had numerous opportunities to immerse himself deeply in Aboriginal affairs had he wanted to, but he had never appeared to carry any particular torch for the problems suffered by the remote communities of the bush and desert.

Labor was desperate to win. The veteran political journalist

Mungo MacCallum presented, with almost knee-jerk antipathy, what he felt would probably be the results of the intervention: 'much despair, and not a little suffering ... it was hard to be optimistic'. MacCallum, like many other Labor supporters, saw this as a 'cunning and devious' plot to wrest the initiative back from Howard; as result, they forgave Labor's acquiescence. They shared a quaint, naive belief that everything would change once their party was back in power.

These old true-believers — the 'luvvies' — steadfastly refused to accept that their party's leader might actually believe in the intervention. Committed irrevocably to Labor, they assumed that he was simply standing close to Howard until after the party won the election when, presumably, normal service would be resumed. There was no suggestion that the new leader may have meant what he said, or even that he might possibly agree with their arch-enemy on this (or indeed any other) issue.

They apparently had no idea (as they sat and pontificated from the bar of the Billinudgel Hotel — MacCallum's watering hole) that many of their own favourite Labor politicians were also concerned about the policy direction the party was taking. Nevertheless, these apparatchiks had already made their own careful and informed calculations. They knew the party desperately required the transfusion provided by regaining office. A new discipline steadied the ranks, keeping them neatly aligned with the leader's new policy direction. Not everyone thought Rudd was the Messiah, but they quickly learned to keep their thoughts to themselves. Some comforted themselves with the thought that the party needed to regain power before it could worry about implementing policy, and that would be when caucus could regain control. Cutting the idea down to its simplest, briefest formulation, expedience came before policy.

Rudd had been handed the political licence to do what was necessary to win. He acted swiftly to take the best and most politically sustainable option available. It was probably also the alternative with which he felt most personally comfortable.

When Rudd had taken over as the Labor leader, he'd recorded a series of television advertisements outside his old school and family home at Eumundi on Queensland's sunshine coast to the north of Brisbane. He'd confidently proclaimed himself an economic conservative, insisting that 'It's a badge I wear with pride'. There seemed no reason to doubt him, yet most party supporters appeared ready to convince themselves that this was all just part of a clever act to lull the Howard battlers back into the Labor fold.

The irony was that Rudd had always asserted that the moleskin-wearing, RM Williams booted ('always have worn them',) country bloke portrayed in the ads was the real thing.

People normally enter politics to try to achieve something. Labor knew that unless the party was victorious, nothing could be accomplished. The coalition had been in office for a long time. There was a growing feeling that unless the opposition regained power, the country might change beyond recognition. The union movement threw all its money behind this attempt to form government. It knew that if Howard won another term, its funding base would be crushed.

The need for restraint won out. Parliamentarians kept their mouths shut and took on the role of police at particularly gruesome road accidents, urging people to 'move along quietly'. Journalists quickly realised there was no story in pursuing Rudd, and the focus returned to Howard. His difficulty was that the intervention provided limited picture opportunities for the media to zoom in on. There were visuals of army engineers erecting buildings. and plenty of opportunities to report meetings … but, after the first stock photos had been taken, it was difficult to keep this story going in the press. It quickly moved off the front pages and the news bulletins.

Social change isn't the sort of subject that the media cover well. Accounts of the effectiveness of the intervention needed to be shrunk and repackaged into tales of individual people before they could be told in the living rooms of voters in marginal seats, but such narratives didn't exist. Soon, the stories that were sent back to the lounges of middle Australia began including pieces of numerical data — a sure sign that they were headed for the inside pages of the paper or the back of the news bulletins.

From a narrow, political framework, the intervention failed to expose any differences between the two parties. Rudd had succeeded in keeping the focus directly on the government. He also implied it was unfortunate that Howard had only now discovered the plight of the original inhabitants of Australia; but, basically, he left the issue completely alone.

The government had managed to outflank the opposition on indigenous issues over land rights — and Rudd was determined that Howard would never do it again. Few of his colleagues might have wanted to go drinking with him, but they knew what Rudd was doing. They could almost smell victory.

More than anything else, Rudd was an ice-cold strategic thinker. He would calmly analyse a problem from every angle, sucking the emotions out of it before tackling it from an unexpected perspective. Howard had attempted to wedge him, but had failed.

Rudd still needed to reaffirm his own bona fides as a supporter of indigenous people; he had to find a way of sending a message to his own base that would reassure them and keep their loyalty. Rudd had avoided being outflanked on the right by Howard's sudden development of the strategy for an intervention. Now he needed to occupy the centre.

This was the opportunity that an apology offered him. Carefully chosen words could provide a way through a policy landscape littered with dangers. In May 2007, he'd spoken alongside Howard while marking the 40th anniversary of the passing of the referendum that gave Aboriginal Australians the vote. At that time, his key message was that Labor would work to cut the 17-year gap in life expectancy between indigenous and non-indigenous Australians.

In particular, Rudd promised 'to at least halve the rate of indigenous infant mortality … within a decade'. Then followed a long string of very earnest but boring numbers that washed over the audience, including funding details like his assertion that there'd be a '$186.4 million contribution from federal funds and $75 million from the states and territories'. The problem — even back then — was that these sorts of promises had been heard many times before. They were not inspiring.

Then right at the end (and almost overlooked) was a broad pledge to say sorry for past atrocities. 'We will do it and do it quickly', he said.

This initial concept of some sort of apology was vague and ill thought out. No mention was made of Wilson's report, and it was an example of the empty rhetoric of the past: a catch-all admission of guilt and regret, going nowhere. Nevertheless it offered a tool that, with further development, would be wielded like a weapon in the political fray.

There was no point in emphasising this during the gruelling election campaign. Rudd's single objective was to shut down any debate about Aboriginal issues. He wanted the campaign itself to focus exclusively on the national mood for change. To risk getting bogged down talking about intractable problems didn't offer the sort of political opportunity that Rudd so desperately craved. Talking about muddy situations risked tarnishing his sparkling-clean image.

Most particularly, it was important that nothing slipped out during those final weeks of electioneering to stop Labor's triumphant march to victory. Rudd acted quickly to quash calls for a referendum on reconciliation, prompting a riposte from Cape York indigenous leader Noel Pearson, who called Rudd a 'heartless snake'. Labor's leader continued to prevaricate, once being asked six times on radio if he'd use the word 'sorry'. Only finally did he admit, 'Of course, the substance of it (the apology) is sorry'.

Then, on Saturday 24 November 2007, Labor was installed as the country's new government. Rudd wanted to find a way of symbolically demonstrating the difference between the way he was going to tackle Aboriginal issues and the way these matters had been dealt with under the coalition. He also needed to reward the party's faithful and show he was not Howard, who had point-blank refused to offer an apology. The earlier general, somewhat fuzzy, concept of an apology was married to the symbolic walk performed by hundreds of thousands of Australians in response to Wilson's report.

Saying 'sorry' was a way of rewarding the party faithful; yet this word, so laden with symbolic significance, was still (in essence) practically meaningless. Rudd could use this as a way of demonstrating to Howard's supporters that, although he represented a change, he wasn't a threat.

The new PM hadn't even sorted out his cabinet when he made two dramatic pledges. One was expected: to sign the Kyoto Protocol on climate change. The second, an apology to the stolen generations, seemed to appear as if from nowhere.

Aware that simply using the 'sorry' word might quickly appear to be merely a change of style rather than substance, Rudd began winding other 'stakeholders' into his production, and elevating its resonance. He insisted it would occur at the commencement of parliament. Yearly reports would measure progress in closing the gap between Aboriginal people and other Australians. The scene was set for what was heralded as a major advance towards reconciliation.

***

The thirteenth of February 2008 was only the second day that a Labor leader had sat in the prime minister's chair (to the right of the Speaker) since the afternoon 13 years earlier when Keating stood in parliament for the last time. Back then, as Keating had swept his notes from the table, the Liberals waved gaily and yelled good-bye. They knew they'd never see him in the house again. Four months later, an unforgiving electorate dismissed Labor with a vengeance. More than a decade later, much had changed, and the body language of both sides was just the start. Now Labor was revelling as it occupied the government benches.

Rudd would never dominate the chamber as Keating had; somehow, he always looked like a bureaucrat as he flicked through his documents or sorted his papers, adorned with post-it notes in a succession of plastic folders. However, this lifeless stationery allowed Rudd to conjure up a remarkable political dynamic. Punctually, at nine o'clock, he began to speak.

'Today', he began, 'we honour the Indigenous peoples of this land, the oldest continuing cultures in human history. We reflect on their past mistreatment. We reflect in particular on the mistreatment of those who were Stolen Generations — this blemished chapter in our nation's history.'

'The time has now come', he continued, 'for the nation to turn a new page.'

From the moment he began speaking, it was abundantly clear that he'd decided to become Australia's storyteller. Rudd was attempting to describe and interpret the world through a narrative structure that he, and he alone, was developing. The most significant power the PM possesses isn't written in the constitution at all. It's the ability to define the terms of political engagement through the media, and by using all the props that surround the office to establish the framework and parameters of debate. Rudd (a sometime winner of the Queensland division of Rotary's 'Youth Speaks for Australia' contest) was about to prove his mastery of the art of rhetoric.

He'd sought input for the speech from four noted speechwriters. None of them has ever claimed credit for any of Rudd's utterances, and one has even gone so far as to deny that his words were used at all. This might give an indication of the workmanlike nature of the speech itself. Nevertheless, if it failed the test of technical brilliance, it achieved exactly what was required.

Rudd said 'sorry'. And, perhaps just in case anyone missed it, he said it again, and again. To Aboriginal people, this was a tremendously significant breakthrough, and a recognition of their suffering and position in Australia.

Gough Whitlam, Malcolm Fraser, Bob Hawke, and Paul Keating sat together in a roped-off area near the speaker's chair. Howard, like three of his former colleagues, wasn't interested in turning up. Wilson Tuckey pointedly walked out. Large television screens transmitted the proceedings to crowds that had turned up to sit on the lawns, or to walk on the dreamtime serpents buried in the tiles outside Parliament House, while they listened to and watched the apology. Others watched (and cried) in Sydney's Redfern and other Aboriginal communities throughout the country. In the heart of commercial centres, others stood to listen silently, some holding the black, red, and yellow flag of the indigenous people, while others clung to their briefcases.

Rudd stood as the applause rang through the chamber and the country. He suddenly reached out and grasped opposition leader Brendan Nelson's hand to shake it, before returning to the front bench.

This surprise action was a political masterstroke. Apparently impromptu, and merely a gesture conjured up in a split second by a man overwhelmed by emotion, it linked Nelson inexorably with the apology. All the divisions within the coalition resurfaced at once. Many were still furious that Rudd had made the apology at all; in doing so, the new PM was grinding Howard's legacy into the dust. Implicating Nelson in the plot to diminish their lost leader seemed like dancing on his grave. There was nothing Nelson could do once the hand was proffered other than shake it; however, many of his colleagues would never move past that moment. They felt he'd allowed himself to be tricked. They felt that Howard, their hero, had been diminished. And they began to realise they were now in opposition. For members of the previous government, it was a cathartic moment. They'd been rendered irrelevant. Some finally realised they no longer wanted to sit through a theatre where they'd been relegated to the bit parts, unable to affect the action, and chanting like a Greek chorus.

Labor was, gloriously and definitively, in office. As far as the new occupants were concerned, the temple had been cleansed. This one energising moment had emphasised that power had shifted — not just political power, but the authority to determine how events would be deconstructed and interpreted. Great hopes had been articulated; could they now be realised?

Meanwhile, back in the Northern Territory, the intervention — Howard's policies — ground inexorably on, despite the change of government. It was almost as if nothing had happened at all.

***

There is little, if any, connection between what occurs in Canberra and in the real world outside the long, echoing corridors of Parliament House. Something happened as the spirit animating the intervention passed through the bush and into the desert sands. By the time it reached the shanties of the communities, thousands of kilometres to the west, the good intentions had become transmogrified into bureaucratic solutions. The ideas that were once invested with so much hope had mutated into realities that bore little relationship to their original aims.

It was almost as if the seeds of failure formed an integral part of the initial model aimed at 'saving the children'. The need was real and immediate, but the workings of government are slow and opaque. Life was quantified into sets of statistics; before any figure could be made to demonstrate results, it was necessary to establish a baseline. One thing the public servants had complete mastery of was the ability to manipulate data so as to prove that the programs were successful. It was, perhaps, unfair to expect them to also have the ability to develop programs that could be implemented effectively.

Less than a month after his election victory, Rudd descended from the RAAF jet that had flown him to Darwin so he could meet with indigenous leaders on their home ground. This seemed to demonstrate his willingness to understand the issues, and television shots beamed back images of a smiling PM being welcomed by traditional dancers. Rudd promised to return soon and to discuss Aboriginal concerns about the form the intervention was taking. As it happened, he never did make it back. Rudd became caught up with other issues, leaving Indigenous Affairs Minister Jenny Macklin to take over as the government's representative from then on. One of those present at that first meeting was later to describe Rudd's contribution as more 'style than substance'. Many of the indigenous leaders became disillusioned. They began to doubt that the new government represented a fresh approach at all.

In 2008, Rudd had made a promise: 'Each year in Australia's federal parliament, the first working day will be marked by a prime ministerial statement reporting on the progress of closing the life-expectancy gap, progress in closing the gap in infant mortality and mortality of children up to five, and progress on closing the literacy and numeracy gap between indigenous and non-indigenous Australians.'

The promise wasn't kept. In 2009, the delayed release of the report card announced that a grand total of 80 houses had been completed in the Northern Territory's remote communities. An additional $50 million was being allocated to fund a new program to tackle eye diseases. As if it came as a surprise, Rudd announced that around 20,000 indigenous children were affected by trachoma, and insisted that 'this should not be the case'.

By 2010, the report had cascaded its way down the list of priorities. Seven ministerial statements took priority before, late in the second week of that sitting, Rudd finally delivered his report. It didn't bother to reveal how many houses had been completed.

When the document was eventually dropped into the boxes of the media outlets, the 74-page brightly coloured essay was festooned with smiling faces and intimations of progress. 'The Apology to Australia's Indigenous Peoples, and in particular the Stolen Generations', the short book insisted, 'created the opportunity for a shared future and a fresh beginning'. The apology had seemingly gained a capital letter and become a proper noun that could unlock the way to a new future. Time was now clearly delineated. It was as if the apology somehow marked Year Zero. Everything before then could be dismissed. The government was now acting to 'close the gap', and creating targets to allow progress to be measured.

As the report made clear, 'without a sound evidence base it was impossible to understand what was and what was not working well: and impossible to track our progress, in closing the gap on indigenous disadvantage'. Numbers had been lacking in the past, and this was anathema to the bureaucratic mind. How could the undoubted results of the intervention be proven unless there were line charts that could visually demonstrate results?

Those people whose lives made up the numbers didn't always appear to realise how fortunate they were to have been offered a chance to start afresh. It was not that the past was viewed with nostalgia — far from it. Nevertheless, the tensions incorporated within this new approach resulted in suspicion and distrust continuing to surround the project.

It had surprised many traditional Labor supporters in the Northern Territory that the new government had not merely continued but extended Howard's policies — not just at first, but subsequently as well. There always seemed to be the feeling that with just a little more regulation, just a slight tweaking of the regulatory parameters, everything would be fine. The results were difficult to measure. The intervention's most radical ideological change — the removal of control from the individual, while making the authorities the repository of power — was still being implemented.

A former chief judge of the family court, Alistair Nicholson, ripped the gossamer-thin fabric of legal legitimacy away from the intervention in early 2010. Accusing Rudd of 'rolling over like a puppy', he accused the PM of avoiding the 'searing moral challenge' of the intervention — the suspension of the Racial Discrimination Act. 'This is disgraceful legislation which perpetuates paternalism and racial discrimination', he said, before insisting that no one serious about Aboriginal reconciliation could possibly countenance such action.

The intervention represented a draconian assault on human rights, effectively eliminating them and allowing the government to prescribe by *diktat* the way that people should behave. This might have been acceptable had it worked — but quite clearly even this had failed, according to a report by the government's own Emergency Response Review Board in September 2008, after the scheme had been operating for a year. Yet, despite this unequivocal finding, the Rudd government ignored calls to reinstate the Racial Discrimination Act.

Nicholson also blasted the government's management of income-support services. The government's review had insisted that welfare quarantining should be abolished, but Macklin's reaction was to ignore these calls and to consider the possibility of broadening the scheme to the rest of the country. Despite protestations that it was 'evidence-based', the government continued to blithely ignore any data that didn't fit in with its previously established assumptions.

A continuing concern in many remote communities had been the extent to which people receiving government benefits had spent the money on grog, drugs, or even just petrol to sniff. For the coalition, there had seemed to be few political downsides to the idea that Aboriginal people should be forced to spend money on food, clothing, or other essential needs. The intervention introduced 'income management' into 75 of the regional communities, effectively policing the way people spent their cash.

This was reminiscent of the 'susso' — the sustenance allowance given out to the poor in the middle of the Great Depression. The St Vincent de Paul Society later told a Senate inquiry that the payment was nothing more than a demeaning version of a 'food ticket', representing an attempt to 'turn back the clock'.

In 2010, a study published in the *Medical Journal of Australia* by Julie Brimblecombe found there was no demonstrable difference in the purchase of healthy food in areas where income management had been adopted. Nor was there any change in tobacco sales. The only significant effect appeared to be an increase in the consumption of soft drinks. The most detailed examination of the policy demonstrated conclusively that spending habits had not, in fact, been modified at all as a result of the policy. Macklin simply dismissed the evidence by referring to an earlier government study based on telephone interviews that, perhaps unsurprisingly, found many people had a 'positive view' of the policy.

Other studies have also raised significant questions about the effectiveness of the intervention. In a presentation to the University of Technology, Sydney, the chief executive officer of the Sunrise Health Service Aboriginal Corporation, Irene Fischer, examined childhood anaemia (an iron deficiency leading to poor growth and brain development) that was directly attributable to inadequate diet. She found that anaemia rates had jumped significantly *since* the intervention, up by 36 per cent to 55 per cent. There was also a rise in low birth-weight, which is linked to poor nutrition amongst mothers. Researchers had no difficulty in finding that income management did *not* reduce either alcohol or drug consumption. Macklin's claims of 'evidence-based policy' were dismissed by Fischer as hollow.

The Australian Council of Social Service insisted that income management would rapidly lead to entrenched social exclusion.

The former Northern Territory (Labor) chief minister Clare Martin launched a vitriolic attack on the policy as both racist and sexist, but the broader public had stopped listening to her. She, like Howard, had become a representative of the past. Her government had singularly failed to come up with any ways of dealing with this corrosive issue. Rudd was not inclined to listen to her now.

In June 2010, legislation applied the measures to broad swathes of those receiving income support, including young and vulnerable people, and those who had been accessing payments for a long time. Martin, now heading the Australian Council of Social Service, again attacked federal Labor. Calling on Rudd to 'halt the scheme', she particularly questioned the supposed 'evidence' used to support its extension. Martin suspected the legislation was intended to effect social and behavioural change — an agenda that was far more conservative than the ostensible reason for the changes. The battle had moved onto new terrain. Now it was not simply over the quarantining of income support; it was also about the extent of control that a government should be able to exert over people's lives

In the communities where income management had been implemented, it mainly appeared to be displacing alcohol drinking, petrol sniffing, and illegal activity to other areas. In many cases, the initiative was coming from the communities themselves, or at least from some of those prominent in local life who believed it would help the transition to a better way. In the broader community, imposing some form of income control had a wide appeal. Many people felt that, as nothing else had appeared to work, this measure was worth a try despite, or perhaps because of, its paternalistic overtones.

By now, the new government's ideology had become clear: it represented bureaucracy in all its glory; it was the modern age writ large. The verdict of those who'd followed Aboriginal issues for a generation was depressing. The editor-in-chief of the *Canberra Times*, Jack Waterford, had been involved with Aboriginal affairs since his time as a young lawyer some 40 years previously. 'Willy nilly' he told me, conjuring up those little circular whirls that shuffle randomly around in the dust of the outback. 'The conversation going on is one in which ... nothing much changes. In the past half-century, in particular, neither politicians nor bureaucrats have learned anything much new about consultation, engagement, or better delivery of goods and services to citizens. We continually reorganise our systems — mostly with terrific intentions — but nothing much is better.'

'Indeed', he continued, 'the incompetence of managing Aboriginal affairs is probably greater now than it has been for decades'.

INTERLUDE

Brendan

It was some months after Nelson had been deposed by Turnbull that I needed to speak to the former leader about another matter. Always polite, he indicated that, yes, he could meet me in his electorate office next week; it would be a pleasure. 'No, sorry,' I responded, 'I meant the next week that you were in Canberra'. Yes, that would be fine, too. When would I like to meet?

It turned out that, with the exception of a couple of party-room meetings, question time and, of course, lunch, Nelson had a great deal of free time — probably much more than he'd had for decades. There's nothing quite as past tense as a 'former leader'. Since September 1914 Menzies has been the only such person who's ever managed to regain the prime ministership. Although (since World War I) six people have led the opposition twice, Howard remains the only one who managed to break the curse and lead the party back to victory. But today the political cycle has sped up. If a leader doesn't immediately impress in the opinion polls, he or she doesn't get a second chance. By the end of 2008, Nelson's political career was washed up. Is it any surprise he seized the opportunity to become ambassador to Brussels when Rudd threw him the bauble?

A prominent doctor (he'd been president of the Australian Medical Association from 1993 to 1995), Nelson was elected in the 1996 Howard landslide and dutifully served his time. He had to wait two terms (until 2001) before the PM finally found room for him in the ministry. Although Nelson did remove his earring before entering parliament, and although in question time he was often the only coalition member — apart from the then prime minister — wearing a double-breasted suit, Howard still appeared suspicious of his talented new recruit.

A degree of wariness might have been appropriate. Back during the bitterly fought election of 1993, AMA president Nelson famously addressed a crowd in the salubrious suburb of Toorak with a loudhailer. 'I have never voted Liberal in my life,' he yelled loudly, to enthusiastic applause. It was the right thing to say at that time, but times change. Two years later, he was seeking desperately to represent the leafy, upper North Shore of Sydney — an area where the Conservative vote is not so much counted as weighed.

Unfortunately for Nelson, David Connolly (who'd entered Parliament in 1974, the same year as Howard) was already representing the electorate. Connolly showed no inclination to move on, and the preselection battle was spiteful. Someone helpfully ensured that all the people on the panel to choose the new MP received their own personal videotape of Nelson screaming his repudiation of the Liberal Party; the doctor responded with a barrage of ideas to impress the preselectors. He declared Medicare unsustainable, advocated a consumption tax and, to finally secure his nomination as local member (offering, perhaps, cream where Connolly could only manage low-fat milk), endorsed Work for the Dole. He managed to topple Connolly by the minuscule margin of three votes out of 189; however, that rapidly became irrelevant. Nelson was on his way to Canberra.

At the ensuing general election, Nelson received a whopping 75.7 per cent of the two-party-preferred vote, making his electorate the second safest in Australia (the improbable Wilson Tuckey held O'Connor by 75.9 per cent). It turned out that Nelson had the capacity to appeal to more voters than the previous member had, as something about him obviously inspired former Labor supporters to switch sides and vote conservative.

His first stint in the ministry was in Education. Here he made some controversial decisions (including nominating the legend of Simpson and his donkey at Gallipoli as the embodiment of Australian values), before eventually moving on to that graveyard of political ambition — Defence. Perhaps sending the doctor there was an unusually weird joke of Howard's to which only he saw the punchline; nevertheless, Nelson remained loyal. When Costello asked Howard to quit in 2006, Nelson unquestioningly supported the PM, although a year later he'd changed his mind.

During the APEC meeting in September 2007, the then foreign minister, Alexander Downer, had called the ministry together at Sydney's plush Quay Grand to canvass them about whether Howard should stand down before the election. Nelson insisted that the prime minister had to be prepared to leave without being pushed. The deciding factor appeared to be that Nelson expected Howard to achieve a better result than Costello would have. There was never much goodwill for the treasurer floating around inside the party — he had a reputation for arrogance and aloofness.

The day after the 2007 election, with Howard unlikely to retain his seat, Costello made the shock announcement that he wouldn't even be standing for the leadership. The party was momentarily thrown into confusion as it looked around for a new chief. No one doubted Turnbull's ambition but, as with Costello, there was a large rump of MPs who were uncomfortable with the idea of the former merchant banker taking over the party. Turnbull had immediately and publicly announced his intention to stand, and conducted his election campaign in the public arena; Nelson preferred to use his time canvassing other parliamentarians by phone. He made it clear that he would love the job and that he had a plan. He spent time talking to people, rather than haranguing them.

When Abbott pulled out of the contest (and with Turnbull already campaigning on radio and television as if he had been anointed), residual concerns about the latter's public announcements helped nudge Nelson over the line by 45 votes to 42. One politician later said, 'Nelson didn't necessarily inspire anyone, but at least he was willing to talk and listen.' These, by implication, were skills that Turnbull lacked.

It's important to realise that Nelson *did* have a plan to knock off Rudd by the end of his first term — he just never got to implement it. He envisaged it, he later told me, as a strategy that would evolve deliberately over three years. Nelson had always been highly attuned to the psychological dimensions of relationships, and he saw the interactions between politicians and the electorate in much the same way. The key was to break down the broader electorate into its different voting blocs, and work out how to appeal to each one. He hoped victory would be delivered by regaining the particular group of swinging voters who'd left Howard in that last term, and the key to this was understanding what had happened during that election.

There were two important points to note about the result in 2007. The first was the fragility of Labor's success. It had benefited from a significant 5.7 per cent swing that allowed the party to take 23 seats from the Liberals. As well as this, the prime minister and three ministers (Mal Brough, Jim Lloyd, and Gary Nairn) had been swept away with the detritus. The new government held 83 seats, while the combined coalition total was only 65. Yet, despite all this, the Rudd-led Labor Party had only managed to inspire 43.4 per cent of the electors to back him as their first choice. This was 1.5 per cent less than Labor had obtained in 1993, the last time it was victorious (under Paul Keating). Only once before, in the 1990 election, had the party received fewer first-preference votes and still been able to claim victory.

Across Australia, Labor secured 159,160 more votes than the coalition, out of a total of 13,646,539 voters. As usual, a far greater number of people had cast informal votes (510,822) than had actually decided the result.

And there was another enormous constituency out there—the 976,789 voters who'd marked a '1' against the name of the Greens' candidate. Nearly four out of every five of these votes returned to Labor as preferences were distributed, and these Greens were vital in determining the result. Labor only managed to win half its seats outright; preference flows were critical. In other elections, a greater percentage of Greens voters had given their preferences to the Liberals. Wooing these voters might also prove a fruitful exercise for Nelson.

The other aspect emphasising the tenuous nature of the victory was that ever since Menzies had left office, the government had lost first-preference votes at the subsequent election. Although Whitlam had only suffered a negative swing of 0.3 per cent in 1974, Fraser dropped 4.9 per cent in 1977, Hawke lost 2.2 per cent in 1984, and Howard's first-preference votes dropped a colossal 7.7 per cent in 1998. Nelson's idea that this could be turned into a one-term government was far from fanciful. The key was to maximise the number of second-preference votes flowing to the Liberals while, at the same time, retaining the party's base of faithful supporters. The difficulty was that these two groups required slightly different strategies to bring them back on board.

Nelson had to distance himself from the policies that the swinging voters had rejected, while at the same time appealing to the party's heartland. Achieving this depended on establishing goodwill that would lead people to overlook minor inconsistencies. The difficult task of walking this tightrope became apparent in December just after his election as leader. In a generally positive interview with Glenn Milne for News Limited's Sunday papers, Nelson stood firmly against gay marriage, adoption, and IVF, yet backed equal (legal) rights for same-sex couples. 'I believe in addressing the social and economic injustices affecting homosexuals,' the new leader insisted—a comment that distanced him from Howard's social policies.

The danger was that Nelson had begun sending out mixed messages right at the start of his leadership, while people were still wondering how to define where he stood on important issues. Complexity isn't conveyed well by the media: nuance can quickly degenerate into confusion. Nelson's distinction was much easier to understand for those who realised that his younger brother Philip had died of AIDS some 17 years previously, but there could be no guarantee that readers wouldn't take out a very different meaning—particularly after living for more than a decade under a Liberal leader who didn't need to concern himself with intricate social constructions. There are both progressives and conservatives within the party; trying to manage the expectations of both groups without the resources of government was like a nightmare for the opposition leader.

This crisis came to a head in January 2008, when Nelson opposed a formal apology to the stolen generations. His initial response was that saying 'sorry' would fuel guilt in middle Australia and engender the negative belief that Aboriginal people were indeed victims. This reaction played well amongst the conservative base of the party: the people who remained faithful to Howard. Nevertheless, it was controversial amongst the progressive members, like Turnbull and others who'd gone public with their support for an apology. There was a lot of pressure on Nelson to take a stand one way or the other; he couldn't afford to prevaricate any longer.

With less than a fortnight to go before the opening of parliament, minor divisions within the party had begun to turn into deep fissures. Nelson couldn't corral his MPs and encourage them to form a united front. On ABC radio, he was reduced to asking rhetorical questions of himself: 'Do we then reinforce, if you like, a culture of guilt … and do we also reinforce the notion that there is victimhood on the part of many Aboriginal people?'

But popular answers weren't going to be found by undertaking deeper philosophical or social investigations. What was needed was a political call, and it was in this forum that Nelson's hands were tied by different Liberal Party factions who were having difficulty coming to terms with the reality of opposition. Neither Nelson nor Turnbull had ever served in opposition before (even Abbott had only been in the parliament for two years before his party shifted across to the government benches). Bereft of a firm leader who could enunciate Liberal doctrine with almost papal infallibility, individual MPs were running everywhere as they sought to get the party to better reflect their own philosophical beliefs. Unfortunately, these were not as coherent as might have been expected.

Every political party represents some form of alliance based around ideas and interests. Often it's only the desire to gain power that's strong enough to trump otherwise large ideological divisions. Labor has its socially progressive left, which regularly falls into conflict with its trade union-dominated Catholic right. The Greens incorporate some who believe in massive redistribution of wealth, together with others for whom concern for the environment is at the forefront of politics. The first Liberal Party (formed in 1909 by Alfred Deakin) was a contradictory mix of free traders and protectionists, united only by their opposition to Labor. What had been Menzies' party of 'forgotten people' now marries conservative, liberal, and free-market streams of thought in a coalition with the Nationals — still described by some as the party of agrarian socialism, although any label quickly risks becoming a mere caricature.

The difficulty this posed for Nelson was the lack of any solid, underlying core of belief that he could fall back on, in the wake of the election defeat, to unite the disparate strands of thought and practice that characterised the Liberal Party. Because this challenge had come right at the beginning of his leadership, it intensified its significance. Nelson had to urgently find a way of keeping the party together. The first dramatic test he faced would come on the morning of the second day's sitting, as Rudd moved the apology on the floor of the house. The new leader couldn't afford to allow his party to split openly — there had to be a unified response.

The problem was Turnbull. From the moment he'd been defeated in the party room ballot, the shadow treasurer had continued to offer gratuitous advice to Nelson about how to 'lift his game'. That morning, soon after having been rejected by the party, Turnbull had charged into Nelson's office, jabbing his right finger in the air and telling the new leader he needed to 'toughen up'. Turnbull even wanted to join Nelson in his first press conference as opposition leader. The shadow treasurer might genuinely not have intended to upstage the new leader, but it was obvious there could never be enough room for two people to stand on the leadership podium. Now the dangerous possibility was emerging that, because of Turnbull, a number of the small-l members of the party might cross the floor unless Nelson managed to associate the party, one way or another, with the apology.

In the end, Nelson succeeded. His own backers — the members who had installed him instead of Turnbull, and who tended to be from the more conservative half of the party — accepted Nelson's decision to offer 'in-principle support' for an apology. Only one of the coalition MPs didn't bother turning up that morning. Nelson sighed with relief. It was close, but the parliamentary party hadn't fractured. But the cost in the broader electorate was enormous: no one was quite sure exactly what the leader stood for.

When Rudd reached across the table in that seemingly spontaneous gesture to shake hands with Nelson, his actions appeared to symbolise the bipartisan nature of the motion. In fact, nothing could have been better calculated to cause angst for the opposition leader. He'd been symbolically placed as one of those dancing on Howard's grave. The party's base — its core — was scathing.

The tactics over moving the party towards the apology had tarnished one of the most precious possessions a political leader has — his integrity. To those who knew Nelson, to those who understood his personal history and who could appreciate nuance, and to those who wished the new leader success, his positioning over the apology made sense. Nevertheless, these ideological and personal divisions within the party were always going to be played up heavily in a media that was also attempting to discover how the new government was going to change the consensus about what represented the new mainstream of Australian thought.

Nelson's leadership was doomed. With every night came the possibility of total eclipse.

Rudd was never going to give him a chance to implement his strategy of uniting different interest groups and sections of society under a common umbrella. No matter what the motivations or the eventual result of Rudd's apology, as a political tactic it was brilliant. It was almost as if it had been designed simply to crush any possibility that the opposition might be able to recover some momentum.

When I finally sat down with Nelson, some months after his leadership had ended in despair, the scars of the battle were still raw. What had finally brought him undone was the polling — although that assertion minimises the critical role played by Rudd in wedging his opponent into impossible contortions. By mid-February 2008 — straight after the apology — a mere 9 per cent of Australians said that Nelson was their preferred prime minister. That figure was disastrous. (Even Beazley was managing to achieve 18 per cent in the days before Rudd challenged him.) As if to grind Nelson's despair into the dust, Rudd at the same time was recording a remarkable approval rating of 70 per cent.

The leader continued setting new records. In March, Nelson slipped again, this time to 7 per cent. A good budget reply brought a little bit of time, but it had become obvious that there was virtually no chance of him being able to remake his public image, let alone take the coalition to an election victory. The only question was who would replace Nelson as leader. Many of the conservatives hadn't forgiven Turnbull for his role in the destabilisation; but, by the time Costello's memoirs were released, there didn't seem to be any other alternative on offer.

In mid-September, despite pleas from many in his party to hold on, Nelson decided he'd had enough. He asked his party to 'draw a line in the sand' by making 'a renewed commitment to unity and discipline, to focus less on internal preoccupations and more on … the important issues concerning everyday Australians'. Whenever a politician refers to the vital matters concerning ordinary (or working) Australians, you can immediately tell there is another agenda going on. The words themselves mean nothing; they are just more of the focus-group pap that both parties prefer to shovel towards the electorate instead of more nutritious policy substance.

Turnbull had been in Italy, and only returned to Australia hours before the vote took place. Nelson gave what even Turnbull backers agreed was a brilliant speech to the party-room, but it seems unlikely he secured any more support. His colleagues had already made up their minds. In the end, Nelson lost by just three votes — exactly the same margin by which he'd won the previous November.

CHAPTER THREE

The Great Escape

'The global financial crisis is the economic equivalent of a rolling national security crisis … (the) worst global financial crisis since the Great Depression'

Kevin Rudd, Canberra press conference, 13 October 2008

Labor was briefed on the contents of the Commonwealth safe the morning after it came to office. The new government's experience was very different from the one Costello had had in 1996. Back then, both parties had veered away from discussing finances during the election campaign: Labor had kept quiet because it didn't want to admit how much government debt had been racked up, and the Liberals did the same because they were worried that drawing attention to the problem would cause concern about where the axe might fall to cut government programs. Neither of these issues was a problem in 2007.

Labor was inheriting a massive legacy worth nearly $90 billion, made up of not just a recurrent surplus ($20 billion), but also three huge infrastructure and future funds. The government was very nicely placed. The only limitation — and it was a minor one — had been the guarantee during the election campaign to match the previous government's promised income-tax cuts.

Costello, who normally disagreed with Howard's desire to hand money back to the punters in small dollops, had for once agreed with the former PM's profligacy. In the run-up to the election campaign, it had begun to appear increasingly likely that Labor would win. The Liberals hoped to constrict Labor's spending as much as possible, boxing in the next government's ability to splurge and spend its way to re-election. The strategy was to hobble the incoming government and force it to dance to a Liberal tune — the idea being that this would mean an early return to government, because Labor would be unable to satisfy its own favoured constituencies' demand for money. Then the economic crisis emerged from nowhere, sending shockwaves through the financial markets. The government was unshackled from the fetters on its ability to spend freely. It could sign blank cheques and still pretend it was being 'responsible', because it was stimulating the economy.

Initially, the origins of the financial crisis appeared to have nothing to do with the real world. They were so completely irrelevant to the massive superstructure of the global economy that they rapidly popularised the 'butterfly effect' of chaos theory. This had its genesis in a meteorologist's comment many years before that 'one flap of a seagull's wings as it flew over the ocean might change weather patterns across the world'. But seagulls aren't nearly as poetic as butterflies, and oceans aren't as evocative as the Amazon; so when, in 1972, Philip Merilees had to give a paper to the American Association for the Advancement of Science, he chose a rhetorical question to popularise the idea, asking, 'Does the flap of a butterfly's wings in Brazil set off a tornado in Texas?'

The idea behind his paper was simple. Chaos theory explains how a single random event (or the repetition of an event — in this case, the continual fluttering of the butterfly's wings) can, under certain conditions, become hugely magnified, depending on the sensitivity of the initial environment. As an explanation of what had happened, this idea quickly became popular; it seemingly explained how, despite the apparent disconnection, house repossessions in the mid-west of America could result in the disappearance of pension funds and investment losses of hundreds of millions of dollars from local councils in Australia.

Although this explanation might have been comforting to those who lost money as the crisis became a crash, the reality has always been that such apparently cataclysmic events are an integral part of the modern financial system. In retrospect, every economic downturn is predictable — perhaps none more so than the original Great Depression of 1929. On every occasion, however, the particular cause of the shock appears to arise 'out of the box' and to come as an unwelcome surprise to those operating the levers of what is a supposedly sound economic system.

It was just the same with the eventual global shockwave that was triggered by the bursting of the US house-price bubble after 2006. Significantly, American mortgages don't operate under the same rules as Australian ones. Here, debt follows the person who has initiated the mortgage like a ball and chain — it's impossible to escape, except through bankruptcy. The situation is different in the US, where it's feasible to simply walk away from a home. This becomes a particularly attractive option if a lot of money is owed on the property. Although householders will lose any money they've already paid towards reducing their home loan, doing this can be a financially sensible option, particularly if the building is worth less than was originally paid for it.

Until late 2005, credit was particularly easy to get for anyone buying a house in the United States. The combination of low interest rates and easy credit was driving prices up, and so more people rushed into the market … until it all began to come unstuck in 2006. Borrowers who'd taken on more debt than they could service suddenly found they couldn't refinance. Interest rates were on their way up. More people began to default, and banks began foreclosing as others failed to meet the extra cost of repayments when their honeymoon rates began expiring. Others, who'd relied on debt-financed consumption, cut back their spending. The bubble began to pop.

But the gurgling sound wasn't just heard in the States. Marvellous financial innovations, such as collateralised debt obligations, meant that investment banks had been able to bundle up huge numbers of dubious (or sub-prime) mortgages into packages that were then sold off to investors around the world.

This resulted in the farcical situation whereby a local council in Australia was happy to purchase huge bundles of sub-prime mortgages from an American financial institution, based on a dubious series of assumptions, despite the fact that they could in no way adequately measure the risk that was contained in the package they were buying.

Investors were making a series of assumptions about issues such as foreign-exchange risk, the continuing state of the American economy, and the likelihood of individual homeowners being able (or even wanting) to continue to repay loans they could walk away from. It's difficult to understand why any Australian local-government body, for example, thought that its own analysis of the risks involved in such investments in the US was necessarily better than those of large corporate multinational institutions; particularly as the value of the American housing market had more than doubled in the eight years up to mid-2006. It quickly became apparent that the so-called financial advisors whom investors were relying on were equally ignorant of the dangers such products posed. They were really just employed to sell products. People around the world, from the individual purchasing a house somewhere in the States through to others who were buying dubious investments, had mispriced risk. The boom couldn't — wouldn't — continue.

American institutions were highly leveraged and, as a result, highly vulnerable. The credit crisis spread like a virus, first through the American, and then the world, economy. The collapse slammed into stock markets, unleashing a crisis of consumer confidence. It spiralled towards disaster. If people were to close their wallets, the miracle of a continually expanding economy threatened to reverse course. Quite suddenly, it looked as if escaping with a mere recession wouldn't be too bad; the real fear was that the credit crisis could become the harbinger of a severe and prolonged depression.

Australia was able to eventually avoid such dire consequences by a combination of good policy and excellent luck.

Ken Henry had been appointed Treasury Secretary by Costello in 2001, but he'd also worked as one of Keating's senior advisers for five years. He had retained his job when Labor came to power. As the swirling crisis threatened to become a whirlpool, his advice to Swan was 'go early, go hard, and go households', and that's exactly what the government did. A stimulus package was designed to pump $42 billion into the economy. It represented a classic Keynesian economic solution to the crisis and, most importantly, it worked.

So what did the government decide to spend its money on? Firstly, and vitally, it bought confidence. Everything else followed from this. The stimulus was skewed towards people who would recycle it straight back into the economy — which meant ordinary workers, part of Labor's natural constituency. This had the added benefit of being good politics as well. As the opposition claimed, the stimulus sent the budget deficit 'soaring' to around 28 per cent of GDP; but, as it normally rests at 25 per cent anyway, this didn't cause a crisis of confidence over the dollar in foreign-exchange markets.

Treasury encouraged federal departments to come up with spending plans, but they weren't as capable of controlling the money as it was flushed out the door. Amongst the allocations that were later to prove controversial was a massive $16.2 billion set aside for school buildings. By comparison, the sum of $2.5 billion devoted to the insulation-batt installation scheme was chickenfeed. Nevertheless, both of these programs helped buy confidence at a vital time for the economy.

The second institution to come to the government's rescue was the Reserve Bank. Governor Glenn Stevens (who'd been putting up interest rates during the previous year in the run-up to the election) slashed rates — a move that, along with the assistance provided by the government's decision to continue giving money to first-time buyers, kept the housing market alive.

Because Australians have so much money tied up in housing (with approximately one in every 10 people also owning an investment property), this proved critical in maintaining confidence. People could attend real estate auctions — which had become a popular Saturday-morning pastime for many — and witness confidence in the future being expressed as prices continued to soar. Those who'd submitted their income tax received a gratuitous rebate simply for doing so. The government was, quite literally, giving away money.

Later, in June 2010, a member of the Reserve Bank board, ANU economist Warwick McKibbin, launched a scathing critique of the government's policy responses at this time. He asserted it had been 'panicked' into over-stimulating the economy, denuding the coffers and spending money on wasteful programs of dubious utility. What had begun to particularly concern him during this period was the way in which Treasury was losing its independent role to become little more than an 'arm of political policy'.

Other institutions, such as the Australian Prudential Regulation Authority, performed their own roles. A series of banking failures in the early 1990s had played havoc with the economy, and APRA subsequently did its part to ensure that Australian financial institutions weren't over-leveraged. However, the critical role here was played early on by the Treasurer, Wayne Swan, when Macquarie Bank was badly hit by the US crisis.

The full story of how close Australia came to economic collapse has never previously been told. In 2007, Macquarie Bank seemed to be a raging success story. Its top 20 executives had split more than

$200 million in pay and bonuses between them (including more than $33 million for chief Alan Moss); but by August of that same year, the bank's shares were plunging (falling by more than 10 per cent, or $8.81, on a single day). The crisis didn't let up. Fourteen months later, the bank was again under intense pressure. Some analysts were even suggesting that the unthinkable could happen: an Australian bank might collapse.

If one did, there would have been immediate contagion in the Australian financial markets. This was something that the government could not possibly afford. On the second weekend of October 2008, Rudd and Henry worked in Canberra, stitching together a vital guarantee worth up to $700 billion for the banking industry as a whole. Only a measure as large as this would have been enough to restore confidence in the sector — because support for the banking system had taken a major beating.

Swan was on the telephone to them from Washington, relaying the news that the International Monetary Fund was concerned that the entire world financial system was on the brink of a complete meltdown; it was vital to inject confidence into the Australian system from the minute that the markets opened on the Monday. Because the Australian markets were amongst the first to open in the world on that morning, a market collapse here might have prompted further crises in other, larger markets. Macquarie's global exposure made it a vital litmus test for the entire financial system.

Policy-makers the world over believed that the situation was critical. The government was told that speculators were poised, ready to pounce, unless swift action was taken. Macquarie was in particular danger of being targeted, and any weakness could see a massive outflow of funds owned by institutions, knowing they'd be able to buy back more cheaply later.

The situation was so desperate that the government even felt the need to urgently brief Turnbull who, as opposition leader, responded by pledging support and promising to smooth the path of any necessary legislation through parliament. This sort of bipartisan political co-operation was more usually associated with military threats to national security, but this was exactly the degree of seriousness with which Rudd believed this threat needed to be treated.

The government's action had the effect of stabilising the financial system. Macquarie was saved; but it didn't take long for the bank to realise that the guarantee could assist it in making a great deal of money. The government's wholesale funding guarantee effectively provided the bank with the opportunity of raising cheap finance. This money could then be loaned, sometimes outside Australia, at a profit that the bank could tuck into bonuses and revenues. Over the next year, Macquarie's revenue surged by more than 110 per cent. Swan was reportedly furious at the way the bank had managed its way back to profitability, courtesy of the government's actions. Macquarie had paid handsomely to use the guarantee (generating about $200 million for the Commonwealth, according to some estimates). But, by using lateral thinking, the company was also able to move quickly to do what it does best — turn a profit.

Today, it's easy to minimise the severity of the dangers that the government confronted as the economic crisis gripped the world, swallowing opportunities and devouring savings in its wake. In the end, the timing and rhetoric accompanying each of the government's measures enabled Australia not just to avoid the worst of the impending depression, but to emerge from the crisis in far better shape than other economies.

Three major factors assisted this escape. The government stimulus, accompanied by interest-rate reductions, worked a treat in boosting confidence and providing genuine indications that policy settings had been appropriately corrected to provide a real boost to the economy at a vital time. Secondly, the intervention was targeted and timely: prompt government action had avoided an impending banking crisis, and the language used by ministers such as Swan and

Tanner reassured markets and consumers. Finally, the contribution of Chinese demand for raw materials and other external factors provided essential support for the economy as it fell to its nadir.

It was difficult for any fair-minded observer not to award the government top marks for the escape, but in the process it had acquired a new problem — managing the transition for a return to normality. The mining sector, for example, has surged ahead because of overseas (Chinese) demand. But the difficulty of finding skilled workers prepared to accept arduous conditions in the resources industry has inevitably led to wage rises and (as Glen Stevens has warned) the emergence of a two-speed economy.

By 2010, the government's net debt had surged to nearly 10 per cent of GDP (Stevens claimed that the country was in 'terrific shape'). By comparison to most other Western countries — which had debt stretching to more than 80 per cent, while in Japan it represented about 113 per cent of GDP — it was true that this figure remained small. This was no reason to spend the money, of course, but it did provide the government with an another reason to assert that investment in infrastructure, or even in simply building educational facilities, could quickly repay the expenditure.

Unfortunately, government debt is often confused with our comparatively high level of current foreign debt, which is known as the current-account deficit. In March 2010, this hit 5.5 per cent of GDP. That's the difference between receipts for our goods and services and the amount Australians paid to the rest of the world for goods and interest on borrowings. By the end of 2009, the total figure in this category was (about) $650 billion, or equivalent to something like six months' worth of production.

Of course, it's companies and businesses that owe this money — not the government — but it still means that (just in the first months of 2010) about $11 billion had to be paid out to foreigners simply to service debts. A further $6 billion (making a total of $17 billion) was added to foreign debt, this last figure being the difference between the value of imports compared to exports.

The other thing to note is that most of this huge amount is denominated in US dollars. When our dollar rises in value against the greenback, it's easy to quickly add to that bill without really feeling it — that is, until the money needs to be repaid. If our dollar decreases, the amount that must be paid off will increase. None of these factors constitute immediate problems, but they will need to be dealt with at some point in the future.

The trouble was that the crisis had completely wiped out the government's savings: the government's overall position went from a surplus of $20 billion to a deficit of $58 billion. Projections for the future ranged from a low of $130 to $150 billion that would need to be repaid to creditors. The turnaround hadn't taken long.

The annual government spend is (around) $345 billion. It's in this context that promises of savings need to be seen. Only a real restructuring can significantly curb expenditure. Against a massive number like this, any attempt to close an occasional government office, or to merge others for savings of a couple of million dollars, can be treated with the derision they deserve. (Nevertheless, every now and then a particularly egregious figure does surface from the deep. In March 2010, it was revealed that it was costing the Department of Finance $37 million a year simply to administer the plethora of benefits and entitlements available to politicians, which totalled $332 million in the financial year 2008–09.)

***

Kevin Rudd played a dramatic role in the resolution of this crisis. He certainly perceived his actions as being vital in averting collapse; nevertheless, it would be incorrect to minimise the continuing role of Wayne Swan in dealing with day-to-day problems — first in prompting Treasury for more information, and then in coming up with suggestions and possible courses of action to avoid the worst of the crisis. Swan provided critical stability as he directed Treasury and funnelled its advice through to the inner cabinet that was making all the vital decisions at the time.

Perhaps overwhelmed with work, Swan did not seek to play up his role in the media. He continued quietly behind the scenes, accepting that Rudd would dominate the news bulletins. Nevertheless, some senior officials within Treasury insisted privately that it would be wrong to minimise his responsibility for ensuring that the right policy prescriptions were implemented. It was only in 2010, during a joint press conference with the PM, that Swan finally insisted he would answer a question on a financial issue, rather than allowing Rudd to dominate the floor.

During this period, Rudd and Swan worked less intensely with Julia Gillard, the deputy prime minister, who was more involved in the design of government spending programs. She was perhaps the individual with the greatest degree of support within caucus — although that didn't mean that she could rely on a majority of the votes. Nevertheless, her popularity amongst (particularly Labor) voters guaranteed that she would be seen as a logical heir-apparent to Rudd.

Whenever she'd appeared on camera on the night of the 2007 election, the crowd at the tally room had burst into loud and spontaneous applause. She'd needed to stop speaking on a number of occasions in order to 'shoosh' the crowd. Upon assuming office, Gillard was instantly recognisable, and received genuine and significant expressions of support that came, perhaps surprisingly, from across the political spectrum. Particularly noticeable were the positive reactions that the deputy prime minister received from businesspeople and others who would not normally belong to a constituency that would back her. This led to a natural expectation amongst the public that Gillard would play a significant role in the government. However, the swift-moving nature of events meant that she didn't initially play a big role in helping avert the financial crisis.

Nevertheless, it had become obvious that cabinet wasn't acting as the government's decision-making body; gradually, a new core group was emerging that was making all the key policy choices. Gillard was the first to join this cadre, with Lindsay Tanner also joining at critical moments — although it would be incorrect to call it a gang of four at this stage. Tanner and Gillard had a history. Both were originally members of Victorian Labor's socialist left … but there are no political divides as steep as the ones over detail and tactics between people who otherwise share a similar general outlook, and during the mid-1980s there were intense divisions within the left about the correct policies to follow.

Tanner (by then an electorate assistant to a Labor senator) was pushing the faction to 'modernise' by supporting the economic and institutional reforms of the Hawke government. Gillard was leading her own grouping, a curious amalgamation of disillusioned former communists and others who believed in a transition to a society dominated by unsentimental economic analysis.

The divide between the two left-wing policy positions may appear to be arcane; but, with Labor in power, and simple ideological solutions to complex modern problems no longer being credible, the instinctive way that the two politicians saw the world became increasingly important. It's been suggested that the new divide is not so much along a left/right axis, but rather a different way of viewing institutions and the workings of society, compared to the role of the individual. This appears to better explain the origin of the theoretical disagreements between the two. Nevertheless, according to others from the Victorian party, the hostility that was engendered between the two young people took a long time to dissipate.

In 1993, they clashed over the preselection of the then safe Labor seat of Melbourne, and Tanner won. Three years later, Gillard had become (the right-wing) Premier John Brumby's chief of staff. When, in 1998, the left refused to back Gillard's attempt to become the federal member for the seat of Lalor, she turned to the right for support (resulting in another split within the party's socialist left, with many individuals supporting her preselection for the seat). This background had contributed to a certain distance between the two in the past, although any lingering tension appeared to dissipate as the government continued.

The key role in policy formation was, of course, Rudd's. He declared that this was a 'rolling economic version of a national security crisis'. On the evidence of Rudd's interactions with other politicians and his staff, there is every reason believe that he felt he played the vital role in ensuring Australia's escape from economic catastrophe.

The duties of a prime minister are not codified. The position is, extraordinarily, not even mentioned in the Constitution. There was never any intention by the founding fathers that anyone would aggregate power to the extent that occurred. Rudd was the first Labor prime minister to have arrogated to himself absolute power to make the ministry and to enunciate policy.

When Rudd did this initially (in opposition), there was no attempt to take on the established power structures within the party. It was very much a loose arrangement. Rudd would announce the decisions of the factions while pretending he'd chosen people all on his own. He did indeed promote a couple of people (such as Peter Garrett) who were bereft of factional support and might otherwise not have received promotion. Nevertheless, it became more and more apparent, as his term in office continued, that he hadn't managed to engender much personal loyalty.

Some close observers suggest it was likely that his method of dealing with the GFC exacerbated Rudd's problem in building support within caucus. The swift pace of the crisis, and the need for immediate responses, demanded an exclusionary attitude. In other words, Rudd (along with Swan, Gillard and, perhaps to a lesser extent, Tanner) decided what to do and then told the others what was happening.

The caucus didn't challenge this working structure while the country was faced with the crisis—nor while Rudd's personal support remained high in the polls. No one was working against Rudd because, while his approval ratings continued to pierce previous ceilings, there was just no point. Any challenge was unthinkable.

Nevertheless, a subtle difference entered interactions between Rudd and others. To some Labor MPs, it almost appeared similar to the strange case of Dr Jekyll and Mr Hyde—multiple personalities within the one body. In public he remained 'Kevin', the marvellously down-to-earth prime minister who always had time for a good yak with any punter about the concerns of normal life. With staff he became 'Prime Minister', a hard-driving autocrat who expected utter dedication, instant obedience, and 150 per cent effort, all the time. He often announced his disappointment with those who were working for him (although he did reward those who met his high standards with what passed for warmth and friendship). For a third grouping (an ever-increasing number of party staff and Labor politicians), he became simply 'Rudd'—but that's getting ahead of the story. At this time, people were still willing to offer him loyalty and respect; often, if they received the opportunity, they'd throw in friendship as well, because it's very difficult to knock back an overture from the prime minister. It was just that he didn't really seem to need many friends.

***

There was one other significant aspect of the Global Financial Crisis. This was a brief (but ultimately futile) attempt by Rudd to inject some ideological meaning into it. In January 2009, the prime minister turned his hand to analysis, writing an essay on the crisis for *The Monthly*. It was, he insisted, an event of 'truly seismic significance ... marking a turning point between one epoch and the next'. He asserted that the 'great neo-liberal experiment of the past

30 years has failed. The challenge for Social Democrats today is to recast the role of the state [with] a ... comprehensive philosophical framework for the future'.

Rudd insisted that he understood the nature and origin of the crisis, and that it was intimately connected with the evolution of modern capitalism. This 7,000-word revolutionary philosophical dissection of the market-dominated system could have read like a demolition job on all the economic reforms of the Hawke and Keating governments, but at that point the wrecking-ball paused, hanging in the air.

There is no great advantage in wading through the unusual interpretations or inconsistencies contained in the economic historical narrative outlined by Rudd; the most significant question was, how did the prime minister propose fixing the system? His system would be both 'compassionate' and 'open-hearted', but there was a surprising absence of specific measures to change things. The entire endeavour represented a breathless critique, but he didn't begin to elaborate in any practical way how his own vision might be brought to fruition.

In a final burst of geographic imagery, Rudd insisted that 'seismic changes are underway, faultlines yielding to fractures which in time may yield to even deeper tectonic shifts'. He asserted that only government was capable of building a fairer and more resilient order: 'How could it possibly now be argued that the minimalist state of which the neo-liberals have dreamt could somehow be of sufficient potency to respond to the maximalist challenge we have been left ... government is not the intrinsic evil that neo-liberals have argued it is.'

Rudd's answer was bureaucracy writ large across the economic landscape, combined with technocratic armies of public servants embracing 'both individual freedom and fairness, a project designed for the many, not just the few'. Like a preacher on steroids, Rudd the denouncer of neo-liberal economics was excoriating the sinners.

On the last day of March 2009, Rudd was in London for a summit meeting of the G20 world leaders. The day before the meeting began, Rudd joined British prime minister Gordon Brown (a dour Scot and the son of a minister in the Church of Scotland) in a simple forum at St Paul's Cathedral. The two men sermonised about the need to reshape the market system to ensure that it incorporated human values, instead of simply being driven by greed.

Both men spoke sincerely; nevertheless, Brown's popularity in the UK was plunging. British observers couldn't help but notice that Brown had been chancellor of the exchequer (or treasurer) for an entire decade prior to his elevation to the prime ministership — a position that should have enabled him to implement reform, if only he'd known how to achieve it.

Rudd had been particularly active in the run-up to the G20 meeting in attempting to shape opinion and develop a working agenda for the leaders. He'd already nominated this institution as the one best able to organise a global response to the crisis, because it included countries that possessed more than 80 per cent of the world's major banks. He'd spent the preceding couple of days working urgently in London with Brown, telephoning other leaders and attempting to broker a consensus.

As a young man, Rudd had been a particularly committed Christian, and at St Paul's he used the tempestuous language of a reformist minister to denounce the modern economic system. 'Unfettered free markets became worshipped as a god,' Rudd declaimed, 'and we know that god was false'.

'It is only by restoring balance between market and government,' he continued, 'between the individual and community, that we can rebuild trust in an economic system that encourages each and cares for all'.

No one doubted the intensity of his belief as he spoke. There was no suggestion that he was making a facile equation by comparing the desire for material wealth with a direct challenge to the nourishing of humanity through transcendental values. The grotesque image of a false god appeared an appropriate metaphor for modern culture's abasement before the desire for wealth and baubles. The attempt to evoke moral values and to incorporate them into a new economy that was more appropriate for contemporary life sounded like a clarion call for the New World Order.

Britain's prime minister insisted that markets need morals. Apparently unaware of the cut-throat, competitive instincts of Australian small and family businesses, Brown even asserted that global markets could benefit by displaying more of their ethical values. His Scottish Presbyterian voice rang clearly through the gilded Anglican cathedral with the stentorian tones of his ancestors as he spoke the words, 'And I say to you plainly, this old world, of the old Washington consensus, is over. And what comes in its place is up to us'.

Brown insisted that Rudd had become 'a prime minister of great courage, a leader of great conscience, and a visionary for reform.' It was indeed a glowing tribute. Yet the rhetorical challenge that Rudd has thrown down was not taken up. In due course, the United States was to toughen the rules governing its financial sector, but the global economic system wasn't reshaped to better 'reflect and respect the values that we celebrate in everyday life'. Nothing was done to fix the underlying problems, let alone address the supposed inequities that Rudd had once appeared so exercised about.

Speeches like the one at St Paul's suggested that the PM had a much broader vision of what life was about. Increasingly, the political debate had been framed around possessions and consumption, but it now appeared that Australia had a leader who was looking beyond material wealth — someone who understood that real meaning had to be constructed out of relationships, rather than bigger TVs, larger houses, and faster cars. The ease and familiarity that Rudd habitually displayed when dealing with religious topics emphasised this dimension of his personality.

Polling showed that Australians liked the fact that Rudd did not present as a 'normal' politician. Focus groups showed that he was increasingly associated with positive attributes — ones that incorporated transcendental values. The danger was that if people ever began to suspect that the values that were projecting onto him were false, they might never believe him again.

***

By mid-2010, global markets were wobbling again, but earlier there had appeared no doubt that the stimulus had supported the economy through the crisis. The Reserve Bank began taking away the fruit bowl at the party by gradually raising interest rates, warning publicly of the increasing dangers posed by the mining boom further skewing the economy. In March, the quarterly current-account deficit had blown out to a massive 5.5 per cent of GDP, or $17.5 billion, fuelled in particular by car imports.

If the deficit increased too much, there was a real risk that a crisis of confidence in the dollar might further erode the government's ability to control what was happening. Rudd's initial promise of a new, creative, sustainable economy had been overtaken by massive Chinese investment; this was delivering vital support to the economy, but at the cost of postponing the necessary adjustments to guarantee a long-term viability for the nation that was not dependent on overseas demand and the ability to dig things out of the ground and sell them.

Raising interest rates is a blunt way of attempting to influence the economy, but it is the only weapon in the central bank's armoury. Increasing rates works to suppress demand, but it also results in a rising dollar. Theoretically, consumers switch to foreign goods, leading to lay-offs in the labour market and a further dampening of the economy. However, this leads to complications, ones that are particularly relevant for a Labor government that must pay attention to the difficulties faced by its core constituency.

As 2010 continued, it became more obvious that the Reserve Bank's desires didn't necessarily reflect the political requirements of the government. Both wielded instruments that could, very bluntly, affect what was happening by stimulating or depressing different aspects of the macro-economy. But the politicians and the bankers found their objectives increasingly divergent. The other problem was that the continuing economic crises were forcing the abandonment of more significant reforms — the very sorts of things that Rudd had advocated in his *Monthly* essay.

By 2010, the detailed qualitative polling being commissioned by the major political parties made it clear that 'the economy' would be a significant factor, but not the decisive issue in the campaign, because both parties were seen as viable economic managers. At a stroke, this deprived the coalition of what had been the most potent weapon in its armoury. It was always going to be difficult for the coalition to capitalise on vague general concerns about debt. The more it jumped up and down campaigning about this issue, the more it increased pressure to identify exactly which areas a coalition razor-gang would target.

Underpinning the incredible economic performance had been the staggering quantity of resources going to China, which had become Australia's biggest trading partner (surpassing Japan and the US). In 2010, a deal worth an amazing $60 billion (Australia's biggest export contract ever) for gas from Queensland was signed by Resources Minister Martin Ferguson in Beijing. This followed hard on the heels of another worth $50 billion for gas from Western Australia.

Perhaps the most startling evidence of Rudd's success at redefining the Australian political debate was buried deep in a Newspoll that sent analysts reeling, if only briefly, as autumn's leaves began turning gold in 2010. For the first time since it took office, voters considered Labor the party best placed to handle the economy, with a record 44 per cent approval. In the depths of the financial crisis, the government had managed to equal the Liberal's traditional dominance in this field, but it never managed to pull ahead before being dragged back. Now, close to the election and at almost the best time possible, in an election year it looked like Labor would finally be rewarded for its successful stewardship of the economy.

Rudd had begun the construction of his own economic narrative striding down a hill at his childhood home in Nambour, declaring himself an 'economic conservative'. His moleskins and R.M. Williams boots — the uniform of the unadventurous National Party heartland — provided the perfect visual reinforcement of the message.

As soon as the financial crisis broke, that narrative became unstable. Rudd's public writing quickly changed as he suggested that he was not a believer in the traditional economic story and that there was an urgent need for change. There was a break in the transmission of his earlier relaxed-and-comfortable attitude to the economy. The screen flickered to introduce a new Kevin, a man who'd supposedly always been aware of the contradictions inherent within the capitalist system. This person had always understood the need to find a new and better way to arrange the economy by making it more responsive to the needs of the ordinary people who made up society. For a short time, it became more and more difficult to reconcile the current prime minister with the opposition leader who had emphasised his economic conservatism before the election.

Then, unaccountably, the crisis seemed to resolve itself. Nothing more was heard of the stinging critique of the economic system that had been delivered so powerfully at St Paul's.

The South Australian Labor politician Rod Sawford claims that his dad came up with a formula that has proven infallible, since it was first applied in 1961, to determine if a federal government would be re-elected. It relied on three indicators: unemployment and interest rates, and inflation levels. According to Sawford's Law, the government would be booted out if any two of these rose over an electoral cycle.

In 2010, although interest rates were kicking up, they were still much lower than they had been when the government came to power in 2007. Inflation was under control, and fears that the financial crisis might again result in huge queues of unemployed people hadn't been realised. Labor thought it had every reason to be confident that the electorate would reward the party for its handling of the economy.

INTERLUDE

Peter

It shouldn't really have been a surprise on the morning after the 2007 election when Peter Costello announced he wouldn't be standing for the leadership. Aside from anything else, such as his sheer exhaustion and frustration after having endured 11 years as treasurer (and the possibility, at the age of 50, just one month older than Kevin Rudd, of beginning a new life and career), there was the problem of Malcolm.

Peter's brother, Tim, had begun describing Turnbull as a 'force of nature' while they campaigned together for a republic. 'When you're on the wrong end of Malcolm, it's terrifying,' Tim told the ABC's *Four Corners*. 'The thunder in the face and often quite spontaneous, (even) over-the-top tongue-lashing. There was irritation, there was annoyance, there was, "If you just shut up and listen to me, you'll understand why I'm right and you're completely wrong." '

The relationship between Peter Costello and Malcolm Turnbull had never been much better. At the end of 2005, while he was still a backbencher, the multi-millionaire had commissioned his own private (and detailed) research paper that recommended 280 possible changes to the tax system. Unhelpfully, from the government's perspective, he'd chosen to release the research publicly and then gone on to spruik the need for further significant changes to the tax system. Perhaps because Turnbull was slightly older than Costello, he appeared to be in more of a hurry and, according to another MP, this 'very understandably got up Peter's nose'.

Malcolm wasn't really the sort of supporter whom anyone would want sitting behind them on the front bench.

Before the election, Costello was well aware there was a significant chance that the government would be thrown out. If the coalition lost, there was little doubt in anyone's mind that Howard would depart. Logically, that would have left the leadership to Costello. The real question was, could he ever achieve anything with Turnbull sitting ambitiously behind him, stalking his every move?

The omens weren't good. Robert Menzies was the last opposition leader who'd taken his party all the way from electoral defeat and back to government again. This meant that since 1949, nobody who's inherited the leadership in the immediate wake of a loss has ever managed to return in triumph to the Lodge. And, of course, the last time there'd been a single-term government was back in the Great Depression. Costello must have believed that if he stayed on, he'd end up working incredibly hard, but only to warm the seat so someone else could take over in either 18 months' time or after the next election had been lost.

On the night of the election, Howard publicly nominated Costello as his successor — but, critically, he hadn't bothered to reconfirm this with the former treasurer. The magnitude of the fall changed everything. Costello spent some time alone, and telephoned the former PM before tentatively deciding to retire. By the next morning, his decision was firm — he'd decided that the chalice he was (finally) being offered was poisoned. The offer of leadership had come too late.

Shortly afterwards, he also rejected an offer from Brendan Nelson to become shadow treasurer, deciding instead to retire to the backbench. But once he was there, Costello loomed like a spectre. His presence was rarely referred to, but surreptitious glances were often cast his way whenever the opposition leadership was being discussed or the debate turned to financial matters. As Australia's longest-serving treasurer, he'd guided the country from deficit to prosperity, navigated through the Asian economic crisis, flicked away concerns about the millennium bug, and created a fund that could be built on for the future. No one could really believe he was just going to sit there doing nothing. No matter how many assurances he gave that he was writing his memoirs and would leave politics, everyone wanted to see the proof. While he retained his seat in the house, the possibility always seemed to be there …

As well as that, Costello seemed to be having some difficulty in packing up and walking off into the wilderness. Word quickly got around that he hadn't been as successful as he'd anticipated in picking up directorships of major companies. It appeared that most of the large corporations had decided that Labor would be in office for quite some time; there was no need to antagonise the new government by appointing a new board member whose utility might be marginal at best.

In addition, there was also another not-so-subtle message emanating from some of the larger companies that had felt the treasurer's wrath or indifference in the past: he hadn't done them any favours in the past, so they weren't going to offer him anything now. Memories are long, in business as well as in politics. The expected plethora of board positions dried up.

Most of the time, Costello sat quietly during parliamentary debates, poring over a computer and occasionally tapping at the keys. Outside the chamber, he was preparing his memoirs for publication, and he managed to appear completely preoccupied with them. Nevertheless, every now and then (and normally when Rudd or Swan were attacking his economic record), he'd suddenly awaken from this apparent slumber to insert a shouted, derisory interjection into the debate taking place on the floor.

It was interesting to watch his face during question time. He'd take his seat, occasionally sharing a word or two with Kevin Andrews, who was sitting next to him. Then, ostentatiously, the laptop would be opened and, as far as any observer could tell, Costello would simply vanish into his own world, completely oblivious to anything that was happening around him.

But his occasional petulant outbursts, when he believed someone was traducing his political record, seemed to belie his carefully crafted appearance. He was paying attention to what was being said, after all. First, his eyes would wander up towards the centre table, and then his head would follow. The smooth gears of his mind would formulate a phrase or a single sentence, just enough to dispatch the long-winded critique of his former policies to oblivion. But it was the next few seconds that best seemed to reveal the seething torment inside.

He appeared desperate to focus intently on the debate, but instead he'd force his head to bend back towards the computer screen. Perhaps it was just my imagination, but his facial muscles seemed to be twitching in frustration. He continued muttering quietly to himself, appearing desperate to participate, yet refusing himself the satisfaction of doing so.

He'd been holding himself in check his entire life, and perhaps this didn't seem to be the right moment to break free. His life had been an ironic picture of restraint in a laissez-faire political party that urged individuals to 'go for it' and to advance themselves. He'd devoted himself to a group that emphasised the central role of individual ambition, yet he was unable to put himself forward, and seemed surprised when the party failed to accept that he was the best person to lead it until was too late for the offer to be taken up.

The tragedy of Costello had three dimensions. The first was timing, as the ambition of an enthusiastic younger man met its match in an older and more skilled practitioner of political art. It wasn't that the youth had any difficulty for his own part in putting others to the sword — it was just that, this time, he'd finally met his match.

In 2008, Costello could still, if only just, remember what it was like to be in opposition. It was in 1990, at the tender age of 32, that he'd stepped over the still-breathing cadaver of Roger Shipton, the sitting member for Higgins in the lovely, affluent, inner-eastern suburbs of Melbourne, to get there. Like Nelson, Costello had fought a particularly vicious battle to enter parliament.

Shipton had proved to be an undistinguished representative of the only electorate in the country that had previously hosted two Liberal prime ministers, Harold Holt and John Gorton. Higgins was a rolled-gold seat, and the electorate seemed ideally chosen to send a third future Liberal PM to Canberra. Costello was a young man in a hurry.

The young man's stellar trajectory continued. Although Andrew Peacock had lost an election to Bob Hawke, this didn't necessarily augur ill for the aspiring young conservative's future political career. John Hewson took over the Liberals in the wake of the defeat, and Costello had a rapid rise through the ranks of the shadow ministry before supporting Alexander Downer to take over as leader in 1994.

Downer's leadership imploded in farcical disaster within a year. At the time, an ambitious Howard had been doing everything possible to regain the leadership — including, as it later turned out, promising that he'd stand down and simply hand over the prime ministership to Costello in one-and-a-half terms, if only he could get a turn in the job first. Young Peter, perhaps naively, appeared to believe him.

Costello backed Howard as the smelly carcass of his one-time colleague was finally cut down, becoming treasurer in 1996. He remained in that job during Howard's second term, beginning in 1998. He continued as treasurer for the third term, beginning in 2001, and then the fourth in 2004.

Howard wasn't stupid. The PM ensured that there were always

other rivals who could be used to divide up the support base of any possible challenge to his leadership. Costello never had a straight run at the prize; there was always somebody else being nurtured as a possible rival to his ambition.

At first it was Peter Reith, who had once claimed that every politician had a field marshal's baton in their knapsack. Maybe that was why Howard appointed him defence minister.

Perhaps by accident, Howard had stumbled on a way of keeping Costello's ambitions in check. After Reith, there was a succession of others (normally moderate or right-wing candidates, whose support base would directly cut into backing that Costello could otherwise count upon), whose aspirations the PM successively fostered before he'd move on to the next one. After Reith came Tony Abbott; then Malcolm Turnbull; and then Mal Brough.

The reality was that Costello never had enough support within the party to challenge Howard until the last desperate days of 2007. In the wake of the APEC meeting in Sydney (with an unpopular Howard publicly ruminating over his own future), Costello might finally have had enough backing to overthrow the prime minister and seize the job for himself. It would have been risky, with an election to be held within months; it would have been touch and go, but it offered the best and perhaps the only chance the coalition had of hanging onto power.

He squibbed it. Some three years later, Gillard decided she wouldn't risk being trapped in the same position when the polls were showing a similar loss of confidence in the prime minister, although that's getting ahead of the story.

At that time, Costello had told the *Sydney Morning Herald*'s Peter Hartcher, 'My view was that there was no point in challenging unless you had a chance of winning. There's no point in issuing a challenge and walking out of the cabinet, weakening the party, and losing.' Perhaps Costello needed to have a chat with Paul Keating, although the former PM had already dismissed any possibility that

Costello had the guts to challenge, 'because he has a heart the size of a caraway seed'.

If the first part of the Costello tragedy revolved around his interactions with Howard, the second part was his failure to build an ideological basis for his ambitions. He'd always been seen as a thrusting, ruthless member of the party, the ideologue who supposedly combined progressive liberal social views with a hard-nosed, new-right economic rationalism. But it was always, in fact, a bit difficult to tell exactly what he stood for.

After it had become obvious that Howard wasn't going to go in July 2006, Costello indicated that he'd be fleshing out a new ideological agenda for the party; but this idea quickly fizzled after a couple of lacklustre speeches. He failed to outline any particular new direction, although this may have been because, although his natural economic inclinations were more to the right, he depended desperately on the left of the party for the votes he'd need to become leader. Certainly, at that time, he injected no significant new ideas into the political debate.

But this wasn't just Costello's problem. In 2008, with the Liberals in opposition, there was a need for clearly enunciated core doctrines that they could articulate and believe in. But a decade of managing government on a day-to-day basis appeared to have sapped the party's ideological unity and strength.

Perhaps the biggest indictment of the failure of the party to base its electoral ambitions on coherent policy was demonstrated in state politics, where the Liberals had enormous difficulty in a string of elections across the country. Despite some tremendously unpopular Labor governments in 2007, the party was out of office everywhere in Australia. Even by 2008, the Liberals were only able to form a minority government in Western Australia with the backing of the Nationals and independents.

The losses continued. In Tasmania, the incumbent Labor Party managed to form a new government by entering into a coalition with the Greens. The Liberal Party did gain a majority of votes in South Australia in 2010, but not in enough of the electorates that would have allowed it to form government. Still, the situation was much better than in the immediate aftermath of the 2007 election, when the highest elected Liberal in the country had been the lord mayor of Brisbane.

In 2006, Costello insisted, 'We have got to get our organisation together, we have got to work on policy'. But there was still one other vital ingredient lacking, and until this could be fixed there was no chance that the Liberals could return to government: they needed discipline, because many didn't yet seem to realise they were in opposition. There was no one with Costello's experience and gravitas who could bring the dissidents into line and focus the party on adopting the policies that it needed to regain government.

These separate problems united in a perfect storm, with each one rebounding on the others, causing further chaos. The lack of a firmly agreed policy base led to bickering, which in turn undermined the organisation, which led to ill-disciplined members. 'At times, everyone seems to have their own idea about policy and believe that their idea is best,' a Liberal who is heavily involved in Parliamentary committee work told me at the time. 'Unfortunately, they don't have a clue.'

This MP believed that if the party made better use of the committee system, they'd have fewer policy disagreements. 'It gives you a chance to examine the flaws of what the government is doing without having to put your own ideology up there.' But in order to do this, the politicians needed to trust and put their faith in the leadership. Unfortunately, none of the putative candidates on offer had managed to build up a large group of cross-factional supporters, and the divisions over matters of principle magnified themselves into personal feuds.

And this was Costello's third fatal flaw. All the time that the Liberals were in government, he'd failed to spend any time building up a support base. Because he never managed to outline a separate ideological agenda to Howard's, Costello had to depend on personal relationships for support. He seemed to find more in common, socially, with the more articulate members of the party's left, a faction that was also frustrated with Howard — although their objections to the prime minister centred on policy issues rather than personal ambition. His policies, however, resonated more strongly with the conservatives in the party.

That's why it was obvious to everyone that Costello didn't have the numbers when Howard finally demanded that he either put up or shut up. As well as that, he'd never get them to back him either. There was just not enough goodwill within the party to support him becoming leader.

Nevertheless, in 2008, while Costello remained in parliament and Nelson was struggling, the possibility that the former treasurer might step back into the fray remained alive. Costello insisted he would not challenge, so journalists immediately asserted that this left open the possibility that Nelson might step aside in his favour. It wasn't until just before his memoirs were released that Costello finally ruled out any possibility that he'd stay in politics. This was the announcement that Nelson had been waiting for, prompting him to ask for a vote of confidence at exactly the same moment. The choice was stark: Nelson or Turnbull. It turned out that Costello had never really been in the picture after all.

CHAPTER FOUR

The Great Moral Challenge

'Climate change is the great moral challenge of our generation.'
Kevin Rudd, opening the National Climate Change Summit, 31 March 2007

'The great moral, economic and environmental challenge of our age is climate change.'
Kevin Rudd, ALP national conference, 27 April 2007

The entire Rudd project was built on one big but simple idea: climate change was real, and normal politics could not deal with the problem. This elevated the issue to another level: it became driven by a moral imperative. From the minute he became leader of the Labor Party, Rudd placed global warming at the forefront of the political debate, asserting it was an issue that could not be ignored. Everything was bundled up in this concept. And at first it paid off, beautifully.

Rudd's first official act as prime minister was to ratify the Kyoto Protocol on climate change. As the news was announced in Bali, delegates who were preparing for the imminent UN conference stopped what they were doing and stood to applaud him loudly. At the time, an organiser insisted that the delegates had acted spontaneously, emotionally inspired by the news from Canberra.

Now that Australia had signed, the US was the only industrialised country in the world still refusing to agree to take action to curb its greenhouse emissions. The omens for a carefully constructed global bureaucratic solution to the issue, involving the trading of carbon permits, appeared good.

A week later, little more than a fortnight after his election, Rudd's RAAF aeroplane touched down at Denpasar airport in Bali, Indonesia. It was his first trip overseas as prime minister and, fittingly, it represented the fulfilment of a promise that had become a major issue in the election campaign. Rudd, Garrett, and Wong (whose appointment as the environment super-supremo had surprised many observers, perhaps even Garrett himself) were joining representatives from 187 other countries to start negotiations for a new climate treaty to replace the Kyoto accord — one that would come into force in the year 2012.

Everyone realised that the initial step would just be symbolic, but that didn't minimise its importance. By travelling to Bali and becoming seriously involved in the negotiations to develop a follow-on treaty, Rudd was asserting that he could forge and then wield a new form of cultural power that saw Australia as a critical broker on the international stage. The country would act to facilitate international dialogue before eventually reconciling the opposing points of view and hammering out agreements.

The ambition was huge, but it didn't seem out of range for Rudd who, as a former diplomat, could be expected to know about such things. Most Australians may not have been certain where their country fitted in global rankings. It would obviously never be a military or financial superpower — but our sporting teams had managed to do consistently well, and the Olympic medal tally always showed Australia near the top. Perhaps the country could become a diplomatic powerhouse as well.

And there was reason for hope. Australia had done well in previous climate-change negotiations. Although most industrialised countries were required to hack away at emissions in 2012 by an average of just over 5 per cent, special pleading had ensured the inclusion of clause 3.7 (later branded the 'Australian clause'), which allowed the country's baseline level of emissions to be set at 1990 — a year in which large-scale land clearing had resulted in a particularly high level of emissions. This meant that the hurdle to be jumped was set at a lower level than for other countries, a compromise that was thought worthwhile back in 1997 during the negotiations leading up to the protocol, on the understanding that Australia would actually sign. Signing was obviously just a symbolic gesture: if emissions remained at 108 per cent of 1990 levels (a target Howard was on track to achieve), Australia would have complied with the treaty. Already it was obvious that the forthcoming treaty would be critical. Unless all parties — developed and developing nations — made deep cuts to their emissions, there was no way that scientists believed the levels of greenhouse gases in the atmosphere would stabilise. If this aim was to be achieved, all countries had to be genuine participants in the treaty negotiations. What was required was a unified international agreement, with every country playing its part. Under Howard, Australia's role in climate-change negotiations had been to surreptitiously block or place obstacles in the way of progress towards agreed reduction-targets. The Australian negotiators had previously been allied closely to the US, but informal contacts with OPEC countries had also been effectively used to slip sand into the slowly grinding wheels of the treaty process. But now all that had supposedly changed.

No one who'd listened to Rudd speak so eloquently and emotionally about climate change before the election had any doubt that he was a true believer in the need to curb emissions. As he prepared to head to Bali, Rudd suddenly announced an even more stunning objective: not simply to sign up and ratify the Kyoto Protocol, but also to go further and 'bridge the gap' between the developed world and other countries. The developed world insisted that everyone had to slash emissions; the developing world didn't want to cut its emissions until its citizens had reached something close to Western living standards. This gap was rapidly becoming a chasm.

'This is going to be tough,' Rudd insisted, 'full of hard negotiations, of course, but I'd rather be around the negotiating table then absent from the field'. The words seemed to promise that the new prime minister would be rolling his sleeves up to do some personal arm-twisting in an attempt to achieve real progress. With his experience in foreign affairs, Rudd was thought to understand the intricate and complex terrain of international treaty-making. Perhaps he would be able to achieve a breakthrough of which the country could be proud. Australia was already presenting a new draft proposal calling for all nations to do more to fight climate change, with rich countries striving for deep cuts to their current emissions while developing nations would act to stem any rises in their emissions.

'We have,' Rudd insisted, 'national and international responsibilities to the next generation. We've got obligations to the region and the planet. We take those very seriously.'

The focus of the conference was very clearly on establishing a framework for whatever international agreement would take over after the Kyoto Protocol ended. Rudd travelled to Bali with an express commitment of slashing Australia's carbon emissions by 60 per cent by the year 2050. This massive target understandably attracted equally huge headlines.

By contrast, the initial European Union proposals, which focused on developed countries reducing their emissions by a minimum of 20 per cent (and up to 40 per cent) by the year 2020, sounded pusillanimous. The difference was, of course, critical. Australian businesses, particularly the miners and coal producers, weren't really all that concerned about the long-term targets. Although they were opposed to the reductions, an important factor for them was to postpone action for as long as possible.

The adoption of out-year targets would postpone the need for action. In Charles Dickens' book *David Copperfield*, the character Wilkins Micawber lives out his life in hopeful expectation, fortified by the firm belief that 'something will turn up'. Once his role in this famous 19th-century novel is finished, Micawber and his family emigrate to Australia. If the fictional character had ever produced descendants, it seems probable they'd now have senior roles in the Mining Council. This organisation perceived any deferment of action as a 'win', because, like Micawber, they were confident of eventual victory. At this time, the government was extremely attentive to the concerns of the industry, recognising its fundamental place in the economy, and bending over backwards to accommodate its concerns. Anything obviating the immediate need to introduce measures that would be harmful to business and the economy was to be welcomed, if not embraced. But it turned out that it was not just the miners who wanted to postpone reductions. There were other significant lobbies at work within the government that wanted to achieve exactly the same result.

The international argument was over timing. America under Bush was completely opposed to any nominated targets. This offered the opportunity for Rudd to play a diplomatic role in attempting to reconcile positions that were diametrically opposed by, firstly, establishing common ground, and then by finding a consensus position that different nations were prepared to adopt.

The difficulty with this approach was that it was based upon a diplomatic negotiator's view of the world. It assumed that the primary goal of the talks was to achieve agreement; but, in order to do this, it was necessary to suspend belief in the science that underlay the need for a treaty in the first place. This was the single greatest problem Rudd would continue bumping into during the next two years. His objectives were based on praxis — the attempt to find practical solutions to intractable problems.

Another point that increasingly rankled with many observers was Rudd's personal style. It was a minor point, but (with the apparent exception of purchasing a dual-fuel car) the PM did not appear to have changed his lifestyle in any way to make it more greenhouse-friendly. Conservative commentators had great fun in pointing out that his own responsibility for generating emissions and damaging the environment as he constantly traversed the country (and the world) by plane meant that Rudd was personally contributing more greenhouse gases than virtually any other Australian. Rudd's weak counter to this charge was that this didn't matter if it was in a good cause and he was managing to achieve something important. This was *realpolitik* on a grand scale: the ends justified the means.

It's been suggested in retrospect that Rudd's entire approach to negotiating a climate-change agreement resembled the diplomatic style of Metternich and Kissinger. Both of these negotiators had been indicted (during their respective lifetimes) for a lack of moral principles. This had become a burning question to many on the left of politics. Was Rudd really engaging in a genuine attempt to deal with an evolving underlying issue, or did his interventions merely represent shallow attempts to preserve the status quo? Was he deliberately trying to forge a treaty — any treaty — simply for its own sake? If so, and if the threat of global warming was real, it would quickly be perceived as an inadequate and conservative solution to a dynamic modern problem.

It's important to note that the head of the US delegation, Harian Watson, was also insisting that 'We're not here to be a roadblock. We're committed to a successful conclusion [of the Bali talks].' Nevertheless, America demonstrated no willingness to negotiate on any significant issues. This begged the question: which was more important, achieving agreement or actually doing something that might deal with impending climate change? Right from the beginning of Rudd's involvement in climate-change negotiations, the Greens began raising serious questions about whether he was genuine about dealing with the problem.

The Australian media, however, didn't attribute any degree of moral ambiguity to Rudd. All his speeches clearly proclaimed his personal acceptance and understanding of the science behind global warming. Once this was established, there could be no doubt that the continued production of greenhouse gases represented an existential crisis for modern civilisation. The domestic political need was to act; the international statesman's need was to ensure concerted action. Bali was the first test of Rudd's ability to achieve a significant breakthrough on the world stage.

As a Reuters report at the time insisted, Rudd stole the show at the Bali climate talks. As well as the initial standing ovation it had earlier received, the size of the Australian contingent appeared to act as a physical demonstration that the country was serious about the issue. This also had an obvious downside, as the media began to calculate the massive amount of gases that had been generated by aircraft flying 12,000 delegates to Indonesia, as well as the surprising use of highly environmentally damaging refrigerants to cool the talkfest. A massive stockpile of hydro-fluorocarbon cylinders near the resort complex at Nusa Dua, where the meeting was taking place, was slowly but noticeably leaking toxic greenhouse gas. It took a fortnight of intense, intricate, and delicate negotiations between the Indonesian delegation hosting the talks, the contracting staff, and delegates before the issue was resolved. It was probably fortuitous that the conference had, by then, concluded; but for genuine environmental activists, matters like this cast a pall over the whole proceedings. It was difficult for many to treat this particular global response as if it was in any way a real attempt to deal with the problems.

The compromise deal that resulted contained no targets and no dates. It did, however, fulfil the normal rules of diplomatic negotiations. The agreement with was 'hammered out' at a 'dramatic final session' that included 'standing ovations' and 'a last-minute plea for compromise'. The US delegation was booed and then applauded after it backed down (supposedly in response to a Papua New Guinean delegate who told Washington to just 'get out of the way'). The negotiators (it would have been inappropriate to call them diplomats by the end of the talks) were exhausted.

A solar-powered taxi had transported delegates to the talks. Unfortunately, this didn't appear to be the way of the future. The (particularly ugly) vehicle cost the same price as two Ferraris. In the same way, it became difficult not to conclude that the entire event represented nothing more than a PR stunt, designed to look impressive, but with no practical effect. Nevertheless, Rudd returned to Australia bearing the equivalent of Neville Chamberlain's statement at Munich: a piece of paper to wave around, this time promising an end to global warming.

The compromise deal did introduce guidelines that extended and strengthened the clean-development mechanism, a dubious system allowing wealthy nations to purchase nominal reductions in emissions from developing countries. Everyone practised chanting the new mantra in unison. There would be 'deep cuts in global emissions', although nobody appeared to need to take much action to achieve this. Reductions would be introduced gradually. In reality, Rudd had failed to bridge the gap between America and Europe, let alone the other countries of the developing world. His first trip onto the diplomatic stage as a serious negotiator had ended in failure. Perhaps more surprisingly, at this stage no one had even begun to focus on the attitude of China and India to the putative negotiations to establish a new global framework to combat increasing CO_2 emissions. This was to become a major diplomatic disaster.

***

None of the obvious conclusions were drawn at the time. After all, Rudd's rhetoric had been unimpeachable — even to lobbies that were extremely concerned about the urgent threat posed by climate change. Polls consistently demonstrated that most people had no doubt that increasing CO_2 emissions were directly responsible for the damage to the atmosphere. The mainstream media reported the linkage as if it was an established fact.

This was more or less where the issue rested. The public was assured that Rudd was continuing to work behind the scenes for the next key negotiation in Copenhagen in 2009. There was little questioning of Rudd's overall approach, in which everything was staked on one single forum and achieving a global accord rather than working locally, within Australia, to curb emissions, or taking action to prepare for climate change. There were continued reports that he was negotiating, behind the scenes, to ensure an accord was reached. As it turned out, he was staking his political career on a successful outcome.

Previous progress in the fight to combat climate change had been measured by two sudden lurches forward; one at Kyoto and the second at Bali. The smooth, co-ordinated approach that might have been expected had been lacking in both instances. Yet no one, and particularly not Rudd, was investigating the possibility that different countries might have objectives that were so dissimilar that a worthwhile agreement might be simply unachievable. The global assumption was that, in the end, altruism would triumph. Rudd ignored the voices that declared his project was flawed in its conception. He'd convinced himself of the worthiness of his cause.

The government continued to ignore other schemes that were proposed to deal with climate change. One represented a simple tweak to the government's commitment to an ETS: a Greens' proposal for a simple tax on carbon production. The advantage of this scheme was that the amount of the tax could be varied as required, allowing it to be hiked up or ratcheted down. The Greens were wary of the government proposal: an ETS would effectively lock in a minimum amount of carbon production, because it would fail to credit people who took personal action to reduce their own carbon emissions by, for example, purchasing something as simple as a solar hot-water heater.

Many others — particularly those involved with agriculture and those living close to the River Murray's mouth — couldn't see that Rudd's scheme would have any practical effect on them. Other countries' emissions dwarfed Australia's, so there was always the potential that global warming would worsen. The PM had no fallback position if this worst-case scenario emerged. Nothing was done to deal with the dry and heat that now enveloped much of the inland in parching drought; there were no new ideas about how to provide water security for people who desperately required it. Everything was being staked on a global agreement, but no actions were being taken to insulate vulnerable areas of the country.

Finally, no significant effort was made to sell the public on the advantages of an emissions trading scheme, as opposed to any other way of dealing with greenhouse gases. Penny Wong has never been a great communicator. She'd been a surprising choice for such a key portfolio; however, Rudd had personally decided he wanted her to steer the ETS through parliament. Openly gay and a practising (Uniting Church) Christian, Wong was born in Malaysia to parents of mixed Australian and Chinese heritage. She became a political activist at university, and worked for a significant traditional union (the CFMEU, which was not a friend of the environmental movement) after studying arts/law in Adelaide. Once she became a senator in 2001, she sat on committees and became a shadow minister; however, there'd been no guarantee (and it came as a surprise to many in the party) that she'd receive an important ministry, particularly as nothing in her background had demonstrated any commitment to environmental issues — indeed, perhaps the opposite was more the case. Although her intellect and ability were not in doubt, she hadn't demonstrated any capacity to communicate complex messages to the wider community. This was rapidly to develop into a major problem for the government.

Rudd and Wong decided to put all their eggs into the one basket: everything was devoted to developing and implementing an ETS. But there was a problem with this: while the government could ram whatever policy it wanted through the lower house, it didn't control the Senate. Because only half the Senate is selected at each election, and because the terms of the Senate and lower house are not synchronised, the members who were elected in 2007 only took their place in July 2008. After the election, there were still 37 coalition senators, but only 32 Labor ones. The balance of power in the Senate was held by seven crossbenchers: five Greens, Steve Fielding, and Nick Xenophon. To pass its legislation, the government needed the support of either all the crossbench senators or, more improbably, the coalition.

Controversially, Rudd decided to ignore the possibility of making a deal with the crossbenchers. There seemed to be two reasons for this: the first was tactical; the second, strategic. The government understandably didn't want to waste its time negotiating an agreement only to find that Fielding (a highly unpredictable character lacking any credibility, whose mind appeared to change from hour to hour, perhaps depending on the direction of each new gust of wind) had suddenly pulled out at the last moment. And yet it was Labor that had been responsible for installing Fielding, giving him their preferences rather than allocating them to the Greens.

Since it had last been in government, Labor had largely forgotten the delicate process necessary to get its legislation through a chamber that it didn't control. Right at the beginning of the term, in the brief interregnum until procedures were established to smooth the path of controversial issues through the upper house, the tactical problem of achieving agreement with the crossbenchers appeared too difficult for Rudd to resolve.

As well as this, there was a more significant strategic issue at stake: the Greens would almost inevitably demand more action on climate change than the industrial wing of Labor was prepared to give. Rudd might have been honest when he declared that the link between global warming and CO_2 emissions was 'beyond doubt'. But this didn't mean that everyone in the party felt the same way — quite the reverse. Human-induced climate change remained a controversial issue in some sections of the party. Although most politicians had by now learned to keep any heretical views to themselves, every now and then a broad Australian accent from the party's union base would be heard making comments that demonstrated they either didn't understand or, worse, had completely failed to believe the new political orthodoxy.

For these people, the idea of dealing with the Greens was anathema. The strategists had another concern as well. They knew that the environmental party would hold out for major reductions in emissions and, as negotiations continued, they'd be publicly emphasising that Labor was not cutting hard enough. The party would have had to fight on terrain that was 'owned' by the Greens; the hardheads believed that no matter how much Labor gave, it would never be enough to satisfy the Greens.

Attempting to do a deal with the Liberals offered two advantages: firstly, power lay with the weight of numbers. Even if the Nationals abstained or the Greens voted against the legislation, Liberal support would push it through. The Greens would be pushed to the margins and denied a public platform on which to mount their arguments. The government would also be able to emphasise the nascent split within the coalition ranks between sceptics and those who believed in climate change. Perhaps most importantly, it would be the government that made the final decision on how far it was prepared to compromise; it would 'own' the new political environment.

Rudd's ETS was a complex scheme that couldn't easily be reduced to a 'soundbite' for radio or television. He could, however, refer positively to noble aspirations, and gloss over difficult realities, and his striking descriptions convinced people that he had a solution to the problem.

The big advantage of Rudd's scheme was that it melded with the European Union's ETS. It eventually envisaged a completely integrated world in which carbon offsets could be purchased to allow emissions to continue being generated by productive industries that had no alternative. Theoretically, it made sense, but the difficulty of explaining its workings meant that, practically, it was a crock.

Part of the reason that Wong had been silent and failed to extol the virtues of the scheme was not just the difficulty of 'selling' it, but also because of the contradictions and absurdities buried within it. The scheme was being foisted on the electorate by appealing to people's altruism, yet its operation was entirely based on the worst of capitalist mechanisms — trading to make money. This inherent inconsistency was easily demonstrated in the simplest of ways.

Many people, encouraged by the government, had already begun purchasing solar-electricity systems, both to satisfy their own energy needs and to eventually return some of their investment by feeding electricity back into the grid. Individuals felt empowered, because they believed their own actions might make a difference. But it wasn't long before they realised that anything an ordinary householder did would free up more permits for the big polluters.

The government appeared to be increasingly on the defensive as the details of the scheme seeped out. This added to rising doubt about the transparency of the system, and raised further questions about the appropriateness of purchasing carbon permits from developing nations.

The concept that a greenhouse producer in Australia might be able to purchase credits from tribesmen in Borneo who were agreeing to preserve pristine rainforests was a robust theoretical concept, but it failed to make practical sense. Few environmentalists believed that real-world methods could be developed to get such a global scheme working properly. And it was also based on an initial idea — handing out permits to large polluters — that stuck in the craw of many idealists.

The ETS—soon changed to the even-more-complex CPRS (or Carbon Pollution Reduction Scheme), a change of nomenclature that failed to address growing concern about what was seen, in shorthand, as a 'tax'—was unintelligible to the majority of the electorate. It's quite possible that this was deliberate. Treasury modelling was released which purported to show that people would be better off once the scheme was introduced; but even before this could be investigated, it failed the obvious commonsense test. How could it possibly not have any negative effect on industry, and result in a bonus for consumers, and yet still reduce emissions?

As 2009 progressed, opinion polling showed increasing resistance to the scheme, although at this stage the growing protest was still quarantined to coalition supporters. Politics is primarily about winning elections, and the government was managing to dominate the ideological terrain over which the contest was being fought. This emphasised the role of polling. As Turnbull's fortnightly approval-ratings continued bumping along the bottom of the range, his lack of electoral appeal extended the opposition's problems.

Rudd drove home his advantage eagerly as the year progressed. Although doubts were beginning to surface about the ETS in the broader community, Turnbull's policy was to back the legislation while articulating his own reservations about particular provisions. Discontent grew as it became obvious that the electorate couldn't see any point in the introduction of minor amendments to supposedly make the legislation better.

Because Rudd had posited this as a life-and-death issue of supreme moral importance, quibbling over detail was pointless. If the legislation was necessary (as the typical Labor voter believed), then it was urgent and should be passed immediately. If it was not the best system (a position adopted by an increasing number of voters, both Liberals and Greens), then 'doing deals' to amend it and make it better was equally futile. Turnbull was caught sitting uncomfortably on a barbed-wire fence, and was in any case already potentially facing a limited tenure as opposition leader because of his blunders over the OzCar affair. Towards the end of 2009, his reactions were being shaped by both the need to protect his party against an early election (which would have been a disaster for the Liberals) and also by his own personal belief in the reality of climate change. As leader, he assumed he could drag his party along with him. This was not, in fact, the case. A succession of crises eventually brought the issue to a head at the end of 2009.

Discontent over Turnbull's leadership had grown inexorably since the OzCar affair in June. The opposition leader had hoped to leave the government reeling by the time the mid-year winter parliamentary recess began, but by the end of June the tables had been turned and the government was in the clear. The subsequent decline in his opinion-poll ratings critically weakened his authority, but Turnbull was unwilling to admit this and continued to push through his own policy positions, regardless of dissent within the party.

This came to a head at the end of September in response to continuing backbench sniping. Although badly wounded, Turnbull was still strong enough to call the party room together and demand that it back his decision to begin negotiations over the ETS. Even though this was an unpopular decision that the leader had made unilaterally, the discontent was still focused on the policy and had not yet bubbled over to become a personal challenge to his authority.

But there was no certainty that this situation would continue for very long. Turnbull risked everything by refusing to change his style or even to slightly amend his negotiating position. 'I will not lead a party', he baldly announced, 'that is not as committed to effective action on climate change as I am.' Instead of locking the party in behind him, statements like this had the unintended consequence of further alienating those who were already discontented.

Psychologists have noted that personal loss resolves itself in a succession of stages. Political parties appear to go through a similar sequence of phases during the transition from government to opposition. It is the speed of progression through these phases that often determines the ability of the party to regain government — almost as much as the mistakes that are committed by the other side.

The initial stage comes with the realisation that the party is again in opposition. It took the Liberals a good 18 months to jettison former ministers and members who were not prepared to make the personal sacrifices necessary to regain government. The second stage is characterised by significant policy debates within the party. Even within the one party, individuals can have many different personal beliefs and 'takes' about what sort of policies are needed to deal with different issues. This is where leadership is critical.

A leader must have the ability to unify different ideological groupings within the party and to convince them to stand behind their banner. They must have the ability to give all the individuals in the party the feeling that their views are being listened to and somehow incorporated in the eventual policy settings — even where this is plainly not the case. If the leader is the beneficiary of excellent polling results, policy differences will not be as relevant as they otherwise would be; however, if the leader is trailing or showing other signs of weakness, gaining their colleagues' support becomes far more important than any display of 'strong' leadership.

It's only in the third stage that the leader can move on to assault the other party. Turnbull didn't realise that he needed to compromise, and wouldn't accept that his decision to defuse the ETS as an election issue had grown into a tactical disaster. His personal authority was no longer enough to staunch the damage to his leadership.

'The party room will support [my negotiated] amendments to the scheme', the leader said, directing resources spokesman Ian Macfarlane to reach a deal with the government. 'Whether my leadership prevails or not on this issue, time will tell', Turnbull asserted presciently, 'but the fact of the matter is we cannot be a party with nothing to say.' He'd chosen the words, but the party was refusing to have them stuffed down its throat.

Macfarlane, a former peanut farmer from Kingaroy, had a voice like a chainsaw, which provided him with his nickname (although he preferred to pretend that this came from his ability to cut through bureaucratic crap). The former minister played up to his simple stereotype as a plain-talking rough diamond. But he worked hard, negotiating with the government on the one hand and corralling renegade coalition MPs on the other. MacFarlane had been through all the stages of grief, and was now working extremely hard to get the party back into office. At one stage, he'd been a serious climate-change denier, but now he threw everything into getting a deal. For others, the ideological compromises being demanded were just too great altogether.

In the end, forcing the government to change its legislation didn't prove to be such an arduous effort after all. It turned out that Rudd was having what one of the Greens later described as 'crazy Kevin's clean-out clearance, where everything must go'. Massive concessions — $7 billion extra to the coal and electricity industries alone — were offered to the biggest polluters. The negotiations offered Rudd the ability to look as if he was serious about compromising to get the legislation through, while at the same time appeasing his own sceptics, and Labor members representing industrial and mining electorates.

At the end of 2009 I met Rudd during a Christmas party at the Lodge. He looked up into the middle distance as we discussed Turnbull's future, appearing genuinely shocked that the Liberals were seriously considering getting rid of their leader. Rudd seemed to believe he'd come very close to gaining agreement on the ETS. In fact, Liberal opponents of the policy were determined to do anything necessary to wreck the deal. If that meant getting rid of Turnbull, well …

The real surprise was that Turnbull persisted in his attempt to force through a policy that, if he had listened, he would have realised was completely unacceptable to many in his party. He never had the moral authority to act as he did. By linking his leadership irrevocably to the ETS, he seemed to be determinedly forcing the assassins to reach for their daggers.

In the end, Turnbull's declaration that he was in control only bought him an extra two months. He called a party room meeting in November to approve the deal that Macfarlane had stitched together with the government. The former climate-change spokesman, Andrew Robb, who'd been on sick leave with depression, flew to Canberra to speak at the meeting.

When the moment came, Robb paused for a second and then began a ten-minute demolition of the ETS, twisting and turning the knife in Turnbull's wound, to loud applause. A knowledgeable Liberal later insisted that Robb's intervention changed nothing; if it hadn't been him, it would have been someone else. The meeting fractured: small differences became unbridgeable gaps. It continued for hours, broke for question time, and reconvened. Sandwiches were sent in, but no food that required a knife or fork to eat. It was far too dangerous an environment for even plastic cutlery to be made available.

Turnbull finally overruled the sentiment of the meeting with what he described as a 'leader's call' for the party to pass the government's scheme. There was an eruption. 'This is not democracy', muttered one member. The party room was furious. 'You're a caretaker leader! You're mad', shouted Tuckey. He'd earlier moved to spill the leadership, but couldn't get support. Now Turnbull's unshakeable arrogance had abruptly changed everything.

Things became ridiculous. Quite improbably, Kevin Andrews soon put his name forward as a leadership contender. This should have been too bizarre to contemplate, but many backbenchers were seething with intense anger at Turnbull. Andrews' move to spill the leadership was unsurprisingly defeated, by 48 votes to 35, but it was a warning that Turnbull failed to heed. The result demonstrated conclusively that the leader was now on borrowed time, yet he still refused to admit that the sentiment in the party was completely at odds with his own desires. Had he done so, he might have been able to salvage his leadership and position himself for the future. But Turnbull had wedged himself in behind the ETS so firmly that he refused to contemplate any other option. The opposition leader refused to bend, even to save himself.

Speculation speeded up as the vortex of the end of the parliamentary year approached. Nick Minchin recognised that the situation needed to be resolved urgently. Another challenge — a serious one this time — developed with Tony Abbott as the new putative leader. Joe Hockey was offered the chance to seize the prize, if only he would agree to dump the ETS. He refused, having surprisingly chosen instead to marry his ambitions to Rudd's policy, effectively opening the door for Abbott to become the new leader of the party. On the first day of December 2009, both Turnbull and the ETS were dispatched by the margin of a single vote.

***

Rudd wasn't able to take any legislation with him as he travelled to Copenhagen for the climate-change conference. Instead, he dragged the largest retinue to the meeting that an Australian prime minister had ever taken overseas. The Australian negotiating position was complex. It included extravagant promises to cut emissions by 25 per cent, but there might as well have been an asterisk attached which noted that 'conditions apply'. The practical effect of these caveats meant that the commitments were worthless; nevertheless, Rudd had invested a great deal of his personal political capital in striving for a positive outcome to the conference.

In the lead-up to the talks, mainstream (Western, industrialised-country) thought was coalescing around two different approaches to the limiting of emissions: either establishing a carbon tax or entering into treaty-based emissions trading schemes. Climate-change activist and NASA climatologist James Hansen insisted on the need for a carbon tax, claiming, 'The approach that is being talked about is so fundamentally wrong that … I think it's just as well that we not have a substantive treaty.' Yet Rudd was still completely committed to the increasingly problematic global approach. He'd been up late at night speaking to foreign leaders before the conference, lobbying them to try to produce his preferred outcome. Perhaps he'd been so busy speaking that he hadn't listened to the increasing number of objections.

Aware of the need to hammer out some agreement, Rudd had begun working on the so-called 'Danish text'. The idea was that this draft could be used to begin negotiations, although it was much more controversial than a simple working document, because it imposed significant obligations on developing countries. When the British *Guardian* newspaper revealed this preliminary document, right at the beginning of the talks, it sent developing nations into a fury because of the apparent double standards being applied. Goodwill immediately degenerated; instead of facilitating the talks and allowing them to begin working on an agreed text, the diplomats involved in the secret negotiations before the main meeting began had managed to derail the process right from the beginning. It gave those objecting a simple platform that would legitimise their refusal to sign any treaty; as well, Rudd's credibility and good faith had been badly damaged because of the part he played working on the text.

Rudd had been given a special role as 'friend of the chair' (as had the Mexican president). The idea was that he'd personally be able to facilitate bringing different countries to an agreement. Within minutes of the leaders arriving in Copenhagen, however, everything fell apart. Instead of Rudd being able to help keep the talks running smoothly, it appears that a number of other leaders had begun to take a particular, personal dislike to the Australian.

There were two key nations whose assistance would be required to nut out any final treaty: India and China. Rudd had never made any particular effort to get on with New Delhi, perhaps unaware that it controlled a significant voting bloc of non-aligned nations; and Beijing simply snubbed his attempts to broker an agreement. At one point during the formal meetings, Rudd became so annoyed that he was reduced to banging his microphone to express his frustration at China's stance and describing the negotiating team as 'rat-fuckers'. The summit careened off course.

In the end, it turned out that Rudd's negotiating skills weren't required after all, because it appeared that a number of nations had turned up determined to prevent any outcome along the lines proposed before the meeting. With the assistance of Mexico (the other co-chair apparently managed to perform a useful service), the US eventually announced that it had reached a 'meaningful agreement' with China, India, South Africa, and Brazil, although the agreement simply recognised 'the critical impacts of climate change'. The accord was not legally binding, nor did it facilitate the introduction of a global ETS. The grand hopes with which people had travelled to Copenhagen had ended in the issuing of rhetorical sops. The government's plan to deal with global warming had disintegrated.

Rudd insisted that the statement released by the US had prevented climate change negotiations from crashing into an abyss. 'We prevailed. Some will be disappointed by the amount of progress', Rudd commented. 'The alternative was, frankly, catastrophic collapse of these negotiations.' But, of course, absolutely nothing came of these talks, which continued, in a desultory manner, until February 2010. They were intended to provide cover, allowing the various national leaders to pretend that something had been achieved. Back in Australia, the coalition insisted it had always known that nothing substantive would emerge from Copenhagen. Meanwhile, the Greens' Christine Milne scathingly accused the government of merely achieving a 'superficial last-minute statement' that didn't represent 'substantive progress on any of the critical issues'.

In the wake of the failure of the Copenhagen talks, it was obvious that the tactical choices made by Rudd had resulted in him leading the government down blind alleyways. By linking the CPRS to the multilateral negotiations, he'd successfully placed enough pressure on the coalition for it to split apart and depose its leader. But he'd also failed to ensure that the legislation could pass domestically without being the beneficiary of a successful double-dissolution election. After the collapse of any early prospect for an international accord, the urgency for any real action on curbing greenhouse emissions appeared to vanish.

Rudd's choice of words — his use of the word 'moral' with its ethical overtones — had imbued the issue of climate change with an almost religious dimension. The actual science was quickly buried in an avalanche of claim and counter-claim in which believers prophesied doom, sceptics revelled in pointing out the flaws in any argument, and the 'fruit-loops' invested everything with millennial overtones. This was about to change, with serious consequences for the government.

***

Climate change (a long-term environmental trend) isn't the same thing as the weather (your guess that it won't rain and soak the washing out on the line). But the weather around the world during Christmas 2009 and the beginning of 2010 didn't help convince the sceptics of any need for rapid action to curb CO_2 emissions: snowstorms blanketed Beijing with its biggest dusting of snow since 1951; winds off the Siberian tundra sent the mercury plummeting to minus 16 degrees centigrade; and Europe shivered in freezing temperatures.

Meanwhile, Australia was being baked. On 5 January, Garrett emerged with the annual climate statement from the Bureau of

Meteorology to announce that the decade to 2009 had been the hottest in Australian history and that 2009 had been the second-warmest year since records began. The next month, a succession of hot nights saw Canberra's average summer minimum soar to the hottest since settlement. But the argument supported by the statistics was losing traction in the broader community.

Floods and heat waves certainly appeared to be coming in more rapid succession than before — but this simply seemed to emphasise the fact that no one really knew what was happening to the climate. People accepted it was changing, but they wanted to know how it would affect *them*. It now seemed that 'global warming' would bring more rain in some parts of the country while other areas were becoming parched. As 2010 continued, so did the bizarre weather patterns. Floods brought water to Lake Eyre in central Australia for the first time in years; tropical cyclones battered the Queensland coast; and Victoria was hit by bushfires and then rain. People turned to meteorologists and scientists for an explanation.

In 2007, the International Panel on Climate Change (IPCC) had issued detailed reports from three working groups, together with a synthesis report on climate change. Thousands of pages clearly linked anthropogenic activity to the changing weather; however, one paragraph went further, suggesting that all the glaciers in the Himalayas might melt by 2035. It was a stupid mistake — something that never should have been allowed to creep into a serious academic document. But it was a scientific blunder, and a serious one. When the error was revealed in January 2010, coming not long after the leaked-emails affair that had implicated the University of East Anglia's Climate Research Unit in the suppression and distortion of climate research, the deniers leapt on the false claim, using it to argue that the rest of the report was also wrong.

One claim was incorrect; but, rather than considering the weight of evidence pointing towards global warming, many people felt that this cast doubt on the entire concept. They forgot to ask what the truth really was. In fact, 90 per cent of the world's glaciers were still retreating and melting at an ever-increasing rate. In 2006, the ice thaw was greater than had ever been measured before, even though three new records had already been set in the years since 1995. The only doubt was about the speed of the warming and its cause. The fact that there were variations didn't detract from the validity of the theory; it just meant that the progression was not in a straight line.

In a possible attempt to convey the urgent need for action, the editors of the IPCC report had ended up ensuring that perfectly reasonable assertions were now being questioned. Most importantly, no effort was being made by Wong to explain any of this to the broader community. The government had gone missing from the debate, confident that it could do a deal with the Liberals to slam an ETS through the Senate regardless.

This was part of Rudd's approach to politics that perhaps originated from his study of China. The so-called Middle Kingdom has never been genuinely democratic. Its size has always made it easier for the rulers in the centre to issue policy edicts and expect them to be obeyed throughout the country. Persuasion had rarely been a valued skill. Rudd attempted to impose a similar political style in Australia. On the positive side, this engaged him intensely in the debate, but *he* needed to be persuaded before anything could happen. Once he had been converted to a particular policy, it appeared to him to be axiomatic that everyone should simply accept that he'd weighed up all the evidence and made the correct decision. There was no room for dissidents and no need for argument. This imperial style, which was entrenched in the public service and reluctantly accepted amongst his colleagues, built up resentment in the wider community, who expected to be consulted and persuaded. This would be ignored as long as things were going well, but risked leaving him without a support base if his method of achieving results became derailed. The risk of this was growing all the time.

The first challenge came from the right of politics. It didn't, at first, appear significant, but as time went on it became obvious that those who didn't accept the reality of global warming had been invigorated as the cold change had swept across the northern hemisphere. In 2010, the bizarre figure of Christopher Monckton visited Australian and leapt onto stages around the country to propound the sceptics' case. Few impartial observers listening to his tirades were convinced by the farrago of dubious statistics he used to deny that climate change was occurring. Monckton had no scientific qualifications whatsoever (although he did possess the lovely ring of certainty that comes with a Cambridge accent); nevertheless, at least he was out there, making a case. No one from the government bothered responding.

In America, it was called the 'tea party' effect. Meetings of small groups of people (at town hall meetings or tea parties) that were provided with only one side of the argument were particularly effective as a method for disseminating political propaganda. This was occurring at a level beneath normal political discourse. The questions were being raised around barbecues and dining tables. This rippled its way through the community, gathering momentum as it went.

The government failed to pick up the reality that a subtle transformation was creeping into the way that Australians viewed climate change. The issue had lost its status as an unquestioned 'fact', subtly transitioning to a new position in the public discourse as a 'debate'. The government, particularly the prime minister, refused to believe that the public consensus was changing, as demonstrated by the polls. This was a major mistake, because the sceptics within the coalition were invigorated. Now they thought they possessed the power to break Rudd's grand plan. Abbott's policy became more hardline as his position in the polls improved. The coalition began offering 'practical action' to combat climate change. If Abbott had appeared to be a genuine believer in the risk of global warming, this might have provided the leverage he required to break Labor's apparent stranglehold on government. Unfortunately for the Liberals, voters who were increasingly abandoning the government were not being captured by the opposition's policies. Instead, they were turning to the Greens. Winning third-party preferences was to take on an increasingly vital significance as the election neared.

The Greens refused to be committed to the unwieldy scheme that Rudd was mandating. This left the government with no fallback position when it couldn't secure an agreement with the opposition. Rudd's decision to work with the Liberals had deliberately closed off the most obvious way of getting an ETS enacted — by doing a deal with the environmentalists in the Senate.

The political problem with this strategy was that it resulted in the government being attacked on both sides. Environmentalists insisted that the legislation accomplished nothing; sceptics attacked it as gratuitous and expensive. The other difficulty was that by refusing to work with the Greens, Labor was undermining its own credibility on this issue.

Normally, in politics, the middle ground represents the strongest position. In this case, however, because of the moral and existential dimensions of global warming, the idea of calling a normal election over this issue was fraught. Rudd would have been forced to continually defend his compromise proposal as being the best available — a defence that would have drawn the limitations of the ETS into sharp relief. It's unlikely that the vote of a single sceptic would have been swayed towards Labor, but the Greens would certainly emerge resurgent from a campaign fought over the environment, and would probably end up with control of the Senate. They would still be in the box seat to block any legislation they didn't like.

Rudd had to call an election some time in 2010. The government was well ahead in the opinion polls, and, as that year approached, the prime minister began to consider the possibilities offered by a double dissolution. If the Senate rejects a bill, it returns to the lower house—which can, if it desires, send exactly the same legislation back to the Senate for a second time. If the upper house rejects it again (or even if it just sits on the bill and fails to pass it), the prime minister can immediately ask for both Houses of Parliament to be dissolved—a double dissolution—so an election can be held to break the deadlock.

A senator's term normally lasts for six years—twice as long as that of a member of the House of Representatives, which is why only half of them face the people at a general election. But if there's a double dissolution, the entire Senate is thrown out at once: everyone faces re-election. This means that, instead of needing 14.3 per cent of the vote to be elected, a Senate candidate only needs 7.7 per cent. Rudd was aware the Greens would easily achieve this result in every state; it was only their second Senate spot that would be in doubt. This option would have effectively handed the balance of power to the Greens, although Labor would almost certainly have done better as well.

Rudd apparently quickly dismissed the possibility of a double-dissolution election. It's not clear why he did this: perhaps he felt it would be easier to work with the conservatives than to place himself in a situation where he had to work with the Greens. Nevertheless, for whatever reason, he ignored this opportunity and decided to prepare for a normal election, rather than opening the way for a poll that would prove to be (effectively) a referendum on his own ETS.

As we've seen, because of the maths and preference flows, a double-dissolution election would almost certainly have resulted in the Greens increasing their Senate numbers. Labor would also have strengthened its position, but it would have been highly unlikely to gain control of the upper house. The real brilliance of the strategy, though, was that by using its likely large majority in the lower house to swamp a combination of the coalition and Greens in the Senate, a joint sitting held right at the beginning of the new term would have allowed Labor to pass any legislation that was being blocked by the Senate. Rudd could have gone to the electorate with his credibility on climate change intact.

Early in 2010, Rudd assessed his options, including specific dates on which a double-dissolution election could have been held. The 'Gang of Four' — Rudd, Swan, Gillard, and finance minister Lindsay Tanner — debated the issue. Tanner was insistent that a policy to combat climate change was necessary, both for environmental reasons and for political ones; he believed that the party could not credibly go to the electorate without a policy to immediately tackle the issue. Gillard and Swan disagreed, and persuaded Rudd to postpone action on an ETS. Swan knew this would mean that the government would be able to announce an early return to surplus, because it would pocket savings that would have otherwise been paid out as compensation to industry participants as the scheme was introduced. At the time, Gillard didn't explain why she argued against taking the issue to the electorate.

What made this a highly significant miscalculation was the way in which Rudd had previously tied his own personal credibility inexorably to the danger presented by climate change, while Gillard and Swan had not. Once set on its course, the government quietly began preparing to dump its ETS as the 2010–11 federal budget was being prepared. The *Sydney Morning Herald's* Lenore Taylor had reported on the politics of climate change for a number of years, and was well capable of finding her way through the detail of such matters. By dint of careful research, she came up with a remarkable scoop: she found out that the ETS had been removed from the budget's four-year forward estimates, at the same time as Rudd was claiming (publicly) 'On the question of climate change, our policy hasn't changed. We maintain our position that this [the ETS] is part of the most efficient and most effective means by which we can reduce greenhouse-gas emissions with the least cost to the economy.'

Rudd wouldn't admit that he'd ditched the idea of a double dissolution or the ETS, and left Wong to continue negotiating (in bad faith) with the Greens to supposedly pass the scheme. His apparent intention had been to slip the news out quietly amidst a couple of big distractions, but Taylor's scoop nixed that strategy. After her front-page story revealed what was really happening, Rudd remained in denial. 'The government's commitment to a carbon pollution reduction scheme remains unchanged. What has changed is the pathway to get there,' he insisted. But, as the polls were too soon to show, the electorate thought otherwise.

Rudd had trashed the one thing that he could never regain — his own credibility. As time went on, the enormity of his failure slowly began to dawn on the party and the electorate. Rudd had attempted to answer the challenge of global warming by backing an international bureaucratic solution to the problem. The failure of the Copenhagen talks means that, globally, carbon dioxide levels will continue to rise. If the science is correct — and Rudd insists it is — it is almost certain that irretrievable damage will be done to the atmosphere, with the potential for bio-feedback pushing this out of control.

Rudd had staked everything on gaining an international treaty, but serious negotiations to achieve this had by now broken down irretrievably. As a result, an international emissions trading scheme would not come into force in the foreseeable future, and Rudd's strategy consequently lay in ruins. Imposing such a scheme on a trade-dependent country like Australia that relied on mineral exports was always fraught with danger. Unless some way could be found to impose a suitable greenhouse penalty on overseas-produced goods, there was always a danger that adopting national curbs would simply result in industries moving offshore, causing more damage to the environment.

There was no Plan B. When Rudd insisted all along that he accepted the science, he could be assumed to have understood his own moral responsibility to prepare this country for a future in which global warming was a reality. But nothing was done in this regard. This is why Rudd's own personal approach had to come into question. It is impossible to both believe in global warming and yet, as leader, not to take action to prepare the country for its effects.

Every day that parliament sat, Rudd was driven into the prime minister's courtyard — a barren waste of light-grey marbled granite — and past what should have been a water feature, one of the many fountains and pools dotted around the building. They'd all been switched off, though, and carried small signs announcing that this was due to 'temporary' water restrictions. For anyone who thought about it, the provisional nature of the restrictions appeared to give the lie to Rudd's assertions that he genuinely believed in global warming. It had now become obvious that the government had been left politically exposed. After insisting for years on the reality of climate change, the government was now forced to admit that it had no plan to curb emissions. Nor was it even investigating measures to mitigate the effect of Australia's shifting weather patterns.

Without enacting a coherent plan to curb emissions, climate change will continue unabated in Australia, and the water nourishing those pools will never be turned back on. Rudd prides himself on being a person who notices even minor details. Was it really possible that, for years, every day that he had been in parliament, he had walked past dozens of these signs believing, as if by some miracle, that the climate would change — for the better?

Equally, Rudd's commitment to a global solution did not have to preclude any effort to ameliorate the effect of climate change nationally. And yet no serious effort was put into efforts to generate power by alternative sources, to reduce the country's dependency on oil, or to deal with the failing river systems of the inland. Instead, during the two-and-a-half years of his term, Australia went backwards as opportunities were foregone. The federal government took no serious steps towards reducing our dependency on coal, one of the most serious contributors to greenhouse-gas emissions. On both international and national levels, Rudd failed to achieve anything to deal with what he once described as the most significant moral issue of his time.

INTERLUDE

Malcolm

The Liberal backbencher sighed audibly. 'Of course, Malcolm never really accepted that first vote straight after the election that installed Brendan as leader.' He shuffled in his chair for a second, adjusting his clothing, before continuing as if he was explaining something obvious to a slow-learning child. 'That vote was too close and Malcolm's ambition always too great for him to ever accept it as final. He was always — always — very focused on exactly when and how he'd be taking over.'

Just three votes had separated the winner from the loser, and everyone believed that a couple of false steps in an interview Turnbull had done just before the vote was taken had weakened his support at the critical moment. As time went on and Nelson faltered, it began to appear obvious (to Turnbull, at any rate) that it would only be a matter of time before he took over the leadership.

Nelson became increasingly annoyed as Turnbull kept up a *sotto voce* running commentary on the leader's failings and, even more insufferably, on what he needed to do to improve his standing with the electorate. There were two ways of interpreting Turnbull's actions: the first was to perceive it as a destabilising whispering campaign, designed to weaken the leader so that, when the time came — sooner rather than later — Turnbull would move straight into the job; the alternative explanation, favoured by those who knew him well, was just that, well, 'that was Malcolm'.

He didn't play by the rules of normal mortals — he'd always been exceptional. I knew this to be true. In fact, I can remember the first time I met him, which is more surprising than it might seem, because I was only 13 at the time. Malcolm had already embarked on a whirlwind university career that would eventually see him gain a coveted Rhodes Scholarship and become a star lawyer, but at that time he was just someone who'd been invited to give a talk at a school speech day to inspire the succeeding generation.

He performed brilliantly. I still remember staring wide-eyed as I watched him speak. Even back then, he displayed the confidence, the assurance, and the certainty that have become his trademarks. Afterwards, I briefly heard some teachers discussing his ability — it was obvious that he was destined for greater things.

As the years passed, the ripples radiating out from Turnbull became stronger. He made an indelible mark on Australia, first as a lawyer and then as a banker, until finally he took over the republic campaign, making it his own. And this was the first time that Malcolm's little problem became apparent to everyone. He didn't have the one vital political skill of being able to subsume his own personality into … well, anything really.

Another Liberal, this time one of Malcolm's opponents, sat back and rocked slightly in his chair. 'Well, Malcolm is Malcolm', he told me, 'and there's nothing anyone can do to change him. He's always been larger than life.'

It may have been this lack of sensitivity that led to his astonishing interaction with Nelson straight after Turnbull had lost the first leadership contest. According to one account, he barged into Nelson's office just before the leader travelled further up the hall to face journalists for his first press conference. Turnbull told Nelson to 'toughen up' and not to use such a sombre 'funereal' manner.

'Apparently, he was attempting to help', says one of those who was there. Those present in the office were shocked. But it seems that Turnbull meant his advice quite genuinely. Perhaps he just didn't think about the best way of persuading other people; he was still too busy trying to lead them.

The thing was, Turnbull believed he *knew* how to win the next election. Uncertainty was foreign to him. He was sure he could triumph. After all, during the election that had swept Howard from office, he'd been the only member who'd managed to achieve a 1.3 per cent swing *to* the Liberal Party, so that he'd won on first preferences. His seat, Wentworth, went against the national trend. He believed his result was marvellous — although perhaps there was no need to share his news so exuberantly with Howard while the prime minister was on his way to concede defeat at the Wentworth Hotel.

In time, Turnbull's strategy might even have worked. The last major poll that came out just before he was dumped as leader encapsulated the conundrum that surrounded his period as leader. The people who most approved of him were Labor voters; it was the coalition's base that had no time for him.

Turnbull had always been driven by the need to win, fortified and sustained by a complete belief in his own ability. Both attributes are political necessities, and when they came together in him they formed a highly combustible mixture that always had the potential to explode with the addition of a third element. Nothing described his personality better than a word used by the English long, long ago: *ofermod*. It denoted not merely pride, but all-encompassing, over-mastering pride. It suggested daring that pushed beyond the normal limit of man; overconfidence taken to extremes. In the old days, it was a word used sparingly to describe heroes — ones possessing a fatal flaw. It fitted Turnbull perfectly.

If he was going to be a hero, Turnbull instinctively understood that he needed a 'big hit', a knockout punch that he could deliver early on in his leadership. He wasn't interested in fighting a war of attrition that would slowly bleed the government of its legitimacy; instead, Turnbull was prepared to charge without delay at what appeared to be the strongest point of the enemy's line and then, by using stratagems to discombobulate his opponents, drive his assault home until victory was his. Anyone who didn't believe in themselves would have thought it impossible. When the time eventually came, Turnbull didn't pause.

After Nelson had signed his exit warrant as leader by demanding a vote of confidence, Turnbull rapidly claimed the leadership. He'd always believed it should rightfully be his; he was utterly convinced of his capacity to do the job. The fact that he'd only just managed to defeat an already mortally wounded leader by a mere three votes was irrelevant; it didn't give him pause to consider his style or the manner of his personal interactions.

The change of leadership stopped the opinion polls from bumping along the bottom of the range, but his position as preferred prime minister wasn't rising anywhere near fast enough. If he remained content with that slow but steadily rising trend-line, it would be years before he overtook Rudd. And Turnbull wasn't going to spend two terms (or six years) in opposition. His reply to the budget went well, but he was on the lookout for something that would tip Rudd into the abyss, a scandal that would dominate the news and dent Rudd's personal credibility at the same time.

In autumn 2009, Turnbull thought he'd got the break he'd been looking for. Because of the credit crunch, car dealers could no longer easily obtain the money they needed to keep demonstration vehicles in the yards. This became a problem for the government, because if people couldn't test-drive cars, they weren't going to buy them. The whole system would gum up, confidence would fall further, and the crisis would intensify. Treasury devised the so-called OzCar scheme, whereby $850 million would be allocated to allow dealers the finance to buy floor stock.

John Grant, a Queensland car-dealer, was enthusiastic about

receiving this financial assistance. He asked his local MP at Ipswich, Bernie Ripoll, to help. Grant also happened to live in the same street in Brisbane as Rudd. While he was just an opposition member, the prime minister had accepted the gift of a 13-year-old Mazda Bravo utility to help with campaigning. Rudd had reported the gift on his pecuniary interests register. Grant was later quick to insist that people would be wrong to assume that he possessed some sort of lifelong commitment to Labor principles, saying, 'If you walk into my office, you'll see pictures of John Howard.' He was, it seemed, first and foremost a businessman looking to operate his business the best way he could.

A senior Treasury official, Godwin Grech, had been put in charge of administering the OzCar scheme. His tousled dark hair, nerdish glasses, and striking features, coupled with a collar and tie that didn't appear to quite sit properly under his conventional dark suit, were soon to catapult Grech to media infamy. *Godwin*, like *ofermod*, is an Old Norse word, meaning 'good friend'. Unfortunately for Turnbull, the allegations that were made by the bureaucrat, while sensational, turned out to have been fabricated. The result would turn out to be anything but friendly.

In early June, Turnbull asked Rudd if his office had ever tried to help Mr Grant by making representations to OzCar. 'Neither myself nor my office have ever made any representations on his behalf,' Rudd responded. To most in the press gallery, the question sounded like an attempt to fossick around to see if any gold turned up. The answer appeared to draw the curtains over the issue: 'Nothing to see here'.

Later that month came the bombshell. Grech, providing evidence to a Senate enquiry, insisted that 'he [Grant] wasn't your average constituent … the initial contact I had with respect to John Grant was from the prime minister's office'.

The Liberals had made sure that influential people in the press gallery were watching the astounding evidence. Senator Eric Abetz knew what questions to ask. The significant allegation was that Rudd's office had pressed Treasury to give special treatment to one of the PM's personal friends. What made the allegation sensational was that Grech alleged there was evidentiary proof: an e-mail that he'd been sent by the PM's special economic adviser.

'My recollection is that there was a short e-mail from the PMO [Prime Minister's Office] to me which very simply alerted me to the case of John Grant, but I don't have the e-mail.' And there, again, things might have rested.

But Turnbull didn't wait for the e-mail to turn up. He attacked at once. 'If the prime minister and the treasurer cannot immediately justify their actions to the Australian people,' he declared, 'they have no choice but to resign.' The opposition leader was preparing to detonate a massive explosion, but the cord to the explosive wasn't long enough to protect him if anything went wrong.

Turnbull's office provided Grech with the telephone number of *Daily Telegraph* reporter Steve Lewis, a journalist in the press gallery. Lewis managed to obtain the complete e-mail, which he'd been assured by usually reliable sources was genuine. He then made four phone calls confirming the details with Grech. The reporter later wrote that Grech 'considered himself a high-level whistleblower … claiming to be privy to a giant cover-up'. Lewis then provided the full e-mail to Rudd's office, asking for an urgent response. He hadn't received one by six o'clock that night, and began writing his story.

'Revealed', screamed the headline, 'E-mail that could topple a government.'

The government was consumed by confusion. For hours, everything hung by a thread as the PM's office went through the office's e-mail trail. It wasn't until 7.30 that Rudd finally told a press conference, 'We cannot find anywhere in the system any such e-mail.' The *Telegraph* immediately changed its lead. Qualifications entered the story: now it was focusing 'on the existence of an e-mail allegedly sent'.

On Monday 22 June, the Australian Federal Police confirmed that the e-mail was a fake.

Two months later, Grech gave the reason he'd fabricated the e-mail. Still insisting that he believed an e-mail did exist, he claimed that he'd made 'an error of judgement' and had simply made it up according to his 'recollection … I thought it would help'. There were many more details, but in August a remarkable edition of the ABC's *Australian Story* was broadcast.

The programme had been filming in Turnbull's office when the revelation that the e-mail was a fake had broken. The camera caught, better than any words could, the consternation in the afternoon as Turnbull's wife and staff suddenly realised the document had been 'concocted inside the Treasury Department'. In other words, it was phoney.

Lucy, Turnbull's wife (herself a Queens Counsel and the daughter of former Liberal attorney-general Tom Hughes), insisted that 'in politics you just put it behind you and you keep going forward'. But voters didn't. There's a big difference between running for lord mayor of Sydney — Lucy's former job — and attempting to become prime minister. The issue raised substantial questions about Turnbull's judgement. His position in the polls collapsed.

Many Liberals felt the entire affair had demonstrated that Turnbull was remote and cut off. He'd insisted on doing things his own way for too long. Instead of bringing Rudd down, Grech's intervention was the beginning of the end for Turnbull.

When, shortly afterwards, Turnbull made his 'leader's call' that the party was going to back the government's ETS, there was no residual goodwill that he could rely upon. Ironically, he ended up staking his own future on Rudd's scheme to combat global warming.

The ETS was notching up a growing list of political corpses.

CHAPTER FIVE

The World's My Oyster

> 'There are still many problems in China. Problems of poverty, problems of uneven development, problems of pollution. Problems of broader human rights.'
>
> Kevin Rudd at Beijing University, 8 April 2008

Rudd's diplomatic background became a marvellous talisman after he took over Labor's leadership in late 2006. It very quickly gave him a backstory: instead of being some kind of idealistic ingénue, he was aware of the way the world worked; he operated meticulously within the system, instead of radically as an outsider. His knowledge of the Chinese language (and particularly his earlier diplomatic posting to Beijing) suggested that Rudd was seriously engaged with the realities of a changing world order. Here was a leader able to confidently navigate the challenging new international environment that Australia found itself in at the dawn of a new millennium.

This is what makes the disaster that engulfed Australia's relationship with the world after Rudd's accession to power in Canberra so absolutely remarkable. By the end of the Howard years, the country was just managing to recover from the disastrous blunder represented by the then PM's comment positioning Australia as nothing more than America's 'deputy sheriff' in Asia.

Yet Howard had slowly recovered from this early gaffe, and by the end of his decade-or-so in power was engaging positively with the countries of the region. Nevertheless, during the election campaign his earlier failure to understand the changing dynamics of the flow of power was contrasted with an image of Rudd who appeared, by contrast, to be integrated into the new century and the evolving world order.

Rudd promised that Australia would once again become a confident nation playing a vital role on the world stage. In power, he devoted a great deal of his time and energy towards that objective; in fact, no prime minister since World War II spent a greater proportion of his time in office overseas than Rudd. By mid-2010, he had spent nearly one-third of a year travelling (or nearly 55 days per year). Surprisingly, at the time of the election that brought Rudd to power, Labor was in the habit of dismissing as a mere 'waste' Howard's foreign-travel expenditure of $13.5 million over more than 11 years. Rudd's spending was set to dwarf that amount.

Foreign Minister Stephen Smith correctly asserted that he ran the department. However,—and this was a problem also encountered by his predecessor Alexander Downer—the prime minister of the day has the ability to slash through all the diplomatic niceties, disembowelling carefully prepared departmental policy positions in an instant with an off-hand comment. Nevertheless, this alone does not explain the increased prime ministerial role in international negotiations and decision-making. There is more to it than that.

Diplomats began to mutter (with increasing degrees of frustration) that the Foreign Affairs department had been reduced to little more than a visa-processing offshoot of the prime minister's office. Funds for the department were seriously slashed in the Rudd government's first budget. Politically, this bore fruit. Whenever any suggestion was made that the PM was attempting to aggrandise Australia's world role, he could just point to the budget cuts, and his point was seemingly made; it looked as if he wasn't grandstanding.

However, what had occurred was a shifting of policy responsibility, away from the diplomats and towards a tight-knit group of bureaucrats supporting Rudd in the Department of Prime Minister and Cabinet.

Rudd emphasised engagement through a stream of bilateral visits and personal appearances at multilateral forums. In doing this, he staked out this arena — the global stage — as his own domain. His policy positions were a confusing mixture of pro-American stances wrapped within the rhetoric of a liberal Social Democrat. The charm that served to protect him like a magic amulet was his knowledge of China. Here, it seemed, was an Orientalist, capable of not merely conversing with the changing world, but taking command of the process. Nowhere were there greater expectations for Rudd than in managing Australia's vital relationship with China.

***

Goodwill from Beijing appeared to burnish Rudd's sheen as he entered office. The first return-trip of the sometime first secretary in the embassy as Prime Minister of Australia was eagerly awaited in both countries. It was probably inevitable that, with such high expectations, there would be disappointment. A more detailed knowledge of Rudd's personal background and inclinations might have lessened those early hopes, but this was not a part of his narrative that anyone had sought to highlight prior to his coming to office.

It's easy to forget there are actually two Chinas. When Rudd was at school, Australia didn't recognise the communists in Beijing, so his first trip abroad was to Taipei — which, to a young student, must have seemed dynamic, vibrant, and prosperous. Taiwan was ruled at the time by the octogenarian Chiang Kai-shek, who'd fled from the mainland in December 1949 when his forces in Chengdu were besieged by the Red Army. Rudd later completed a thesis on the protest movement within China, and revisited Taiwan when he was posted to Beijing. As a young diplomat, it was also Rudd's task to meet with Chinese dissidents who'd begun to come into the open as the central government had begun to countenance the possibility of reform.

That blooming of dissent didn't last long. Rudd had left Beijing by the time the crackdown ended its most significant phase; nevertheless, during the mid-1980s the continuance of monolithic control by the Communist Party did not appear as inevitable as it came to appear later, after the suppression of the students at Tiananmen Square.

The important point about his personal experience was that it provided Rudd with a remarkable insight into the complexity, or duality, of China. This understanding is a vital part of deconstructing Rudd's method of dealing with the superpower. The ancient Taoist concepts of yin and yang offer a simple example of how different forces nonetheless remain interconnected and bound together. Although these two concepts are often considered to represent good and evil, it is perhaps better to understand that they are two different forces which continually interact — hence the importance of balance.

The important point is the need to understand the complexity of what China meant for Rudd. There was a tendency for many Labor sympathisers to assume that Rudd was completely sympathetic to the aims of Beijing. This was not correct.

The Chinese government believed it had treated Rudd with warmth both before and after his election as prime minister. That's why there was some confusion when he gave a provocative address to an elite audience of students at Peking University during a visit in April 2008. Normally, such lectures are anodyne: they extol the strength of the relationship, gloss over differences, and ignore any real problems. Rudd broke the rules.

His speech would have been surprising in Washington or London, but in Beijing it represented an exceptional challenge to the authority of a state that imposes its own method of interpreting events. In particular, Rudd referred a number of times to Lu Xun. A significant left-wing writer, Lu had died before the communists had achieved power in China; he was, however, a liberal, and a serious critic of authoritarianism. This made Rudd's repeated references to the writer somewhat ambiguous. Then came Rudd's assumption that he could be a *zhengyou*, or a 'friend who disagrees'. Arrogating that role to himself, the prime minister implied that he could 'engage [with Beijing] in a direct, frank and ongoing dialogue about our fundamental interests and future vision'.

The problem is one person can't create a relationship by himself. There'd been no indication that the Communist Party felt any desire for Rudd's friendship in this way. Meaningless platitudes may have characterised the relationship in the past, but there was a sound reason for this. It's difficult to know why Rudd spoke the way he did. He may have been motivated by a genuine desire for honesty and the hope that his speech could do some good in the evolution of this country that he thought he knew well. It seems unlikely that he was motivated by a desire to demonstrate to Australians that he was no 'puppet' of Beijing. It would have been irredeemably stupid to use a speech in the Chinese capital to posture to a domestic audience back home.

Whatever his motivations, Rudd certainly managed to surprise his hosts. Unfortunately, 'surprise' isn't always perceived as a virtue in China. Speaking out, particularly in public and especially at a significant forum like this, came as a shock. Rather than respond at once, Beijing held its counsel, waiting to hear what extraordinary thing might next come out of this Australian's mouth. But soon after Rudd's visit, some non-Australian analysts in the Chinese capital reported that a significant message had emanated from the top party leadership. Beijing (and Beijing alone) would decide who was a *zhengyou*. The Communist Party didn't require any self-appointed 'friends' pointing out its flaws. If the party wanted to engage in a self-criticism session, it could do so without assistance from outside.

When Rudd had been posted to the Chinese capital as a young diplomat, Australia did have a significant role as an interlocutor between West and East. A lot had changed in the subsequent quarter of a century, though, and Australia had lost any connection that might have permitted this sort of talk. Although Beijing valued Canberra, the leadership had decided that if it was to continue, in future this relationship would be marked by respect, not intimacy. Top party officials felt that Rudd's words had lacked this vital ingredient. The increasing disparity in size and power between the great East Asian giant and the little Australian gnat came into play. Rudd's comments were brushed away, dismissed as 'ignorant' and, even worse, 'impolite'.

The first opportunity for Beijing to respond came a couple of months later. At the beginning of June 2008, with no diplomatic preparation whatsoever—without gently floating the idea in foreign capitals or even seeking to obtain some feedback on his idea—Rudd blurted out a grand new idea for a new multilateral organisation in a speech to the Asia Society in Sydney, just before heading overseas (to Japan, this time).

His idea was simple: a new institution, the Asia-Pacific Community, was going to be established. Everything, from economic to security issues, would be on the agenda for the new body. It was going to range widely and become the pre-eminent forum for enhancing a co-operative agenda (and even freeing up trade—this was before the global financial crisis had led to Rudd's almost Damascene conversion to beat the scourge of free markets).

If Rudd had expected his revelation to be embraced, he was rapidly disillusioned. For a start, it was discourteous to unveil this proposal to a domestic audience without having previously sounded out other countries about it. The almost unanimous response from Asia was, 'This is an interesting idea that should be considered further.' For anyone with even a basic understanding of diplomacy, such an oblique endorsement was the equivalent of throwing it into a coffin, and slamming the lid shut and hammering it closed with so many nails that it could never arise to disturb a tranquil world. It seemed that Rudd was a slow learner.

As a junior diplomat, his precocious ideas had been welcomed by his ambassador, Ross Garnaut, who'd seen the merits of some of his proposals. Garnaut had encouraged the young Rudd by lending him, for example, books on economics so the junior staffer could introduce himself to concepts that he hadn't come across at school or university. Rudd was no polymath; his academic career had been dominated by a focus on particular subjects in an attempt to master them. He'd done well, of course, but so had others, and there were rumours that he'd only swapped from Chinese to Asian Studies so he'd be guaranteed first-class honours, rather than a second.

A fellow student at ANU's Bergman College insists that, when he was younger, Rudd had flirted with the idea of becoming a missionary, and that this had been a partial inspiration for his later studies. This person suggests that religion provided Rudd with the certainty he craved at this period of his life.

Subsequently, his experience of working for Queensland premier Wayne Goss had catapulted him into an extremely senior position in that state's civil service. As a result, he'd leapt straight from being a junior diplomat into a job where no one dared to contradict him — as long as he maintained the backing of his political master. This had continued until Goss's destruction after merely two terms as premier. Part of the reason for Labor's fall had been perceptions of authoritarian behaviour at the top. Some internal critics had linked this directly to Rudd.

From then on, Rudd had involved himself in developing his own political career. An analyst who saw Rudd operating at close range during this period suggests that he lacked substantive experience in government (or diplomacy), where he'd had to negotiate the terms of a proposal by listening to other people's concerns and then being malleable enough to achieve an objective. If Rudd had power, he'd force a proposal through. If he didn't, he'd drop it. There was no negotiation or discussion.

The foreign affairs community was shocked by Rudd's Asia-Pacific Community announcement. None of the young diplomats wanted anything to do with it. In the end, Rudd chose the experienced but octogenarian Dick Woolcott to shuttle around the Asian capitals in an increasingly futile attempt to breathe some life into the proposal. Woolcott, a former boss of Rudd's at foreign affairs, had been involved in the establishment of the Asia-Pacific Economic Co-operation organisation. He should have known better. APEC had previously been derided as a collection of words in search of a noun, yet the APEC leaders' meeting had become an important fixture on the diplomatic calendar. No one wanted to risk that forum.

There was no international desire for Rudd's vision, although no one would admit it publicly. The bizarre manner of its birth had virtually guaranteed that it would be stillborn, and indeed it went nowhere. By 2010, the PM had finally recognised that there was no enthusiasm for his new international architecture. Woolcott received a 'no' wherever he travelled as he continued his lonely campaign as Rudd's frontman for over a year. When he eventually submitted his report to Rudd, it contained upbeat and positive beginnings and conclusions — but the main body revealed that there had been no progress on the idea whatsoever.

Amazingly, the PM didn't give up. He instead decided that APEC was the problem. Instead of accepting this successful forum, he began attempting to downgrade it to a mere meeting of foreign ministers. This was so national leaders would have 'more time available' to participate in his own grandiose idea. There was immediate opposition from South American nations and Taiwan (which would have been eliminated from the new forum), but Rudd kept pushing. Some other countries grew frustrated with the man who simply wouldn't take no for an answer.

By now, Rudd had changed his proposal to reflect reality, but it was difficult to see exactly how any advantages would cancel out the anger he was generating elsewhere. He had finally accepted that ASEAN (the Association of South-East Asian Nations) was the core grouping that needed to be brought on board, but he attempted to browbeat the national leaders within the regional grouping without managing to offer them anything in return. The last thing that many of the smaller South-East Asian countries wanted was to swap their own tight regional grouping, which had proved so effective in the past, for a slightly larger group that would be dominated by the US, China, Japan, and Korea, leaving aside India and Russia. Japan also had its own proposal — different from the Australian one, because it left the US out in the cold. Behind Rudd's back, Asian diplomats based in Canberra trashed the proposal. It was going nowhere.

Yet the PM still refused to admit that all the effort had been wasted. It was not until Singapore's foreign minister, George Yeo, visited the Australian capital in June 2010 that Rudd was finally forced to accept defeat, although he was still not prepared to administer the funeral rites. It was left to the visitor to state that ASEAN would decide if there was any need for another expanded Asian community. The failure of the initiative was barely reported.

In fact, by the end of 2008, Rudd's international credibility was already on thin ice. The time had come to start repairing already fractured relationships. That's why the release of Australia's Defence White Paper came as such a shock, particularly in Beijing.

Rudd had always been interested in strategic affairs. Indeed, he'd begun writing a thesis in this area before he'd dropped it because of political work pressures. While he was foreign affairs spokesman, the party had developed a strong critique of the then government by insisting that the coalition had failed to provide any co-ordinated approach to dealing with military affairs. The last Defence White Paper had been prepared back in 2000 by Hugh White (who'd earlier worked with Beazley, and later went on to be a professor at the ANU). Although the Howard government had issued updates since then, no overall strategic framework had been developed to explain the force structure that Australia required.

While in opposition, Rudd had insisted there was an urgent need for a new White Paper. Very early during the term, defence minister Joel Fitzgibbon had commissioned Mike Pezzullo (who'd also worked with Beazley) to prepare a report. According to one story, an early draft was shown to Rudd, who looked at it briefly before announcing definitively, 'No, this won't do!' This account of the meeting has it that Rudd then said, 'If you want to know what I want, listen to what I say in Townsville.'

It's important to note that this story has been absolutely and flatly denied by Fitzgibbon.

Rudd did, however, make a speech to the RSL National Congress in September 2008, prior to the release of the White Paper, in which he warned of a 'substantial arms build-up' in the region, and emphasised the need to 'make sure that we have the right mix of capabilities to deal with any contingencies that might arise in the future'. At no stage did the prime minister ever mention China (or indeed India), but it was difficult to make sense of his comments in any other context.

What had become absolutely clear was Rudd's determination to ensure that Australia was properly defended. The White Paper had a remarkably lengthy time-horizon, a factor that might have explained the trepidation with which it viewed the future. It was, in fact, a realistic rather than pessimistic analysis of potential future threats and the military capabilities necessary to deal with them.

Prior to the paper's release in May 2009, Pezzullo went on a 'road trip' around the region to brief other countries on its contents. This was a sensible way of preventing any untoward reporting of aspects of the report that might skew an important point: this was a proposal for *defence*. Australia wasn't anticipating any immediate threat. He was attempting to build confidence by making sure there were no unanswered questions about the new defence posture.

Nevertheless, according to one analyst, the Chinese reaction was 'incandescent'. The assessment made by senior Chinese academics instead suggested that the Australian military was about to begin a significant expansion of capability, directly intended to counter China. Beijing had already begun boosting its own forces, expanding its naval force as well as the technical capacity of the other arms. In 2008 alone, the budget allocated to the military increased by almost 20 per cent; although it's difficult to measure Chinese military expenditure accurately, according to most accounts it had risen at least fourfold since the year 2000. Officially, this now represents 1.4 per cent of GDP, but most analysts believe that it is closer to 2 per cent.

The issue that was most infuriating to the Chinese was a startling development intended to provide Australia's forces with a razor-sharp deterrent—a dozen massively capable submarines—an idea initiated by Rudd himself. China possesses 55 submarines (including ballistic nuclear missile-armed boats) and has a number of more advanced models under construction, but it was still concerned about Australia's build-up. The vessels that Rudd was proposing to build (small enough to be hard to detect, but large enough to carry guided missiles that could be launched from underwater) represented a new capability for Australia. These vessels could secretly remain on station in the South China Sea for long periods, with their missiles posing an implicit threat to the Chinese mainland. Although there were obviously no plans for Australia to develop nuclear weapons, the submarines alone were intended to have a significant deterrent effect. This gave the paper a tough edge that made it unpalatable to Asian tastes.

It is easy to see how the (perhaps paranoid) overseas analysts had joined the dots to come up with a negative assessment. Nothing the Australians said changed their view. For a start, this represented a doubling of the country's submarine fleet. Second, the envisaged submarines were significantly larger than conventional submarines operated by other advanced Western countries. The assumption was that this was intended to increase their range so they could operate a great distance from the Australian mainland for extended periods of time. Third (and surprisingly, given the disastrous experience of building the Collins-class submarines), the submarines were to be designed and manufactured in Adelaide. The Chinese assumed that the desire to retain an Australian shipbuilding industry wasn't enough to justify the extra costs of doing this — there had to be something else behind the desire to develop the submarines. They quickly conjectured that this was intended to threaten China's hegemony.

There is no need to attempt to examine this belief critically. The vital point was that China's relationship with Australia could no longer be automatically assumed to be friendly.

As Rudd was well aware, context is everything when interpreting a foreign language. Suddenly, it seemed to some analysts in Beijing that Rudd had offered them a key to understanding his earlier statements at Peking University. He was reminding them that there were still two Chinas — the mainland and Taiwan — and that while Australia was prepared to deal with the great emerging superpower, it would do so on its own terms. As far as some of the political autocrats who governed China were concerned, Rudd had presented them with a Rosetta Stone through which they could decipher the meaning of his earlier comments: Rudd was just being rude.

An Australian analyst of the relationship believes the Chinese leadership felt that the prime minister was behaving like a crass barbarian, a *gweilo*. Although this term (meaning 'ghost-man') is Cantonese, it provides a good description of Beijing's reaction to what it saw as the uncivilised nature of Rudd's interactions.

The most significant breach in the bilateral relationship came in July 2009, one month after Rio Tinto had rejected a Chinese bid to increase its shareholding in the company. One of the company's senior negotiators, Stern Hu (an Australian businessman of Chinese birth), along with three other Chinese colleagues, was taken into custody as a result of investigations by China's State Secrets Bureau in relation to the stealing of secrets and the receiving of bribes. It was alleged that Hu's computer, seized at the same time, contained evidence that he was engaging in bribery.

It took some time for charges to be laid. The Chinese legal system is different from Australia's: charges are not normally formalised until the prosecution is certain it has the proof necessary to obtain a guilty verdict. There is no point in going into any great detail about the case; suffice it to say that events can be read on a number of levels.

A simple explanation of what happened is that the Chinese legal landscape is different from Australia's. The evidence adduced in the court conclusively demonstrated that the employees were involved in demanding bribes and suborning Chinese executives. Rio accepted the verdict, terminated the employees' contracts, and attempted to restore its relationship with China. Anything else would have been commercially suicidal. It remains to be seen what the company's reaction will be once the former employees have been released.

A slightly more complex explanation views the case as having been constructed to send a message to other (often Chinese) employees of Western firms who were involved in contract negotiations with Chinese government companies. The legal intricacies of this particular case are less important than the fact that this action sent a shudder of apprehension through the foreign business community. Certainly, the apparatus of the state was being used to monitor commercial transactions. It appears that, so far, only the one Australian and other Chinese Rio employees have been charged in relation to the case; at the time of writing, there have been no reports of charges being laid against those offering bribes.

A third — the most sinister — layer of complexity is dependent upon well-sourced reports that link the decision to prosecute the case with the very apex of the party hierarchy. It seems unlikely that the Shanghai bureau would have unilaterally decided to embark on a case like this, with such major international ramifications, without approval. According to well-sourced information from Beijing, the decision to initiate the indictments came from not just the top, but the very top. The decision to trash the value of an Australian passport was, according to this analysis, seen as a bonus rather than a reason not to go ahead with the prosecution.

Rudd did not personally intervene in the matter. Given the apparent guilt of the executive, this would have been difficult. He did, bizarrely, refer to 'possible economic consequences' as a result of the case, although he gave no indication what these might be. It appeared unlikely that Australia would refuse to sell minerals to China, or harm trade in other ways. Beijing responded immediately. 'I've noticed', a spokesman commented (in an off-handed sort of way), 'that in Australia recently some people have been making noise ... we're firmly opposed to anyone deliberately stirring up this matter. This is not in accordance with the interests of the Australian side.'

You didn't need to speak Chinese to interpret the blunt directness of that message. Comparing Rudd's carefully chosen words to 'noise' was an intentionally insolent dismissal. The message for Rudd was simple: he had no right to make any comments about what was happening in China. The world had changed significantly since the mid-1980s, when Rudd had been posted to the Middle Kingdom. Beijing had grown tired, very tired, of the Australian. Enough was enough. Beijing had decided it would to teach Rudd how to behave. The relationship would continue, but the 'close and warm' friendship was over.

***

During the 2007 election campaign, Labor had made two significant assaults on the coalition's international credibility. The first was in regard to Australia's relationship with Asia; the second dealt with the country's increasingly invisible position on the world stage. This latter criticism asserted that multi-level forums are significant institutions that can shape events, and that the country needed to become more engaged in these arenas. As you'd expect, the key institution that was singled out was the United Nations.

Visiting the UN headquarters in March 2008, Rudd announced that he was making a bid for Australia to become a temporary member of the UN Security Council in 2013–2014. The council has five permanent members (Britain, China, France, Russia, and the United States), and 10 other members, each serving two-year terms. The council is chosen by all 192 member states, and the success or failure of Australia's bid would be determined by a vote to be held in 2012. The country has been represented on the Security Council four times, the last time from 1985 to 1986. In its previous attempt in 1996, Australia hadn't been successful: Sweden and Portugal were chosen instead.

Six months after announcing that the country would try for a place on the council, Rudd was in New York again, this time to speak at the UN General Assembly. Fifteen-minute speeches are normally given by foreign ministers, although occasionally other leaders talk. In that particular year, speeches were given by leaders such as Libya's Mummar Gaddafi and Iran's Mahmoud Ahmadinejad. In previous years, Howard had also given addresses to the Security Council and plenary sessions of the UN.

Rudd had to wait, because previous delegates went over time. When he finally got the chance to speak, he laid out a program to increase financial stability and to warn of the dangers of climate change. Unfortunately, by this time most of the world wasn't listening. The room was later described as being 'near empty'. Diplomats were always polite about Australia's important role in the world; however, when it came to the hard choice between canapés and champagne, or listening to words of wisdom, the diplomats in the New York forum preferred to party hard.

Rumors circulated freely within diplomatic circles that the real reason for Australia's desire to obtain a seat at the UN was to allow an 'escape route' for Rudd in case he ran into domestic problems at home: while sitting at the high table, he'd have a brilliant opportunity to lobby for the UN's top job, the secretary-generalship.

The current secretary-general, Ban Ki-moon, was appointed in 2007. Although his five-year term would normally end in 2012 (and most are reappointed for another five years), the former Korean diplomat and foreign minister would be 68 by the time he'd come up for re-election. Within diplomatic circles, there were various permutations being discussed that would have allowed Rudd to succeed Ban — although all of these required, at least to some extent, the suspension of credulity. In any case, by 2010 it appeared extremely unlikely that Rudd would ever receive anywhere near enough backing to allow him to slip into the job. By then, the focus had returned to merely attempting to grab a Security Council seat. There were fears that even this might prove (in Rudd's words) to be a 'bridge too far'. The PM's lobbying effort appeared to have generated its own backlash, although Foreign Minister Stephen Smith acted to reverse this trend.

Making a bid for the Security Council isn't cheap — approximately $35 million, at least, is needed to lobby for votes (although only $11.2 million was officially allocated directly for the bid, with the rest going in 'aid'). Finland and Luxembourg were Australia's rivals for a seat on the council. Finland's reputation as a good international citizen meant it almost certainly would receive one of the seats, but it was initially considered that the Grand Duchy would be easy to beat. As time went on, however, it became clear that the European city-state was receiving a strong sympathy vote because it had never previously sat on the council and also, perhaps surprisingly, because there was a significant anti-Rudd sentiment emerging at the United Nations.

Australian diplomats became worried as they realised that a country of barely half a million people — little more than a train stop on the route from France to Germany — had begun to firm as a favourite. It turned out that there were fewer votes we could count upon in the UN than expected, but a serious lobbying effort was continuing, which involved a considerable amount of both time and money.

In an extraordinary move, the government even apparently asked Governor-General Quentin Bryce to travel to seven African countries (nine in total, including stopovers, at a cost of $700,000) to lobby for support for Australia's contentious UN bid. At the time, the trip was dismissed as little more than vice-regal tourism, although diplomats who'd seen their departmental travel-budgets cut back because of lack of funds were privately angered. It appears dubious that the governor-general will have proved more successful in obtaining support for the bid on a fly-in, fly-out visit, but that can't be judged until the vote is taken in 2012.

Australia's bid for the council seat later came under threat when Mossad (Israel's intelligence agency) carried out a 'hit' in the Gulf state of Dubai while using four fraudulently manufactured Australian passports. At the time, Rudd insisted that 'we will not let the matter lie'. Later, Australia abstained from a motion in the UN condemning Israel for the attack, instead of voting against the resolution, as it normally did. However, while Britain (which had its passports similarly abused) took swift action to expel a Mossad agent, it took five months before the Mossad representative in Canberra was also expelled; there were suspicions that other concerns, such as obtaining a seat on the Security Council, were the primary factors influencing Australia's actions.

Rudd had always been a friend of Israel, having travelled there a number of times, and he was apparently unwilling to take any action against that state. But it was made clear to the PM that the Arab countries had a significant lever over his pet project to grab a seat on the council. If these, with their other proxies, were to vote against Australia, they'd stand a very good chance of blocking any hope the country might have of winning a council seat. Subtle lobbying by the Syrian ambassador to Australia was behind the dawning implications of any failure to condemn Israel further. Because the ambassador had previously been posted to the UN, he understood Rudd's ambitions and, according to some sources, cleverly parleyed the threat of withdrawing support for the council bid into action against Israel and, specifically, withdrawing accreditation for Canberra's local Mossad officer. Nevertheless, it's important to note that many on the left of the ALP have long been frustrated by Israel's hard line, and were also calling for action as a result of the abuse of the passports.

Rudd again condemned Israel at the beginning of June 2010, when an Australian was wounded and two reporters were arrested by Israeli commandos while on the high seas heading to Gaza. This close to an election, both major political parties just wanted Middle East concerns to simply 'go away', because both were aware that wealthy individuals were liable to withhold donations to election-campaign funding if the government adopted what they perceived as 'bad' decisions. On the other hand, Rudd faced intense pressure from the broader public, and particularly within his own party, to act in ways that might have challenged his natural inclinations.

Before the 2007 election, Rudd had told the *Australian Jewish News* that 'we would like to initiate legal proceedings against (Iran's) President Ahmadinejad (in the International Court of Justice) on a charge of incitement to genocide'. This statement had gone down well amongst many in the Jewish community. Nevertheless, as a former diplomat, Rudd must have realised this was rubbish as he said it, because this particular court doesn't judge individuals; it tries nations. Needless to say, no action was taken after the election.

Rudd had suddenly dumped his past support for Israel as he took actions that ensured there would be no reason for the Arab nations to vote against Australia. A senior diplomat I spoke to could find no easy explanation for the way Rudd seemed prepared to deal so instinctively (and impulsively) with Middle Eastern issues. 'It doesn't make sense that a trained diplomat would act in such a disjointed fashion,' she insisted. 'There must be some other personal factor involved; he has a real blind spot in this regard. There is no co-ordinated approach … It's difficult for a peripheral player like Australia to have influence in an uncertain environment,' she says. 'Our [diplomatic] missions are being asked to achieve something they can't.'

The chaotic effect of these prime ministerial interventions was to become most readily apparent when the words 'Middle East' and 'nuclear' were put together and mixed into a diplomatic cocktail. The problem for the missions dotted throughout the region was that Rudd would often highlight one issue or 'fact', using this as a prism through which he'd then promote his own wider interpretation of events.

Another experienced regional analyst finds it difficult to accept that Rudd approached the Middle East with an open mind. He suggested to me that the PM insistently deconstructed the myriad problems and concerns surrounding the Middle East through his own predetermined perspective: 'Don't forget that Rudd's not new to thinking about this region — but remember how he first engaged. He was a very earnest young Christian at university.' Personal views formed in his youth may be critical in understanding the way Rudd approached problems in an area that is, after all, the crucible of Christianity. This may have explained his initial approach, but the need for Arab votes appears to have substantially altered his thinking.

A second foundation to the PM's analytical approach was his intellectual placement as a diplomatic 'realist'. This is a particular way of viewing the world as an anarchic society of states (in the categorisation of Hedley Bull, who was professor of international relations at the ANU while Rudd was studying there). But it's worth noting that even realism has its divisions — the main one being between those accepting pluralism, and others who believe that more should be done to foster particular universal 'goods', such as human rights and democracy. Recently (and particularly in the wake of the collapse of the Soviet Union), there has been considerable argument about this approach to international relations. This debate has increased, particularly as disagreements about the 'realism' of particular courses of action have intensified.

The situation in East Timor clearly demonstrated the limitations of realism. As an opposition backbencher, Rudd had been particularly keen to involve himself in the development of Labor's international policies. However, the opposition spokesman at that time, Laurie Brereton, had unilaterally decided to make a significant change to the party's policy, and mischievously asked Rudd to organise a function in Brisbane to allow him to announce that the party would support self-determination and independence for the island state. According to one observer, Rudd was stunned and horrified when he heard of the change to Labor's position. He had apparently been an enthusiastic supporter of the previous policy formulated under former Labor foreign minister Gareth Evans.

Evans describes himself as a realist. As a minister in the Hawke government, he'd asserted his judgement that Indonesia would never be prepared to give up the island, despite the continuing guerrilla war that had been responsible for many tens of thousands of deaths in the tiny country. Evans decided to deal with the occupying power, even though the UN had failed to accept the incorporation of the territory into Indonesia. Most infamously, he was pictured toasting Indonesia's foreign minister with champagne as the two flew above the Timor Sea while signing a treaty to divide the oil wealth of the area between the two countries. Evans described the

1991 Dili massacre (in which hundreds of people were killed) as 'an aberration, not an act of state policy'.

Grass-roots supporters, particularly those on the left of the party, had become furious with the leadership's refusal to change its position on this issue, despite continuing evidence of Timorese animosity towards Indonesian rule. The realists, however, could see no advantage in challenging the integration of the island, because they could see no prospect of Jakarta ever relinquishing control. As far as Evans was concerned, it was his opponents who were guilty of naivety.

This changed radically in 1999 when president B.J. Habibie decided to allow a UN-supervised referendum. The result emphatically demonstrated that, despite nearly 30 years of integration, the islanders were desperate to regain their independence. It suddenly appeared that it was the realists who had failed to give appropriate weight to the violence and brutality with which the Indonesian military had enforced its rule. The effect of international condemnation, and turmoil inside the province, had played their role in finally convincing Habibie to hold a free ballot. After the election, as retribution and violence engulfed the island in chaos and bloodshed, there were popular demands for Australia to send troops to intervene. If Jakarta had failed to restrain its military, to accept the result of the ballot, and to withdraw its troops, it's not inconceivable that relations between the two countries could have come close to war. As it was, ties between Canberra and Jakarta very nearly broke down.

This incident raises questions, not about the virtue of realism per se, but rather about the rigour with which the 'Evans school' interprets the facts on which it attempts to base policy. The significance of this was that Rudd positioned his policies very much within the Evans intellectual tradition. Indeed, one of the new PM's acts was to ask Evans to head up a new commission on nuclear non-proliferation and disarmament.

The idea for the commission was originally announced during a visit to Japan on 9 June 2008. That country was asked to provide a former foreign minister as Evans' co-chair, and the idea was to work on shaping consensus before a meeting of an international conference on proliferation in 2010. However, everything began to unravel virtually immediately. There is no need to go into the intricacies of the increasingly difficult relationship between Rudd and two Japanese governments. The real surprise was that, despite the emphasis that Rudd appeared to give to preventing nuclear proliferation, he pointedly refused to go to President Obama's Washington nuclear summit in April 2010. The summit made genuine progress towards disarmament, but Rudd may have realised he wasn't having much effect on the world stage. Instead of a disciplined approach to foreign affairs, Rudd was displaying alarmingly sloppy tendencies in an area that should have been his strength.

By mid-2010, even the relationship with Japan had disintegrated — this time over the issue of whaling. The embattled left-wing government in Tokyo could not risk alienating any domestic constituency and, behind the scenes, begged Australia not to introduce further complications into the relationship. Peter Garrett, the environment minister, had insisted that legal action should be taken to try to ban whaling completely. Rudd agreed, even though there was a considerable risk that if the case failed it would permit the resumption of unrestricted whaling.

***

At the end of February 2010, Rudd finally released the government's (long-withheld) Counter-Terrorism White Paper. Within the bureaucracy, even the way the paper had been formulated almost entirely from within the PM's department had been controversial. It was quietly put about that Rudd's need to oversee every paragraph had been the real reason the document hadn't been ready earlier.

This reasoning appeared validated by the slim nature of the final product, which had apparently been rapidly altered to stress potential dangers to the nation, making it more significant for the media.

It detailed predictable threats — dirty bombs and the probability that terrorists would not just come from overseas but would increasingly include other, home-grown threats. Crucial details were, however, lacking about the $69 million funding boost that was scheduled to accompany the release.

One of the headlines the paper generated was that people from 'around ten' countries would be measured biometrically to ensure that their identities matched their passports. This vague requirement allowed the government to look tough without having to risk saying how the idea would be implemented or, vitally, which nations it would apply to. Unfortunately, by now the relationship with South Asia had already washed onto the rocks, and neither Pakistan nor India appreciated being singled out as problem states.

The relationship with India had already plunged to its nadir: were potential students now to be slugged with another requirement, simply ensuring that they felt like suspects? Or were Pakistani nationals to be singled out, when it was Saudis who had provided the bulk of terrorists attacking the US on 9/11? The very idea of a 'list' of nations capable of producing potential radicals represented a diplomatic disaster in the making.

However, Australia's international relationships were fraying badly even closer to home. Rudd had paid little attention to the nations of the Pacific as he flew around the world. The relationship with Fiji, wracked by coups, had deteriorated markedly. Diplomats on the island nations rarely found they were troubled by enquiries from the prime minister's office. Rudd's vision appeared to be much broader than the local neighbourhood. More importantly, the relationship with Indonesia has been fitful at best.

President Susilo Bambang Yudhoyono (SBY) had originally

been scheduled to visit Australia in 2009. He never came that year, because too much was happening at home. When his plane finally touched down at Fairbairn airforce base, both Rudd and Governor-General Bryce were out to greet him. Their joint appearance served as a reminder that SBY does the job of at least two people. The Indonesian president combines the roles of both head of state and leader of government as he balances on the tightrope of politics in the archipelago to our immediate north.

Geography alone ensures that our relationship with Indonesia will remain one of Australia's most critical. Strategically, it's vital.

It's easy to reel off the litany of reasons for this. The world's fourth most populous country and largest Muslim nation (with 135 people to every square kilometre) shares an enormous and porous border floating somewhere in the Timor Sea between those 17,508 islands and our own. Australia ranks about 14th in the world in terms of gross domestic product and similarly in terms of per-capita GDP (the IMF says we each produce about US $41,982); Indonesia is about 19th, producing $2,224 per person, and growing at 4.4 per cent in 2009 (the third fastest in the world). In the same year, our growth levelled out at just 0.8 per cent. This is one international relationship that's crying out for emphasis. Unfortunately, under Rudd it was left to drift, with less prospect of ever reaching the shore than a people-smuggler heading for Christmas Island.

Years before, when Rudd worked for Wayne Goss in Queensland, he'd authored a major report on Australia's vital need for increasing Asian-language acquisition. This followed on Goss's election pledge to introduce these languages into every state primary school. The study of four languages (Chinese, Indonesian, Japanese, and Korean) was to be given priority, and every student was expected to be able to speak a bit of Bahasa Indonesia. The more intellectually able were to be introduced to the rudiments of Putonghua (Chinese). In his report, Rudd had proposed that *every* child should learn another language until year 10, and that 60 per cent of students would acquire one of the priority Asian tongues.

Today, fewer than 15 per cent of students leave school after studying another language, and only a tiny portion of these people work on one of the 'priority languages'. Even back in the (supposedly culturally sterile) Menzies years, close to 40 per cent of students acquired at least the rudiments of another language. The government dedicated some money ($62 million) to raising the number of Asia-literate school graduates (to 12 per cent by 2020), but specialists in the area insist this is pitifully inadequate. This collapse of interest in our surroundings has been reflected in the universities, where fewer than 500 people across Australia are studying Indonesian. More than double that number are now learning how to be journalists, even though it's been estimated that there aren't enough jobs to employ even one-third of the number of people who'll graduate with this particular qualification.

It wouldn't matter too much if a failure to institute language-training in Indonesian was the only issue bedevilling the relationship. However, Rudd's apparent refusal to prioritise the bond engendered hostility amongst some in Jakarta's political elite; that's why, when SBY finally came to Canberra, the mood amongst those in his delegation remained cool and reserved.

It's not the Javanese way to air grievances openly: this is seen as embarrassing, and leads to a loss of face all round. But behind closed doors, the Indonesians had plenty to talk about. There were the 254 Tamil asylum-seekers who'd been towed to Merak (Java) nearly half a year earlier, but who were still refusing to disembark. There was the continuing flow of boats apparently transiting the waters of the archipelago. There were questions over the fate of prisoners like the condemned drug-courier Scott Rush, who would face a firing squad early one morning unless he was suddenly granted a presidential pardon. There was the continuing irritant of military repression in West Papua, and environmental differences. All this, coupled with the Department of Foreign Affairs' refusal to remove an utterly bizarre travel warning — grouping our neighbour in the second-most-dangerous category — which suggested that travel to Indonesia was more dangerous than, for example, India (despite the more recent terrorist attacks that had affected many Australians in that country), and on a level with the Congo, Lebanon, Nigeria, Pakistan, Sri Lanka, Yemen, and Zimbabwe.

Yet, as SBY pointed out when he visited Australia, his country is one of Australia's top-ten tourist destinations. In 2009, 567,000 Australians travelled to Indonesia. Perhaps the moral is that no one believes anything a diplomat says. Certainly, nothing Rudd was doing on the international stage appeared to be having any effect — either overseas or in the way that ordinary Australians interacted with the world. A great deal of sound and fury had ended up signifying nothing.

SBY gave a speech in perfect English to the Australian parliament. Unfortunately, no leader of any party was able to reply in fluent Bahasa.

INTERLUDE

Julie and Joe

Straight after Brendan Nelson took over as Liberal leader, there was another ballot to decide who would be deputy. Of the three candidates, Christopher Pyne (sometime president of Adelaide University's Liberal Club) received 18 votes; Andrew Robb (formerly chief of staff to Andrew Peacock and federal director of the Liberal Party) obtained 25 votes; and surging through, slightly to the right of centre, was Julie Bishop, the former education minister under Howard, with 44 votes.

Bishop was a former lawyer who had managed Clayton Utz's Perth office and had attended an advanced-management program at Harvard. Talent spotters had noted her arrival in Canberra, although it didn't appear she'd be receiving rapid promotion. To gain her seat, the well-groomed Bishop had to defeat Howard's friend Allan Rocher (who'd defected from the Liberal Party to stand as an independent). More importantly, she didn't bear any resemblance to other well-known Howard favourites such as Jackie Kelly. Nevertheless, Howard eventually left his reservations behind and promoted the woman who attempted to describe herself as economically dry yet socially liberal. She hadn't really made her mark in parliament so far; some thought that perhaps this would give her the opportunity to shine.

In time, after Nelson was defeated, she became Turnbull's deputy. She held on to the job as he, in turn, was overthrown. At a news conference just after she'd pledged her complete loyalty to Abbott (her third leader in two years), Bishop was asked about her apparently transferable loyalty. She insisted that 'it was clear to me that my party wanted a deputy that would work with the leader and show absolute loyalty to the leader'. She insisted that this had been the case 'under both Brendan Nelson and Malcolm Turnbull. I'm now serving the party as deputy to Tony Abbott.'

Her choice of words gave a slightly second-hand aura to her protestations, and she appeared oblivious to the fact that her own image was becoming tarnished as her leaders fell around her.

Following on from Nelson's election as leader, Bishop took over as the spokesperson for workplace relations. It was a tough gig — the introduction of Work Choices was seen as one of the prime causes of the former government's defeat — but, even so, Bishop didn't manage to shine. Turnbull had been shadow treasurer before he became leader, and it's been a Liberal Party tradition for the deputy to choose his or her own job. Bishop wanted it. She felt that she had the experience and ability to do it, and to do it well. It solved Turnbull's problem of not wanting to initiate a major reshuffle. Finally, she'd been dealt into the main game and entered the big league at last.

But it wasn't in Turnbull's nature to share the spotlight. In opposition there's not really much opportunity for anyone other than the leaders to make their mark in the media; certainly not unless they're significantly adding to the debate by presenting new ideas or damning critiques. Bishop didn't do this — a point that Labor emphasised with carefully chosen words suggesting she was out of her depth. For once, her stylish appearance wasn't an advantage. The government relished the opportunity to attack her credibility, and a whispering campaign began to gain traction, suggesting she was 'all beauty and no brains'. What should have been an asset had been turned into a liability. Unfortunately for Bishop, her mannerisms simply reinforced the government's message.

Question time remains the major forum (outside the media) for politicians to get a chance to shine and to impress their colleagues. For an hour, between two and three o'clock when the house is sitting, this becomes the theatre where everyone evaluates how well their peers perform under pressure. The highest-level skill for an opposition MP is the ability to ask tight, short questions about, say, an egregious disaster, and pinning it to a specific minister. The skill is to wrap up the denunciation within the question so that any response becomes irrelevant. However, before you can ask the right question you need to know the answer, and that requires a lot of work.

But Bishop didn't seem to fit into the schoolyard brawls. She certainly failed to nail the treasurer. She didn't seem to be deeply across the issues, and some Liberals didn't feel she was contributing a great deal to the policy debate, either.

In the media, Bishop appeared to struggle with details of the portfolio. She proposed simply waiting, rather than doing something to avert the worsening financial crisis, leaving the coalition looking like helpless spectators. She then called for substantial tax cuts on the grounds that this would boost revenue. Her own colleagues worried that Bishop lacked the weight that the opposition so desperately needed in such a vital portfolio. She was faltering.

After five months, the party had had enough. As 2009 began, while the waves of the financial crisis washed around the Australian economy, the coalition was surprisingly hopeful that it might be able to turn things around and make Rudd a one-term prime minister. It was evident that as the crisis started to change the landscape, the party had to ensure it had a strong performer in the shadow treasury portfolio. That person needed to be entrenched by the time of the budget, due in early May. Bishop was told she had to go.

She wanted to keep the job, but she'd become a liability. According to one source at the time, Bishop's only support was fellow West Australian Wilson Tuckey. (However, that comment may have been meant simply to twist the knife in the wound.) The time was soon coming when no one would consider Tuckey's support anything other than a liability.

By Valentine's Day 2009, it had become clear that Bishop wouldn't be receiving any cards. There was a flurry of negotiation behind the scenes, and two days later she bowed to the inevitable. Joe Hockey took over as shadow treasurer, and Bishop switched to foreign affairs.

Much later, after Turnbull had been mortally wounded by the Grech affair, Bishop delivered a stinging rebuke to her colleagues, accusing them of acting like a rabble. She stressed the need for the party to back the leader, and suggested that this was an important cause of the Liberals' poor showing in the polls. By now, though, her style was beginning to let her down. She spoke to her colleagues like a schoolteacher would, but they weren't paying attention.

That was because she'd misdiagnosed the situation. The problem wasn't just the appearance of squabbling MPs: it was about leadership. She was right to note that the party lacked discipline, but she was only highlighting the superficial aspect of the underlying problem. Individuals were nurturing their own ambitions at the expense of the party, and there was no unifying ideology articulated to bind them all together. To many, it seemed that the deputy hadn't done much to help.

Finally, at the end of May 2010, everything came together for Bishop in the worst possible way. During a television interview she blundered badly, asserting that Australian intelligence services forged foreign passports. The comment was a political disaster, but it wasn't just the words she'd used. She'd accompanied them by throwing one of those withering looks, where her eyes fixed the interviewer (Fairfax TV's Tim Lester) as if he was dull and naive not to have realised this already, when he was having difficulty believing she'd made such a blunder. When she subsequently realised her gaffe, she simply attempted to deny her words. Doubts about her suitability crystallised. Bishop would not be retaining the deputy's position under the next leader.

* * *

On the last day of November 2009, the afternoon before Malcolm Turnbull's leadership smashed into the brick wall of party-room opposition to the government's proposed emissions trading scheme, Joe Hockey seemed to be vacillating. He hadn't even announced if he'd be a candidate for the leadership, although it was just hours before the vote due to be held the next morning. It looked as if he couldn't decide what to do. His nickname, 'Sloppy Joe', didn't just refer to his size, but also to his perceived lack of attention to detail.

Turnbull declared he was standing, Abbott had been doing the numbers carefully, and Liberal senator Nick Minchin was being even more precise. But Hockey was still trying to negotiate. Although he wasn't going to challenge the leader, he was intending to stand if Turnbull was forced to commit to a ballot. He was prepared to allow a free vote on the ETS. Hockey was ambitious, but he was also a committed family man, married to an extremely successful woman who had just given birth to their third child.

Just a few days earlier, it had appeared that Hockey was the consensus candidate and that the prize was his. Abbott had announced he wouldn't stand as long as Hockey guaranteed that he'd oppose the ETS. Abbott's offer was apparently genuine. But Hockey refused to do this, because he'd already declared he was in favour of the ETS, and he decided that he couldn't abandon his principles and change his position — even if this meant he had to forego the leadership.

His position was completely unacceptable to the sceptics. Later that night, Abbott withdrew a pledge not to stand against Hockey and threw down the gauntlet, announcing that he was determined to grasp the leadership and block the legislation. Hockey wanted to eliminate climate change as a political issue because he could see it was destroying the party. He thought the best way to do this was simply to pass the ETS and move on to other subjects, but many in the party were implacably opposed. The price of their support was the death of the bill. Abbott realised that this battle presented the opportunity to lever himself into the top job. Turnbull (who earlier that day had given one of the most impressive press conferences of his leadership, outside the doors of the House of Representatives) insisted that he'd fight. He'd been working his numbers hard. The Liberals had two clear choices, with Hockey standing apparently irresolute in the middle. But the party wasn't in the mood for compromise.

In the end, Abbott and Turnbull both had the numbers when it counted. No one doubted that Hockey was the most popular consensus candidate, but he couldn't get past first base. The Liberals wanted a leader, not a conciliator.

Hockey was eliminated in the first round. He lost by three votes, receiving 23 votes to Turnbull's 26 and Abbott's 36. In the deciding vote, eight of his supporters switched over, handing victory to Abbott by exactly one vote. Fran Bailey, one of Turnbull's supporters, was in hospital and absent. But there'd been one other surprising slip-up: someone, disgusted by the choice between the two, had just scrawled 'no' on the paper. No one has ever admitted to casting this decisive informal vote.

As he flew back to Sydney, Hockey was reportedly extremely angry with Turnbull.

This disaster added another small chapter to the party's sorry recent record of infighting. Since 2007, it had been led by John Howard, Brendan Nelson, Malcolm Turnbull, and now Tony Abbott. One putative leadership contender, Mal Brough, had fallen at the election. Peter Costello had rejected the chalice and left parliament, as had Alexander Downer. Now Julie Bishop and, later, Joe Hockey, had been found wanting.

The Liberals were finding it impossible to develop a workable policy, let alone to present a coherent message to the electorate on the environment. This was a fundamental issue for Australia's future, yet the party continued to effectively deny that it required a policy on the subject.

It appeared that the only way the opposition could conceivably return from the political wasteland it was inhabiting was if the government began to self-destruct.

CHAPTER SIX

The Program

'I think it is quite plain that one of the problems that we have had as a government, for which I accept responsibility, is that we didn't anticipate how hard it was going to be to deliver things ... We didn't properly, I think, estimate the complexity of what we were embarking on.'

Kevin Rudd on ABC TV's *Insiders* programme, 28 February 2010

The last week of February 2010 witnessed a dramatic rhetorical *volte-face*. Previously, Rudd had presented a picture of confidence, insisting he was in command of the detail and that the government was heading in the right direction. But, suddenly, this had all come unstuck. Very publicly and suddenly, people knew things had gone bung, and the reason they knew was because Rudd himself was telling them.

For any other politician, the risks of admitting such culpability could have been disastrous; but even at the beginning of 2010, Rudd knew he still had an enormous reservoir of goodwill out in the electorate. His storyline was simple. He pre-empted any assault by getting in first, acknowledging mistakes and promising to fix things. For the first time, he publicly accepted that there were major problems with Labor's program. It was such a complete confession that it would have made his old childhood priest proud.

But there was a significant difference between Rudd's confession and the type that used to be heard at Saint Ita's Catholic Church in Eumundi during his youth. He was neither requesting forgiveness nor admitting to specific failings of his own; there was much more to it than this. The wider community was well aware of the government's mistakes, so Rudd intuitively understood it would have been naive to expect voters to simply forgive him. He was engaged in something far more substantial: a recasting of the entire project.

The confessional practised by the Eastern Orthodox Church stresses not merely repentance, but also progression from the mistakes that have prompted the original confession. In other words, the admission of failure is just one part of the journey towards a better life: the acknowledging of a mistake that can then be corrected. Rudd was doing much more than simply confessing his sins to restore his connection to the electorate — he was promising to change the way the government was working so as to avoid trouble in future. This enhanced the resonance of the simple message.

The polling demonstrated that his continuing commitment to avoid problems in future sparked forgiveness instead of opprobrium. Voters knew that mistakes had been made, but they were prepared to accept Rudd's assurance that he'd personally ensure they didn't occur again. It was a powerful message.

Nevertheless, the series of interviews that the PM embarked on represented a huge risk in an election year. It required voters to accept that, despite Rudd's own admission that there'd been serious problems with a large number of the schemes his government had introduced, he remained the right person to solve the problems. The message was simple, personalised, and much the same as the one he'd used to win victory in 2007. Rudd was saying, quite plainly, *Trust me, I'm the person you want on the job to fix things.*

How had the shiny new government come to be tarnished so badly?

The specific cause of the *mea culpa* was the disastrous implementation of the pink-batt insulation scheme, but Rudd knew there were a number of other problems that remained just beneath the level of public consciousness. Labor had come to office with a big agenda for reform, and the government's entire method of operating was being increasingly called into question. Things were beginning to go wrong, and the public wanted to know why.

The question was: where did responsibility for the stuff-ups lie? Although the PM was demonstrating an inordinate control of decision-making, he insisted he had been quite prepared to leave the specifics of detailed policy implementation completely in the hands of the relevant minister. His 'confessional' relied on the idea that he couldn't be implicated in the succession of disasters. He was coming in with clean hands; his intervention would bring things back on course.

The idea was that, in future, Rudd would ride his cabinet with a tight rein. He was suggesting that in the past, once policy had been decided, he'd simply thrown away the reins and left it to the relevant ministers to follow through with implementing the details. This came as news to some of those ministers; nevertheless, they understood the media strategy that Rudd was pursuing, and no one complained.

In off-the-record conversations with me, two senior ministers (operating in areas where the PM had a specific interest) both contradicted the assertion that Rudd interfered with the administration of their portfolios in any way. This supported Rudd's new narrative. Senior public servants in a number of other ministries also denied that the PM was riding roughshod over policy settings in any way.

Perhaps it would be more accurate to say that nothing could happen without Rudd's approval, but any perception of the PM's hands-on role also depended on exactly where an observer sat. People in positions at or below the level of deputy secretary seemed to find much more of their time being occupied in dealing with either the prime minister's office or requests emanating from there. They'd been increasingly frustrated by these because of the urgency with which briefs were demanded, only for them to be left unread for ages before any decision was taken. No decisions could be taken without Rudd being actively engaged in the issue. In his absence, everything simply ground to a halt.

Towards the end of 2009, Dennis Shanahan from *The Australian* newspaper reported a story going around Labor MPs that revealed much about Rudd's style. Late in the evening, South Australian ALP politicians were meeting with the PM in his Parliament House office to discuss, amongst other issues, Adelaide's transport needs. The discussion became far more intense than expected. Rudd's viewpoint was, apparently, being articulated quite forcibly. Soon, a map of the city was called for, as the PM demanded to see the detail of what was being proposed. In the end, pages from a photocopied street directory were laid in front of his gleaming eyes before the debate could continue.

A similar story is told about the decision-making process prior to the later rollout of the National Broadband Network. Rudd insisted that his office be provided with detailed technical information about various alternative high-speed broadband alternatives. Perhaps significantly, he didn't request this through the minister, but commissioned his own study — one that he demanded be completed within two days. This deadline meant that the resulting document bore far more resemblance to a school project (even including excerpts from Wikipedia) than it did to an in-depth study of the most expensive infrastructure project ever undertaken by an Australian government.

These incidents encapsulate much about the way the Rudd government worked. Things happened at the periphery, and the routine drudgery of process continued much as it always had. But always in the centre was the PM, guiding some actions and propelling them forward, while holding others back or vetoing ideas he disagreed with.

This is not a description laden with moral values: it simply *is*. Some politicians liken Rudd's method to that of a dictator attempting to control everything; these tend to be people whose projects were put on hold, often indefinitely. Others breathed a sigh of relief that someone was finally able to finally cut through complex, knotty problems and make a decision. The surprising result is that, on so many issues, Rudd became the crucial decision-maker.

Bureaucrats tended to find his interventions more frustrating. Rudd was not prepared to simply accept options that were put to him by civil servants. Instead, he often wanted to see evidence, proof, to be convinced himself that particular options were the right ones to proceed with. And if he wasn't convinced, Rudd was not afraid to decide on what the correct alternative was, and to send the work back until he got something he was happy with.

His desire for intervention could be seen in the massive expansion of the prime minister's department. Unsurprisingly, Rudd reserved the right to contribute his personal input into the crucial decisions his government was making. Some — but not all — observers believe that this led to two significant problems becoming institutionalised. The first was gridlock and deferral, as decisions banked up awaiting the PM's approval. The second problem (somewhat ironically, given Rudd's insistence on evidence-based policy) was a concern that, occasionally, prime ministerial caprice could skew outcomes, as well as the way issues were addressed.

As a very senior public servant put it to me, 'His word is the word of God. Nothing can happen in Canberra without his personal okay.' Another senior officer from the PM's own department was sent on an odyssey flying around Australia, accompanying Rudd in a desperate effort to obtain some 'face time'. He knew that without doing this he'd never be able to receive the direction he required as he put a vital document together. This led to the quite bizarre spectacle of policy literally being made 'in the air'. Politicians also found that this could be the best time to get Rudd to focus on an issue.

Although public policy is supposed to reflect the best thinking of experts, bureaucrats in the senior levels of the public service soon came to realise that Rudd believed only he had the ability to quickly understand the competing requirements of different policy areas and to come to a correct decision on the issues involved. This meant, inevitably, that he was the person best placed to arbitrate and choose which policies to implement. The role of the public service was reduced to simply administering his decisions. Many found this frustrating.

Added to this was the spreading reputation of the prime minister. *Herald Sun* columnist Andrew Bolt referred to his image as a 'particularly methodical Christian dentist [and] publicly prissy churchgoer', but insisted he was, 'privately a foul-mouthed, arrogant, paranoid and abusive control freak'. This made staff particularly reluctant to deliver bad news to Rudd.

Wherever possible, public servants also began to keep their interactions with the PM to a minimum. He also gained the reputation of having a particularly nasty and vindictive personal streak. This was reinforced as a result of one incident in which a diplomat appeared to have his appointment as ambassador to Germany blocked by Rudd.

Hugh Borrowman had known Rudd since they'd both stayed at Burgmann College as students. He then became a diplomat, and was working in the international division of the prime minister's department when tensions with Rudd appeared to erupt. The foreign minister, Stephen Smith, subsequently endorsed Borrowman for the position of ambassador to Germany, but this was blocked by the PM himself. He bizarrely chose to insist that, 'when it comes to foreign diplomatic appointments, I do place priority on languages, as does the minister. And last time I looked at Germany, they speak German'.

This was a particularly flagrant insult because, in fact, Borrowman did speak German fluently (as well as French and Swedish). Rudd appeared to believe he had the ability to alter reality whenever he wanted, simply to suit himself. Borrowman was sent to Stockholm instead.

The toll on ministerial advisers was also tough. By early 2010, more than half of the 444 ministerial staffers who had come in with the government had departed. People privately began referring to Rudd's own personal office as the 'transit lounge' after he'd lost 28 staff, a turnover of nearly one a month. 'It's just not worth working there,' one normally loquacious individual told me, before quickly insisting, 'and that's all I'm going to say.' It became difficult to work out to what extent the exodus was attributable to Rudd's personal workstyle, how much of it was just part of the normal turnover that results from people moving to a new job, or whether it was due to the fact that some people couldn't keep up, as Rudd himself implied publicly.

It was perhaps unfortunate that the PM later compared his staff to dogs, when he noted that the enormous stress they were placed under while working for him was similar to a 'dog's year' — or the equivalent of seven human years. 'So folks stay with me for three or four years, that's probably 28 or 30 years more in actual time', he suggested. 'Look, it's a tough environment.' Presumably, that comment also went for Air Force stewards who dared to serve the wrong meals.

Advisors quickly learned not to cross Rudd, even when the PM was making mistakes. As a result, he became increasingly surrounded by a coterie of courtiers. This tendency appears to be inevitable in any prime ministership; however, it is not normally noticeable until the second or third term, as with Howard and

Hawke. The last Labor politician who built a personal office around himself was Keating. But, as one Labor politician commented dryly, 'Of course he's surrounded by yes men. I'm one myself whenever I'm around him! Do *you* want to be the first to give him the bad news?'

Ministers also developed their own different ways of interacting with the PM as a result of this tendency to use their few moments of 'face time' as positively as they could. One, sometimes portrayed as being henpecked by Rudd, told me that he disagreed with the assessment that the prime minister controlled everything. 'You can talk him around,' the minister said. 'He's got ideas, but if you front him and argue a persuasive case, he'll listen to your argument and change his mind. Perhaps those who've said this is not the case have just been putting forward bad policy.'

'I remember one case in particular', the minister continued. 'Rudd outlined his point of view right at the start of the meeting, but indicated he was flexible and open to persuasion, and he was. He was convinced by other arguments that his initial idea wasn't the best one. He contributed ideas, but there was nothing dogmatic about his position — and this was an area about which he knew a great deal.'

Some ministers learned to carefully time their plans around Rudd's movements, such as when to hand in a submission that needed approval. Apparently, things could sit in Rudd's in-tray for ages; the word quickly went around that it was far better to submit minor issues whenever he was out of the country. At least Julia Gillard would deal swiftly with proposals, instead of postponing decisions or asking for more information.

***

Not long after the 2007 election, it became apparent that not all of Labor's election promises would be followed up. The most obvious initial casualties were the 'Watches'.

The government announced 'Grocery Watch'—a website that would allow shoppers to compare grocery prices—in August 2008, the day after the Australian Competition and Consumer Commission insisted that there wasn't enough competition amongst supermarkets. Grocery Watch was a straightforward populist response by a government that was intended to provide more information to the public; nevertheless, analysts suggested that the solution being proposed by the ACCC was itself flawed. The website would simply allow the major supermarkets to benefit most, because they were the ones with the ability to manipulate information and prices most effectively.

There was, understandably, a great deal of deeply entrenched opposition to the idea. The smaller retailers, in particular, insisted that the government was just 'beating up' on the middleman. By February 2009, the site had become embroiled in claims that it was neither specific nor up-to-date. The consumer group Choice was going to take over the site when, just days before the website's scheduled re-launch, the government decided to abandon the scheme. The entire concept had turned into a disaster.

The debacle demonstrated conclusively that nobody in government was properly overseeing the project from conception to execution. As a result, what had seemed like a good idea at the time wasn't thought through properly, and no one had acted as a devil's advocate in pointing out the problems with the scheme. In announcing the idea, Rudd had posed as the consumer's friend; but gradually, as the problems had become more and more obvious, the PM withdrew his support to leave it to others to bear responsibility. Consumer Affairs Minister Craig Emerson was left to quash the scheme, asserting that it wasn't feasible to generate reliable or timely data which would allow people to make meaningful comparisons.

What made the disaster more ominous was the fact that it followed the earlier announcement of a similar scheme which would have allowed consumers to work out where the cheapest petrol was available. The idea for what later became FuelWatch was generated at a Sydney cabinet meeting in April 2008. Without developing the idea of the scheme, Rudd walked straight out to announce his desire to 'put the maximum pressure on retailers' to ensure that fuel prices were kept low. This was intended to be another important method of easing the pressure on 'working families', as well as of increasing competition.

Unsurprisingly, the move accompanied a spike in the price of oil, and unleaded petrol cost more than $1.70 a litre two months later. The action was announced quickly to demonstrate that the government was concerned about the rising cost-burden for families. Soon the government's action looked more like a PR scheme, because — again — the way the scheme would work hadn't been properly thought through. As the year went on, the price of oil began to retreat, and the urgency left the debate. However, by November the scheme had been blocked in the Senate, while the opposition argued that they had evidence which clearly showed that FuelWatch would result in less frequent petrol discounting.

Senator Nick Xenophon insisted that the scheme was merely a distraction. 'If the government is serious about cheaper petrol for motorists, they must address the cosy buy-sell arrangements in the wholesale fuel market', he said. He compared the scheme to the bobbing head of a plastic dog on a car's dashboard. 'A distraction,' he said, 'but it doesn't really do anything'. Motoring associations agreed that the way the scheme was constructed contributed to **its** failure, having the perverse effect of making it anti-competitive. They also insisted that it would lead to higher average fuel prices.

Admitting defeat, Competition Minister Chris Bowen insisted, 'FuelWatch wasn't the be-all and end-all. Obviously, it was important, but it's not as if it was all we were doing.' Ironically enough, earlier that same year he'd been the one who'd insisted that the scheme would help people 'find the cheapest petrol prices and make significant savings'. Some observers noted acidly that while it was Rudd who'd announced the scheme, it was the ministers who were left to clean up the mess afterwards.

Just days after the election, Rudd had nominated education as his 'agenda item number one'. It seemed a worthy choice. Education, after all, enables individuals to fulfil their potential, and it is the bedrock of future productivity. The resonance of that particular message was, however, diluted three months later. As the Reserve Bank began to publicly mutter about the dangers of rising prices, the PM announced that his new 'number one priority' would be 'the war against inflation'. Nonetheless, by the end of that year, in the middle of some of the dire economic prognostications, he changed to insist that saving jobs had become 'our first national priority'.

Despite this evident confusion, Rudd certainly gave the impression that he would be an education-focused prime minister, although the implementation of this noble desire was left almost entirely to his deputy, Gillard. It wasn't long before she'd seemingly taken over full responsibility for overseeing everything in this area. She apparently didn't need to tell him to 'butt out' — Rudd was sensitive enough to understand that the amount of support she commanded within the party meant that he should not attempt to interfere with her handling of the portfolio.

When it was finally inaugurated, the 'My Schools' website represented a major, albeit qualified accomplishment for Gillard. She had pushed ahead, against quite considerable union and teacher opposition, to get the academic test-results of schools around the country published online. However, it was as if the battle had so exhausted her that the government was now unable to follow through immediately with any plan to either focus on schools that were falling behind, or to identify and reinforce success. At the same time, she guaranteed there would be no cuts to Commonwealth funding of private schools. It was difficult to see where the extra resources would be obtained.

Additionally, no changes were introduced to the funding model for either public or private education. This appeared particularly surprising if the government really did intend to invest substantially in the public sector. The government was failing to communicate messages effectively to the broader community.

However, it was the test results, and the comparisons they enabled — together with their palette of colours from relaxing pale-green to the urgent red of danger — that fascinated everyone. The trouble was attempting to make sense of the results. In their book *How Australia Compares*, Rod Tiffen and Ross Gittins noted, for example, that while the share of spending on private education in Australia is among the top three countries' in the OECD, expenditure on public education remains 12 per cent below average. Yet the website disregarded differences in the individual school-funding model, preferring to concentrate on the children's results. Instead of providing holistic comparisons, the website ignored other vital aspects of the educational experience and the inputs that the children were receiving.

Nevertheless, parents now thought that they had a handy extra guide allowing them to compare schools. This was indeed useful for those who were prepared to swap schools, pay more, or travel to ensure that their children were educated in the best establishments possible. Unfortunately, changing schools was not an option for many families. Students found themselves trapped in under-performing schools — so easy to identify, thanks to those same red (seriously under-performing) or pink (mildly concerning) labels appended to class results. The problem was not that schools were being classified (people already had a rough idea of which schools were poor, and which were performing exceptionally); it was that there was only a sketchy plan to do anything about the results.

When the site was launched just after Australia Day in 2010, Gillard insisted that, 'By comparing statistically similar schools, it will be clear which schools are doing well and which schools need an extra hand. The Rudd government is standing ready with new money and new targeted programs to help schools which are found to be struggling.' Although $550 million had been allocated to improve the 'quality of teaching and school leadership', it was not clear how this would be spent to assist particular schools. Unless this was genuinely new money, it appeared as if any plan to help the laggards would effectively punish the good performers. If any plan had been formulated to assist failing schools, it would have made far more sense to have released it before the testing system began, and to couple the announcements of the results of the exams with financial commitments.

After more than 1.5 million hits on the first morning, technical problems plagued the website, and it temporarily broke down. This certainly demonstrated that parents were incredibly interested in the information. It didn't necessarily mean, though, as Gillard later tried to claim, that all those who used the website approved of it.

To some extent, the website avoided the creation of 'league tables' by doing the job itself. It grouped so-called 'statistically similar schools' to enable different institutions to be judged against one another. Nevertheless, teachers reacted angrily to the website — not simply because it existed, but also because they alleged it didn't achieve what it had set out to do.

There were significant problems with both what was being measured and the 'comparisons' that were being made between different schools. Some institutions claimed that their scores didn't properly reflect their students' attainments: a teacher at one small school pointed out that because it had one disabled pupil (who scored extremely poorly), the school's other students were stigmatised as poor learners. Stories spread of particular children being encouraged to stay home on the day of the test. Parents and teachers argued, additionally, that schools which were meant to be similar, according to the website, were radically different. The scene was set for further confrontation that might have been avoided if a more co-operative approach had been adopted to begin with.

Some schools, both public and private, were obviously underperforming; the real question was how to raise their standards. It's invidious to pick on individual schools, but the publication of the results certainly raised significant questions about funding that remained unaddressed.

A second major problem was that the schools' website focused exclusively on academic attainments. Multiplicities of other attainments were also referred to in an introductory paragraph; however, anything that couldn't be quantified was, by necessity, ignored. Because only some attributes were measured, others were by necessity downgraded in importance. The world has entered a period where rote-learning skills (while remaining very important as a measure of student success) are not the only vital skills. Some parents' groups argued that creativity and analytical skills, together with the ability to reason, were the building blocks for success in the 21st century. Unfortunately, these are difficult to measure in a test environment.

All of these differences of opinion became acute later in the year, when the Australian Education Union — by now entrenched in its opposition — ordered its teacher members not to hand out the tests that were to form the basis of the website's results. Arguments rapidly escalated, with threats of fines, disciplinary action, and loss of pay bruited. In a popular but bizarre move, Gillard appeared to be prepared to recruit parents as strike-breakers to administer the exams.

Gillard had developed a rhetorical style of beginning answers with the word 'obviously', as if her particular preferred solution was self-evidently the only possible answer to any problem. Convinced that the website was the right thing, she had pushed ahead, regardless of opposition from well-meaning educationists and unions. Both were promised that changes would be introduced to the most egregious aspects of the site; but it was surprising that, in public, Gillard's negotiating style had been so intransigent.

As part of an unusual codicil to this affair, representatives of the so-called 'elite' universities (those belonging to the Group of Eight) urgently telephoned Gillard, asking her to construct a similar website for the tertiary sector. Confident in their own superiority, they believed this would emphasise the difference between the quality of their own degree offerings and those of other tertiary institutions.

Gillard was also lucky that the blame for mishaps in her other major scheme, the 'Building the Education Revolution' — otherwise known, in another addition to the acronym-rich practices of the government, as BER — didn't manage to attach itself to her. Although the government insisted on getting the credit for every building (ensuring that large billboards were erected outside each school while construction continued), it turned out that there were also a significant number of problems with the implementation of the idea.

The program had initially been rolled out as part of the government's stimulus proposals in an effort to kickstart the economy and to boost consumer confidence. It achieved this objective brilliantly. It pushed money out into the community, and everyone saw the dollars being spent; it is difficult to measure the effectiveness of this in keeping the economy buoyant, but undoubtedly it had a significant effect. The difficulty for Labor crept in later as the scheme continued rolling out.

It was a problem with administration. Firstly, and perhaps inevitably, people criticised particular projects with which they disagreed — for example, a tuckshop rather than a library, or buildings rather than books or computers. The second problem was the time it took to get many of the projects developed. Often, by the time the program was kicking in, the need for the money to be spent in the community had disappeared. Long lead-times and rigid bureaucratic procedures caused angst, and the involvement of the different state bureaucracies quickly became seen as an extra layer of complication, rather than something that facilitated a better product. However, the third and most serious problem was with the cost and administration of the scheme. Parents could rapidly find out how much the particular projects at their children's school had cost, or if the builders employed were local or from elsewhere. Concerns like these animated concerned parents and, if they saw any money being wasted or people coming in to work from outside their own town, they would often complain — animatedly. These effects must have cancelled the earlier positive feelings engendered by the stimulus.

Gillard attempted to stare down the grievances. It was claimed that findings from an Australian National Audit Office report vindicated the program, but the government was using selective quotations. When it was eventually released, after being sat on by the government, the report found that the primary aim of the program had been accomplished — but that was to stimulate the economy rather than to get value for money. This latter goal appeared to have been achieved in far fewer cases. Parents (and the media) were able to compare the much-higher costs of buildings in public schools than those in the private and Catholic-education sectors, which imposed tighter controls over costs. Gillard, though, continued defending the program. This was a surprisingly inept political judgement, because individual parents had already made their own decision about the value that the BER was providing, and were not going to be persuaded by anything she said to the contrary.

The BER's positive effect was always going to be engendered precisely because it quickly spread the money throughout the community, and enabled people to see that the government was stimulating the economy. The negative for Labor was that, in many cases, people saw large sums of government money being misused — as was inevitable in a program this large. Simply telling people that they were 'wrong' wasn't the best way of dealing with the problems, yet that's what Gillard did as she continued to face down critics of the 'revolution'.

This was a serious mistake. She was denying the reality of many people's personal experiences. The art of successful political communication is, at least partly, to shape the way the audience receives the message, but Gillard failed to engage positively with any criticism. It defied belief to assert that such a massive expenditure of money (which also depended on state government administration) could be rolled out without a glitch. Nevertheless, Gillard dismissed concerns while she continued to receive positive results in the polls, which suggested that voters didn't blame her too much for the waste or extravagance.

Gillard's other sweeping change was far more positively received. She moved quickly to roll back the politically poisonous swag of industrial-relations reforms that Howard had introduced once he had acquired control of the Senate in his final term. These changes were swiftly introduced and implemented by the incoming government, which needed to keep faith with the union movement, while endeavouring to maintain competition in the workforce.

On 19 March 2008, Gillard introduced her 'Fair Work' bill to replace the 'WorkChoices' legislation of the previous government. Despite its horrific name (governments in the past decade have seemingly done everything they can to realise George Orwell's fear that politics would pervert the English language beyond recognition), she'd worked hard to achieve a positive outcome for as many 'stakeholders' as possible. The new system was bedded down effectively and without any immediate problems. The government's only (minor) problems came when Gillard continued to insist — against the balance of probabilities, if nothing else — that *everything* had changed for the better.

Just after the government came to power in March 2008, Sky News' Kieran Gilbert asked Gillard if she'd guarantee that no worker would be worse off under the new system. She replied, 'They will be substantially better off', and later reiterated this assurance. 'I can give a guarantee that no worker … will be worse off.'

Such a blanket guarantee only required time to pass before it was proven incorrect. The coalition was able to find a multitude of instances in which people were adversely affected by the changes. Liberal parliamentarian Stuart Robert, for example, brought up the alleged case of meter readers with the Spotless Group who'd previously been paid a total of $716.98 a week, but who were now paid $563. Spotless had insisted to the workers who were losing money that it 'did not implement this modern award. This is a government issue.' Robert insisted that this was happening 'across the country'; however, by now he'd begun spinning his own tale. Predictions of widespread discontent failed to materialise; in this case, the legislation had obviously been carefully formulated before it was introduced.

Nevertheless, the government was quite certain that industrial relations remained a strong suit that it could use to batter Abbott, in particular. Attempts were made to link him with the possibility that WorkChoices might be reintroduced. Given the fights that Rudd's government had already engineered with the unions, it needed to do everything it could to ensure that workers would remain faithful to it.

A difference was becoming apparent in the degree of latitude that different ministers were allowed in both making public comments and implementing policy. Outsiders noted that while the deputy prime minister was allowed to run her portfolios without any apparent interference, other ministers (perhaps, in some cases, understandably) were supervised far more closely. Some ministers further down the pecking order found their inability to contribute to policy particularly frustrating.

As 2009 wore on, it appeared that the department of the environment under Peter Garrett had failed to effectively oversee a government-funded program to provide insulation for houses. The original idea behind the scheme (funded at $2.45 billion) came as part of the government's programs to combat the financial crisis.

Departments had been asked to consider ways of pumping money into the economy, and this idea quickly received Treasury backing because it seemed to tick all the right boxes. The general idea was worthy, because it would reduce energy consumption, leading to long-term environmental benefits. It also had the advantage of getting money into the economy speedily by putting it in the hands of the very people who were likely to spend its fastest — tradesmen.

The environment department was essentially responsible for formulating policy, and didn't have a great deal of expertise in implementation. This isn't, however, an adequate explanation of why things turned sour so quickly. Given its policy expertise, the department should have been able to ensure that the systems worked right from the start; however, these turned out to be the basis of many of the subsequent problems. Some later measures, cobbled together as the extent of the catastrophe became apparent (such as providing the money as a rebate rather than offering it directly to the installers), should have been introduced from the start.

On 10 February 2010, the day that Garrett, finally, was due to announce changes to the insulation-roofing scheme, it became obvious that the minister would be subjected to intense questioning from the media on the subject. Instead of allowing adequate time to answer all such questions, Garrett gave the press gallery barely five minutes' notice before a news conference he scheduled for 1.40 pm; then he turned up five minutes late, with barely 15 minutes left for him to answer questions about the scheme before he had to rush away for parliamentary question time. In such a tight timeframe, and with so many issues to be dealt with, it was impossible for reporters to gain a true understanding of what had occurred — and who was responsible for it. Only much later did it emerge that there had been a very good reason for the government to prevent reporters from questioning the minister: Garrett's scalp was being offered as a sacrifice. It wasn't the environment minister who had failed to act — it was Rudd himself.

As soon as the deaths of four people were linked to failures in the scheme, it became obvious that the subject would remain a bleeding sore for the government. These were facts that could never be batted away, and that's why Garrett was overturning his previous position to agree that all homes with foil insulation would now be subjected to a safety inspection. But vital questions remained unanswered: in particular, when was he advised of the safety risks, and had he informed the prime minister that he wanted to close the scheme? On these answers hung the far more serious question of whether he bore any personal responsibility for the people who had died.

In fact, his office had been informed of the risks in March 2009, but he didn't ban the use of metal fasteners until November that year, after the first two deaths. It wasn't until another two months had passed, and another death had occurred, that he finally acted to suspend the rebates for foil insulation. By early 2010, the deaths of four people and as many as 200 house fires had been linked to the scheme. However, key details in this devastating timeline were not revealed at the time.

As the minister responsible, Garrett had written to the PM, warning of the 'unacceptably high occupational health and safety risks', four times the previous year. His last letter, in October 2009, warning the PM's office of the dangers accompanying the rollout of the scheme, was sent weeks before anyone had died. These letters were only released to the Senate months after Garrett had been demoted and forced to shoulder the blame for the government's failure to implement the scheme properly, and for the consequent deaths of installers.

Because of Rudd's subsequent words and actions, the minister had effectively been blamed for supervising the scheme inadequately. It turned out, though, that he'd advised on measures that, if they'd been acted upon promptly, might have saved lives. Apparently, no alarm bells had run in the PM's own office and, as a result, the matter hadn't been treated as urgent. It is unedifying and pointless to attribute blame for the failure of the scheme — it will not bring back any of those who died — but it appears that the culpability was spread more widely (or perhaps more narrowly) than Rudd had first suggested.

Bizarrely, instead of facing questions on the subject, Garrett spent the third weekend in February looking at rare angle-headed geckos and golden-crowned snakes. He continued to guard his privacy jealously, never once mentioning that he'd lost his own mother in a house fire when he was 23, being badly burnt as he attempted to rescue her from the second floor of their house in Sydney's Lindfield, even though this fact might have demonstrated how deeply he felt personal anguish over the installers' deaths. Although, at times, his responses appeared jerky and awkward, nothing was able to stop the flow of smooth verbiage that covered up the massive flaws in the scheme.

It seems impossible not to conclude that the minister had decided to lie low, deciding to sacrifice his own credibility in the interests of the party. Whether this was also in the interests of good governance was left for others to decide.

The solar-panel rebate also had to be abandoned after another blunder that cast a pall of possible incompetence over both the minister and his department. This scheme had offered householders a rebate of $8,000 for installing environmentally friendly equipment. The rebate had been so popular — some 55,000 people made claims worth $440 million in the last two weeks of the scheme alone — that it had run $850 million over budget. That's why the door had to be slammed shut three weeks early, with only one day's notice given for people to lodge their claims.

Even at a theoretical level, there were qualms over the widespread introduction of household solar panels. Green economists pointed out that individual households didn't represent the optimal way of generating electricity: it would have been far better, from an environmental perspective, to pour the money into large-scale generators — possibly using wind power. These concerns were swiftly brushed away. The big advantage of pushing the money out to individual householders was that it meant they could immediately see that the new government was doing something for the environment. The advantages of this appeared to outweigh any benefits over the longer term of keeping electricity prices down.

Green Loans proved another debacle. When people were offered a no-interest loan of $10,000 to improve energy efficiency, they rushed for assessments to allow them to qualify for the scheme. Once they qualified for the money, householders would then be able to use the money to purchase water tanks or solar-generation systems.

The government had anticipated demand for the scheme to require 360,000 assessments over four years, although it's extremely difficult to see how such a low estimate could possibly have been arrived at. When 22,000 requests were booked each week (and the number of assessors exceeded the government's expectations by a factor of twelve), the department quickly realised it had massively underestimated the appeal of the scheme. Yet, for some unexplained reason, one assessor, Field Force, was allocated nearly one-third of the funded work as the scheme rolled out. Such mistakes couldn't be explained away simply by the department's theoretical policy-bias.

The schemes were obviously intended to be popular, and yet the department had been caught completely unprepared. There was obviously going to be a massive, batt-led expansion of the roofing-insulation industry, for example, and yet the department put no measures in place to either ensure the maintenance of quality or that safety procedures were enforced. The scheme was intended to significantly boost one sector of the building industry, and yet no method of minimising this structural dislocation was considered. Greens Senator Christine Milne had been initially positive about the government's ideas; however, once she saw the way they were put into practice, she insisted it had been 'turned into an utter debacle through gross mismanagement by Peter Garrett's department'.

Garrett's first brush with politics had been in 1984. Although he was then still the lead singer of the band Midnight Oil, he stood as a member of the Nuclear Disarmament Party for a New South Wales Senate seat. At the time, Labor refused to give him preferences, directing them instead to the coalition. In 2004, he'd been recruited to the Labor Party by Mark Latham, announcing at the time that it was better to attempt to influence government from the inside rather than by remaining pure (but impotent) on the sidelines. Much later, as a minister, Garrett continued to refuse to accept any personal culpability for the disasters he presided over; however, he also failed to explain how, if the government had taken the sorts of actions he was advocating, the problems wouldn't have spiralled out of control. (It was later to turn out, as we've seen, that he'd been sending letters to a prime minister who'd failed to respond.) Perhaps more significantly, he also appeared to have failed almost completely to change Labor's policy on a number of issues that he'd previously been closely identified with.

Rudd rapidly quashed Garrett's raising of the possibility that the traditional owners might be able to ban climbing on Uluru, or Ayers Rock, in central Australia. There was also controversy in October 2008 when Garrett slashed $2.6 million allocated to fund the Melbourne-based Australian National Academy of Music. Although the money was later reinstated, no clear reason was given for either the decision to remove funding or to restore it. As minister, Garrett also announced the approval of a potentially environmentally damaging pulp mill for Tasmania, and encouraged a major expansion of uranium mining in South Australia. All these decisions were made with Garrett sitting around the cabinet table, so one can only assume that he was happy and content with the results.

On the emotive issue of whaling, Garrett actively sought a ban, in the face of two major diplomatic problems that this approach came up against: the Japanese government indicated privately that this was likely to severely affect its relationship with Australia, and it was likely that Japan would be able to obtain the numbers in the relevant international forums to allow the continuation of whale hunting. For some time, Garrett's complaints remained unheard within the government, but by mid-2010 Australia decided to bring Japan in front of an international court over this issue. This honoured an election commitment, but at the cost of New Zealand's refusal to join the lawsuit because it believed the chances of success were negligible. Australia's neighbour warned that an unsuccessful case would result in more whales being killed; nevertheless, the government decided to plough ahead, regardless of the danger that it might backfire.

A meeting of the International Whaling Commission in June 2010 turned into a showdown between pro-whaling nations and those wanting to ban this activity. Japan was firmly committed to the resumption of whaling, but proposed an alternative that would have permitted some commercial whaling (including of endangered species), but would have reduced the overall numbers killed. This split opponents of the hunt, with New Zealand and other nations prepared to consider the proposal while Australia remained firmly opposed to any killing of the mammals.

This caused a serious breach with Japan.

Despite Garrett's attempt to take action on whaling, Paul Watson, the captain of the controversial Sea Shepherd Conservation Society, insisted that the minister's tenure had been highly disappointing for the environment. During his travels around Australia to boost support after the whale-hunting season had finished in 2010, he happily volunteered a damning epitaph for Garrett to the media: 'After all those years of singing about it, he finally gets the opportunity to do something real, and does nothing at all.'

On the other hand, a politician I spoke to — one who didn't get to sit around the cabinet table — was more sanguine about reconciling youthful aspirations with the realities of politics. 'There are limited opportunities to contribute to the formation of policy,' he told me. 'That's what you expect when you move from opposition into government. There is much less time available for those in the hot seat to speak to other people. It depends on the issue, I guess.'

Nevertheless, this explanation failed to satisfactorily encompass the apparent inability of a minister sitting around the cabinet table to influence events in his own portfolio. It was becoming difficult to work out exactly how the Rudd government worked.

***

This book is specifically about Kevin Rudd's 2007–2010 period in office. It doesn't aim to detail the ins and outs of decision-making over the multitude of programs that the Rudd government initiated. Nevertheless, it's become obvious that particular factors had a major influence on the formulation of policy.

Most significant of all was the central position of Rudd in the entire project. He firstly ensured that he was fully briefed on all the factors he considered relevant in order to make a decision on the broader policy settings that surrounded any issue. Because of the demands on the PM's time, this could often take a long time. He also appeared to have a predilection to unconsciously sift out evidence that didn't appear to point in the overall direction that he wanted to go. There was a tendency for even relevant and important information to be discarded as Rudd whittled things down to his own satisfaction.

Exceptions to this pattern occurred when Rudd was unwilling to interfere with other ministers. He kept his hands well clear of Gillard's portfolio responsibilities, and also appeared willing to delegate power to people such as Simon Crean, Kim Carr, and Martin Ferguson. Some members of caucus noticed that Rudd appeared to be reluctant to meddle with any ministers who had their own support bases within the party.

Understandably, Rudd ensured that, wherever possible, he was associated when the government was announcing 'good' news. When Carr, for example, announced that some of the money originally allocated for developing clean-car technologies would be given to Holden so that the company could research a conventional four-cylinder engine (on the grounds that it would be more fuel-efficient than, presumably, a six-cylinder car), Rudd was happy to be associated with the move. After that time there was little media interest in the story, and it appeared to closely match the reduced amount of concern that Rudd showed about the subject.

In March 2010, a story surfaced in the media that Rudd had called Senator Stephen Conroy in for a 'roasting' over problems regarding the National Broadband Network. Previously, Conroy had been allowed to run this extraordinary and costly scheme to stretch cable around the country without any detailed oversight. He appointed a Labor insider, Mike Kaiser, to a top job with the company, and had been allowed to roam unfettered through the policy landscape, despite the $43 billion cost of the project. Strangely, this massive project — the biggest such in Australian history — hadn't even been flagged before the election. It had just been allowed to grow after Telstra initially proved unwilling to work with the government. By building its own network, the government effectively committed itself to deliberately devaluing the investment of individual Telstra shareholders, who thought they'd been buying into a monopoly asset. No other private company was prepared to take on the huge task that the government had subtly announced it was willing to throw taxpayer dollars at. This was reflected in the share price of the telco, which initially dived as news emerged of its rift with the government, only recovering later once the two institutions had done a deal.

Only in 2010 (after the scheme was already being rolled out in Tasmania) did the government finally provide a consultant's report that declared the scheme viable, although this depended on a large number of assumptions. By then, Labor was already committed to the network, and it was politically virtually impossible for the government to withdraw from the project. Communications wonks had known for a long time that the beleaguered scheme was in technical trouble; however, it wasn't until two particular problems became widely raised in the media that Rudd acted.

The primary problem appeared to be American concerns about Conroy's Internet 'filter'. The minister had been determined to retain the filter to siphon out objectionable material, even though the barrier was more like a sieve that could be circumvented easily by people with a basic level of technical skill. Most people were concerned either about the Internet slowing down as a result of the barrier or, alternatively, the possibility that appropriate websites might be banned by accident, leading to censorship. Conroy brushed away these concerns as irrelevant.

What caught Rudd's attention, though, was the US State Department's announcement that the filter was contrary to American policy encouraging the free flow of information throughout the world. Rudd had seemingly been unconcerned about this issue prior to it becoming an irritant in the press, even though many Internet users had complained about Conroy's high-handed attitude for more than a year.

Conroy had become increasingly concerned to avoid sensationalist media claims that the network would bring 'porn to the home', just as the economic case for the high-speed broadband began to collapse. At the time, the minister was sitting on an implementation study into the network by McKinsey and KPMG. This had not been released, amid a swirling undercurrent of rumours that the expensive report had thrown significant doubt over the critical economic viability of the entire scheme, particularly as it was being developed as a direct rival to Telstra.

Because large numbers of Australians own shares in the former publicly owned telecommunications company, there was the risk of significant public concern suddenly erupting as people began to realise that the government's network would effectively be cutting the value of their shareholding. There was a concern that this issue was a 'sleeper' that might suddenly awaken if concerns about censorship or the enormous cost of the project were given oxygen in the press. The cost was the real problem — particularly because it depended on large numbers of people buying into the expensive wiring simply to begin to pay the interest cost on the borrowings.

As a result, Rudd had apparently suddenly interested himself in the way the project was being implemented. And, according to reports from the meeting, he didn't like what he saw.

It was difficult to understand why it took so long for him to become aware of the problems surrounding the network. Right from the beginning, the idea had been troubled, and analysts doubted Conroy's capacity to create a workable plan. Initially, it was hoped that the cost of establishing the network would be shared by a private company, and that a partnership would be established. The government spent $17 million in a fruitless search for such a partner before scrapping the tender and instead plumping to develop the $43 billion fibre highway itself. There'd been numerous indications that the rollout would be beset with difficulty; it almost appeared to telecommunications observers as if Rudd felt that his determination could 'will' these problems out of existence.

Rudd didn't have the caucus numbers to dump Conroy from the ministry, and so he apparently postponed any confrontation with him. Nevertheless, the minister didn't lead a quiet lifestyle, and he began appearing in the media for all the wrong sort of things — for example, meeting the owner of the Seven Network, Kerry Stokes, while on overseas holidays, and appointing former Queensland ALP state secretary Mike Kaiser to an unadvertised job (but one which ppaid $450,000 a year) with the government's own National Broadband Network.

Perhaps the most unusual thing about Conroy's decisions to slip down the slopes with Stokes, to relax at the races, to admire the AFL, and to goggle at the Grand Prix was the petty nature of it all. The thought that such small trinkets could buy favours should have been ridiculous ... so why did Conroy accept these tiny tokens of media bosses' largesse? Did he really, honestly, think that they liked him so much that they just wanted to share the pleasure of his company in the corporate boxes?

Everything did appear to have been properly disclosed by the senator — even Foxtel's gift of an English football team's signed jersey. But why did the pay TV operator hand it over to him? What was in it for them? Apparently, Conroy didn't feel he needed to ask the question. Neither did Rudd.

In the new millennium, parties on the private yachts of media moguls had been replaced by visits to exclusive snow resorts at Vail, Colorado. In the media, Conroy appeared to have been captured by the moguls, accepting petty gifts that were obviously not intended to be bribes but that carried the odour of inappropriateness. [text obscured] convincing people of his innocence, Conroy's brusque [text obscured] ed to scream out that he could measure power down [text obscured] tion, knowing exactly how much of it he could

[text obscured] obsession with other policy areas left the [text obscured] inister free to develop policy as he saw fit. [text obscured] minister a long time to realise that there was a [text obscured] his intervention in this area. Unfortunately, by [text obscured] isions had already been taken, making it [text obscured] tional Broadband Network and admit [text obscured] right at the start.

[text obscured] cut a deal with Telstra. It's difficult [text obscured] he failure of both sides to bargain effecti[text obscured] ad already begun stringing wires across the coun[text obscured] talk had led to a bizarre situation, whereby the government and a private company became locked into a disastrous confrontation that, unless averted, would obviously have left both sides badly wounded.

INTERLUDE

Tony

'Sometimes it's better to ask for forgiveness rather than permission.'
Tony Abbott, after making a 'leader's call' on paid parental leave, 9 March 2010

Tony Abbott phoned as the Commonwealth car drove him into Parliament House from the airport in December 2007. Shortly, he'd be fronting a news conference to admit that he didn't have the numbers to run for the leadership. Nevertheless, he was philosophical as he spoke to me on his mobile phone.

'It's not my time now or even the next time the leadership comes up', he said. Then came that odd noise he makes, somewhere between a slight grunt and an ah-ha, pausing for thought. 'But maybe the time after that.'

I didn't respond, because there didn't really seem to be anything sensible to say; I thought he was dreaming. If he couldn't win now, how on earth would he manage to increase his support for some implausible future tilt at the leadership? Both Nelson and Turnbull had more support than he did, and at that stage the party appeared to have many other potential leaders. It was difficult to see how this could change.

In the immediate wake of Howard's defeat, I was writing a book about the reasons for the Liberals' loss of power. We returned to talking about those last days, when the leader had suddenly got the wobbles and briefly considered standing down. With refreshing honesty, Abbott continued explaining exactly what had happened.

Howard had asked for his opinion about retirement. Abbott told me that, as well as canvassing various backbenchers for their views, he'd also spoken to a couple of non-political friends, asking whether they thought the seemingly doomed government stood a better chance of holding on under Costello's leadership. This was another surprise. Most people in Canberra wouldn't have bothered asking for strategy advice from anyone outside the beltway. Abbott did. He couldn't help himself. Although he'd been deeply embedded in politics since 1990, when he was John Hewson's press secretary, he still wasn't a creature of the machine. He was too genuine for spin, but that wasn't what people wanted. He genuinely believed in particular principles — but, unfortunately for him, they were based on values that not everyone shared.

Back in 2007 he'd urged Howard to remain, genuinely believing that this was the coalition's best hope of holding on to power. What surprised me at the time was his apparent willingness to sublimate his own ambitions for the good of the party. He personally would have had a far better chance of becoming the leader if Costello had taken over, lost the election, and then departed. Seemingly, Abbott really had acted in what he felt were the party's best interests.

Many years before that vote, Howard had (briefly) nourished Abbott's own desires for leadership, even if it was simply to act as a counterweight to Costello's increasing desire for the top job. Howard had always been careful to assemble an intricate pattern of pretenders as a defensive measure to protect his throne. No one was ever strong enough to challenge him, but all of them were powerful and ambitious enough to stop Costello from having an unobstructed run for the leadership. Howard always made sure there was an ABC — Anyone But Costello — candidate. He'd be just enough of a rival to prevent anyone else challenging, but not dangerous enough to threaten Howard's control of the party. The problem was that his failure to ensure succession planning left the party tearing itself apart the minute that he departed.

When Rudd had taken over as Labor's leader, he'd focused everything and everyone on one goal: achieving government. This unity of purpose had ensured that only one united message escaped into the public arena. Like a single beacon of light, Rudd's words came to represent exactly what the party stood for. He became the sun: everything else was sublimated to the leader. After Howard's defeat, the Liberals had become a constellation of stars, each little pin-prick of light apparently heading in its own direction. This appeared to guarantee the party a long period in opposition.

Howard had been defeated. Costello left of his own volition. The party burnt out Nelson and Turnbull as the bickering continued. Bishop stumbled as deputy, and was no longer a plausible candidate. Hockey might become a leader in the future, but a reputation for sloppiness surrounded him. If Abbott went down as well, Rudd might have commissioned a special belt, just like the brave little tailor in the Grimms' fairytale, proclaiming 'seven with one blow'. The continuing leadership turmoil was Howard's responsibility: he'd refused to leave for too long, and now the party had lost policy direction as individuals destroyed each other in a struggle for personal power. When Turnbull faced the backbench revolt over his support of Rudd's ETS, Abbott finally got his chance. Hockey's vacillation and Minchin's desire to stop the ETS at all costs ensured there was a gap big enough for Abbott to slip through.

His leadership began well. The party knew that Abbott's strengths were deeply intertwined with his weaknesses. He had a polarising effect: polls showed that people either liked him or not. Worse, party research showed that most people already had an opinion about him, with comparatively very few claiming to be undecided. Voters believed that Abbott was a 'real' politician who, very differently, stood for something. The trouble was that many didn't like what he stood for, and it was going to be difficult to persuade them otherwise. It also meant that most of them were already well down the path of working out who they'd vote for.

Abbott realised that he urgently needed to make a splash. He had to grab the electorate, and wake the sleeping voters up and convince them that he represented a new and better way of doing things. However, in order to be credible, any strategy had to be based around his own personality—and this represented a significant risk. When Rudd had taken over as opposition leader, he remained something of an empty vessel into which voters poured their own hopes and desires. Abbott didn't have that luxury, because he was already a known quantity to the electorate.

Back in 2008, Abbott tried to explain why he was a conviction politician. He'd written that it 'was a waste of time asking Howard to pose as something he was not'. After the 1995 budget, Abbott recalled, 'I had waited for the then Opposition leader to arrive at his office. "Let's block the partial sale of the Commonwealth Bank and torpedo Labor's budget strategy," I urged … he patiently heard me out before saying [that] whatever credibility he had rested on not playing that sort of political game.'

Abbott says he learned from this; however, he still appeared to find it extremely difficult to forego a tactical opportunity to cause mischief, as his series of positions on the idea of reducing greenhouse gases (discussed later) showed. He appeared to be announcing politically palatable policies, rather than the ones he really believed in.

Balancing this was another character trait: whenever he was asked what he thought about a subject, he actually attempted to answer the question, instead of merely repeating motherhood statements in an effort to ensure that everyone kept sleeping soundly. This meant that his honest message cut through in the media. But there were two problems with this approach: many people didn't agree with his ideas in the first place; second, when he changed his message — sometimes fundamentally, in ways that couldn't be dismissed as a simple, pure 'change of heart' — he cast doubt on his entire strategic concept.

Abbott did things his own way, relied on himself, and pushed ahead regardless. From the outside, it appeared as if he was attempting to reprise the techniques that Rudd had used so effectively to bring Howard down within a year. And, at first, they seemed to work.

Abbott spent the Christmas-holiday period at the end of 2009 working and travelling. The leader later told a private partyroom meeting that, 'We won't win the next election by adopting a small-target strategy'. His message — *I'll do whatever it takes* — was crystal clear. Without delay, Abbott sought to engage Rudd at a deeper level, below the surface of the traditional media. He started getting out into the electorate and meeting people. The theory was that this would generate a 'ripple effect'. People he'd met would spread the news that the opposition leader was an 'okay sort of guy' by word-of-mouth — something that was much more positive than having a message modulated through the traditional media.

He'd travel, for example, to a coal mine in the New South Wales Hunter Valley, promising that *he'd* be the one protecting workers' jobs, and trying to convince them that Rudd's ETS threatened their future. But, while effective, these tours also appeared to lack method. The chances of swinging the votes of enough miners to make a difference was virtually nil. Abbott didn't have enough time to continue wandering around the country, convincing everybody he met to vote for him. He went to some marginal electorates, but Labor observers took heart. They found it difficult to detect a pattern in this burst of activity.

One event emphasised that whatever Abbott did or said, it simply appeared to reinforce stereotypes that had already been constructed in the observer's mind. He was asked by the *Women's Weekly* what advice he would give to his daughters about sex before marriage. No one had bothered asking Rudd a similar question; he almost certainly wouldn't have answered it if they had. Abbott did. He gave an honest answer, but the particular words he used created an immediate furore.

Abbott suggested that his daughters should be very certain of someone before they had sex with them. He went on to say, 'It [virginity] is the greatest gift you can give someone, the ultimate gift of giving, and don't give it to someone lightly'. A cursory reading suggested that he was urging everyone to remain a virgin until marriage, which was not the case at all. Gillard rushed to the attack, suggesting that Abbott's words confirmed women's worst fears about the opposition leader. 'Australian women want to make their own choices,' she said, 'and they don't want to be lectured to by Mr Abbott.'

Nevertheless, Liberal polling (which had seemingly previously been in an almost terminal state of critical decline) suddenly began to look up. There was a growing anger with the government, which was having difficulty implementing its grandiose programs. In late February 2010, Rudd issued his public *mea culpa*. He was beginning to feel threatened, and wanted to put the bad times behind him. Rudd's apologia was believed. Voters still trusted the PM, and felt assured that he'd be able to turn things round. Labor polling appeared to recover. The pressure was now back on Abbott. Desperately needing something else that would allow him to break through to the voters, he cast round for new ideas.

Abbott had blocked the ETS, but that was a negative policy; now he needed to define a positive difference between the opposition and the government. That's why he announced a radical $2.7 billion proposal offering six months' fully paid leave for parents, to be funded by slugging the country's top 3,200 companies with a 1.7 per cent levy. Labor's reaction was incandescent. The workers' party suddenly realised it had been completely outmanoeuvred.

The volume of political debate quickly rose from shouting to screams of disbelief. An Abbott quote from 2002 was rapidly dragged up: as employment minister, he'd asserted that paid maternity leave would only be introduced only 'over this government's dead body'. He now insisted that he'd had a slow conversion in his thinking on the subject over a long period, emphasising that he'd advanced the idea for parental (not just maternity) leave in his book *Battlelines*. Abbott referred to a reply from John Maynard Keynes to a critic, after he'd changed his monetary position during the crisis of the Great Depression: 'When the facts change, I change my mind. What do you do, sir?'

Abbott stressed the very personal nature of this conversion on *Lateline*. He said that a 'deeper understanding of women who are trying to juggle families and careers [and] thinking more deeply about the sorts of choices that I would like to be available for my own daughters' had led him down the road to Damascus until, finally, he'd seen the light.

What he didn't talk about was the private polling that Bishop quietly referred to in the closed partyroom meeting on the Tuesday after his announcement. She noted that there was still one vital group that steadfastly refused to demonstrate any inclination to vote Liberal, particularly after Abbott had taken over. Women, predominantly those under-45 with children, had not budged; even worse than that, they were increasingly supporting Labor.

They'd become Tony's little problem. Hence the 'solution'.

Parental leave certainly turned the tables, upsetting the cosy tea party of ideological disagreement and sending the occupants racing in every direction, spluttering and coughing with indigestion. Unions NSW and the Greens — dealing with the issues — applauded Abbott's policy. The ACTU's Sharan Burrow and the Australian Industry Group's Heather Ridout engaged in a bizarre coupling as they united to attack the proposal. Labor had a scheme of sorts, but not one that contained the benefits of the Liberals' policy. At question time in parliament, coalition women rose to ask Rudd why he was 'supporting big business over working families' by rubbishing a scheme that would 'help up to 146,000 families a year'. Labor's women wanted to know why Abbott was hurting big business.

The opposition's tactics were shaking the comfortable foundations of Labor's dominance. Liberal strategists asserted that it was 'getting through where it counted … to the people in the marginal seats'. The suggestion was that these electors could work out how much they'd benefit from the policy and would vote accordingly. The problem was that, because business organisations hadn't first been massaged (and brought on-side), their immediate reaction was to condemn Abbott's proposal. This significantly confused the message being sent out to the electorate.

It would have been far better for the party to have selectively briefed a couple of companies in an attempt to get a few supportive comments into the public arena, but this wasn't done. The Liberals weren't displaying the tight professionalism of a skilful team engaged in a professional campaign. Instead, the policy was dismissed as one of Abbott's thought bubbles. This set a pattern for the electorate to dismiss the messages with which the Liberals were desperately attempting to woo the public. Serious initiatives were soon being discounted as ideas that hadn't been properly developed.

Abbott's support appeared to have a natural cap that limited his appeal. The Liberal base, its core, had been re-energised, but he was still having difficulty in convincing enough swinging voters to switch over. Many still harboured negative perceptions of him from his years in government. This was to become a critical issue in 2010 as the election approached.

Abbott unveiled a new indigenous policy, utilising his previous experience as shadow minister for indigenous affairs. He threw a grenade into the land-rights debate, suggesting that part of the problem was communal ownership of land which was vested in land councils. 'If Aboriginal people want to be able to use their land as an economic asset, they must be able to do so,' he said. Raising the possibility that land councils were effectively barring Aboriginal people (the traditional owners) from developing their land, Abbott suggested that, unless individuals could develop their land, native title was just 'a sentimental version of Aboriginal land ownership'.

It was an idea directly targeted at the core beliefs of ordinary Australians who aspired to own their own houses. The implicit suggestion was that the 'Aboriginal industry' could somehow stand in the way of allowing traditional owners to develop their land as they wanted. Abbott didn't articulate any alternative, but he did manage to raise a complex issue in a way that identified him with a fundamentally Australian way of viewing the world; at the same time, it forced the government to defend the problematic status quo. It was another way of very effectively running rings around Rudd — but always moving on quickly, before Liberal policy risked becoming the target.

Abbott knew which Aboriginal groups he could tap to help propel his proposals into the public sphere. To demonstrate his credibility while announcing the policy, he visited two elders, the traditional owners of the Watarrka-Mereenie country about 250 kilometres south-west of Alice Springs. They whisked Abbott off on a serious quad-wheel motorbike tour around their land and the sacred sites that their ancestors had used for traditional ceremonies. But when the group went missing for hours, his message was derailed as well. Slight hitches like this should have been irrelevant, but they combined to make Abbott the story, rather than providing reassurance to voters that he wouldn't do anything rash.

Abbott was asking people to trust him, which merely encouraged Labor to trawl through his record to cast doubts on his honesty. In 1998, on the ABC's *Four Corners* programme, he'd denied any involvement in legal action against Pauline Hanson; later, in 2003, he'd had to admit that he'd lied on air. 'Misleading the ABC is not quite the same as misleading the parliament', he'd said at the time. But facts couldn't be airbrushed away like that. He'd been caught out being untruthful to the Australian people. Those who were inclined to forgive him did so; however, not everyone accepted his easy dismissal of an issue that went to the heart of his credibility and character. For many people, honesty doesn't depend on who you happen to be talking to at the time.

In October 2009, Abbott had told an audience in the Victorian countryside that 'climate change is crap', while insisting that 'the politics are tough [because] 80 per cent of people believe climate change is a real and present danger'. The implication was that he'd mask, or even change, his personal beliefs in order to get elected. Later, Turnbull declared that Abbott was a 'weathervane', twisting and turning in the winds of political reality.

All this provided a context to an extraordinary interview that Abbott gave on *The 7.30 Report* in May 2010. 'All of us' Abbott said, 'when we're in the heat of verbal combat, so to speak, will sometimes say things that go a little bit further … the statements that need to be taken absolutely as gospel truth are carefully prepared, scripted remarks'. This astonishing admission had followed questioning over why Abbott had decided to breach a commitment (given in February) not to introduce new taxes, only to shortly afterwards slug Australia's top companies with a levy enabling the government to finance a parental-leave scheme.

Searing honesty has its own appeal, but Abbott's remarks simply served to accentuate the polarisation of the electorate's views about him. Those inclined towards Labor saw his comments as proof that he could not be trusted; those tending towards the coalition excused his 'honesty'. The irony was that, this time, in formulating his answer, Abbott had the dial set to truth, rather than to political astuteness. His insistence on being a real person with his own ideas and beliefs was forcing people to commit to or against him; he was not allowing his personality to acquire the malleability that Rudd had managed to achieve while in opposition.

Abbott had begun 2010 by running rings around Rudd, but

there were serious questions about whether it would last. Abbott continued to give the coalition a lift in the polls, providing a much-needed transfusion of hope for the conservative cause as he won back disillusioned supporters. But there was always going to be a natural cap on this new buoyancy. The increased support for his party was not being transferred to him as an alternative prime minister. He carried a lot of baggage: too many people still suspected him of misogyny, and his support of the monarchists' cause during the Republic campaign had identified him not simply as a traditionalist, but also led to him being grouped with the 'wacky fuddy-duddies'. Labor polling was showing that the electorate didn't regard Abbott as a safe conservative choice for PM. Even in the depths of the government's low ratings in April–May 2010, it still felt to pollsters and Labor insiders that there was too much ground for the coalition to make up. Many of the policies on which Abbott chose to differentiate himself were not likely to appeal to those who had deserted the government. Indeed, as the election approached, some of the policy positions that the conservatives emphasised — such as opposition to Rudd's mining tax — appeared doctrinaire and reactionary, rather than likely to gain the support of fresh voters.

With tactics like this, Abbott had arrested the slide in the coalition's polling numbers that had destroyed Turnbull's leadership, but he appeared unable to pick up many of those who had become disillusioned with Labor. Polling by Essential Research in June 2010 highlighted this at a time when support for Rudd was plunging. Its research suggested that Abbott himself was the problem, with director Peter Lewis noting that 'the real leadership story in Australian politics is that Abbott is unelectable'.

This appeared to tie in with the detailed qualitative research that had been done by the Nielsen company, which had been one of the first to discern the Liberal recovery. Director John Stirton noted the difficulty that Abbott was having in converting alienation from

Rudd Labor into positive support for the opposition.

Depending on who you chose to believe (and on the eventual result of the election), Abbott's leadership was either a mistake or a brilliant and necessary change.

CHAPTER SEVEN

A Big Country

'Well, first of all, Kerry, let me just say: I actually believe in a big Australia. I make no apology for that. I actually think it's good news that our population is growing.'

Kevin Rudd on *The 7.30 Report*, 22 October 2009

'Many Australians have legitimate concerns about the sustainability of the population levels in different parts of the country ... particularly its impact on urban congestion, its impact on the adequacy of infrastructure, its impact on the adequacy of housing supply, its impact on government services, its impact also on water and agriculture and on our regions.'

Kevin Rudd announcing a new population ministry, 2 April 2010

Between the end of 2009 and the beginning of 2010, Kevin Rudd must have had an epiphany. There was simply no other way of reconciling his various pronouncements about population growth and asylum-seekers. The earlier Rudd was seemingly 'relaxed and comfortable' about both issues. He apparently had no difficulty with the idea of a 60 per cent jump in Australia's population over the next four decades, and was similarly relaxed about asylum-seekers, confident in the knowledge that he had absolutely the right policies in place to deal with the issue.

Less than six months later, a panicked Rudd was suddenly creating a new population ministry and had introduced a harsh new detention-regime, focused on dissuading Sri Lankan and Afghanistani asylum-seekers from hopping on boats headed for Christmas Island. Despite the foreign minister's claims to the contrary, Australia was the only country in the world to make the arbitrary judgement that conditions in those two countries had changed enough to justify the suspension of considering people from those states as genuine refugees. It was impossible not to conclude that the country had changed its stance for domestic political reasons.

The reality was that the government needed to do something to quickly stop the flow of boats filled with asylum-seekers. It believed that votes at the next election depended on it. Despite these changes, Rudd still wasn't prepared to admit that he might have introduced the wrong policies to deal with the issue in the first place. He had begun to personify George Orwell's 'Big Brother' from the book *1984*.

In this novel, set in the fictional nation of Oceania, Winston Smith labours hard at the Ministry of Truth, changing history to reflect the current political reality. Facts become irrelevant to the inhabitants of this superpower, because no individual has any ability to change anything; the past is perpetually rewritten according to the dictates of the present. Society exists simply as a life-support system for the economy of the super-states as they engage in their perpetual wars. Meaning is destroyed; the purpose of life becomes simply to exist.

A similar economic determinism appeared to underlie Rudd's initial reaction to Treasury predictions that Australia's population could explode by 60 per cent to 35 million. Costello had initially introduced these reports, ordering his department to produce them every five years. But it didn't take the politicians long to work out how useful they could be in shaping public debate.

In 2007, Costello used the release of the report to provide a platform to extol the coalition's record in improving Australia's economic situation. By the end of 2009, Swan had realised he could use the statistics in much the same way, saying, 'Projections suggest that Australia's population could be larger and younger than presented (previously)'. Even though the predictions were accurate — they were straight lines drawn from current data to provide trends to the future — this meant that a small change to the underlying assumptions could result in a massive blow-out at the other end. And that's why the predictions were so dramatically different from the previous years' reports.

But Rudd didn't bother to qualify this in any way. When Treasury head Ken Henry had released the startling new figures, he quickly qualified the limitations of such projections, whilst also noting pessimistically the big challenges they represented for the future of the environment and country. Rudd, however, had no qualms in endorsing such a huge population.

'This government', Rudd opined, 'is building for the future; we call it nation-building for the future. Let's be optimistic about the fact that this country is growing. So many around the world are heading the other way.' The message was simple: the country was growing, and that was good. This meant there would be new challenges; however, Labor was ensuring that the country would be able to cope with any difficulties.

Rudd burst into this stunning verbal endorsement of unrestricted population and economic growth on the same day that Henry suggested that the population expansion raised profound issues for society. 'Where will these 13 million (extra) people live … how will cities cope … what types of services will our governments of the future need to provide (and) are Australia's natural resource endowments, including water, capable of sustaining a population of 35 million?' he asked. These appeared to be significant questions that demanded at least some indication of how the country could cope.

Henry himself insisted that he was pessimistic. 'Our record has been poor, and in my view we are not well placed to deal effectively with the environmental challenges posed by a population of 35 million.' Rudd simply brushed away these challenges without bothering to answer them.

The significance of Rudd's comments went far beyond the immediate issue of what Australia's population might be at any point in the future: it represented both a political and personal message that went to the core of the way he viewed the world.

Rudd was optimistic: any challenge could be faced and overcome. Australia would need to confront the changing world, and he believed this could be done without any need to alter any of the government's main policy settings. What was required instead was a government that prided itself on its technocratic excellence. With Rudd's hands on the levers, everyone could look forward to a prosperous future.

Firstly, and most surprisingly, there appeared to be no room in Rudd's unique vision of the future for the emergence of any environmental or resource scarcities. Presumably, his assumption was that harvests would continue to increase, boosted by some sort of new agricultural revolution. Surprisingly — especially given that the government was warning that, unless an ETS was passed immediately, the world would face dire environmental consequences — even the need for enormous quantities of extra water didn't figure in the prime minister's vision of a big country.

Rudd's surprisingly naive approach simply focused on the benefits coming from this 'necessary' increase. He pointed out that more people would obviously be needed to look after retirees as the population aged. This was half correct and half remarkably stupid. Exactly the same straight-line predictions that produced the 35 million figure for 2049 would have necessarily produced an amount of more than 70 million by the turn of the century, and 140 million a few years after that. At some point, a limit would have to be reached in this continual process of expansion or (if you prefer) population pyramid scheme, whereby there was always another, larger generation of people available to look after their predecessors.

Simply insisting that he was positive about a big Australia wasn't a particularly sophisticated response to the question of how many people the country could 'carry'. And even a cursory examination of the so-called 'need' for the population to continue expanding didn't suggest that there was any need for it to continue doing so at the projected rate. The whole idea was, ironically, closer to the worldview of people like developers and businessmen, who did not normally form part of Labor's natural base, although they did have an important role as donors to the party. But Rudd's rhetoric left the government wedged in an extremely awkward position, particularly in regard to the environmental movement.

Two linked factors quickly became obvious in the so-called population debate that followed these comments. The first was that people already had relatively fixed ideas about the population-bearing capacity of the country. Despite what Rudd had claimed, there was no commonly accepted view about the need to increase the size of the population. In fact, the more people thought about the issue seriously, the more pessimistic they became.

The immediate effect of Rudd's comments was to further boost the real estate market and to endear him to developers, but he had gotten way ahead of public opinion. One of the disadvantages of his self-confidence (or conceitedness, as MPs from his own party were increasingly labelling his behaviour) was that Rudd increasingly believed his instinctive call would prove to be correct. The PM was beginning to attribute to himself an almost divine ability to understand the world — even when, as one Labor politician said at the time, 'He doesn't have a clue what he's talking about.'

Bernard Keane in Crikey.com.au dissected the farcical nature of the predictions. 'There is a useful graph', he wrote, 'in the report appendices that gives the lie to this.' In other words, the first point that Rudd should have made was that the predictions were anything but inevitable; the corollary of this was that political settings were vital in determining the future environment that would be faced by young Australians.

It didn't take long before there was an increasing and understandable uncertainty about exactly what Rudd stood for when it came to the future make-up of the country, or indeed if he had any idea at all. Three months later, it became apparent that Big Brother had mis-spoken.

By the time he next appeared on *The 7.30 Report*, in January 2010, Rudd significantly qualified his remarks to a somewhat confused Kerry O'Brien. 'You're comfortable about a big Australia within 40 years of around that number of 35, 36 million,' asserted the host, only to be corrected in short order by the PM: 'This is a challenge of national preparedness ... Let's also put the other side of this question as well.' Suddenly, the PM was far less willing to assert that a big Australia was inevitable.

Normally, Rudd was capable of presenting himself as holding a 'commonsense view'. He'd previously found a way to triangulate issues, appearing to represent a reasonable compromise between different alternatives. But this was an issue on which that particular political tactic was destined for failure. The polling demonstrated that people were seemingly irrevocably fixed — one way or another — in their views about future population growth for the country. But a vital sector of Labor's support held the firm view that the inevitable constraints that resources were placing on the environment placed an absolute limit on the country's population.

Cynical commentators were convinced that this sudden change of opinion was driven by the polls. One survey had asked Australians if they felt positively about the proposed increase in population to 36 million by 2050. Across the board, 48 per cent were negative about such a swelling number of people on the continent, compared to 24 per cent who indicated they felt happy about the proposed growth. What was perhaps more significant was the political breakdown of respondents: 52 per cent of coalition supporters and 58 per cent of greens opposed a larger population — the greens more vociferously than any other group. Labor voters were most positive about such growth (even though this was a low 32 per cent of respondents), suggesting that Rudd may have been unconsciously reflecting one particular part of his own constituency; but, by the time undecided voters were removed, opposition to the population increase ran at something close to two to one.

The genesis of the popular mood was easy to understand. The nation's state governments were barely managing to keep transport networks and hospital systems running as it was. Doubling the numbers that would compete for living room simply appeared to be a method of compounding myriad existing problems. Many politicians, however, saw the comforting revenue-streams that the flood of newcomers would bring, particularly easing demographic problems that might otherwise require serious changes to be made to the status quo. The healthy projections meant that the magic pudding would continue to succour the economy, providing continued healthy growth without a real need to address fundamental underlying problems.

In an old *Yes Minister* programme, the bureaucrat Sir Humphrey (played by Nigel Hawthorne) informs the minister's advisor, Bernard Woolley (Derek Fowlds), that their political leader 'must obviously follow his conscience, but he must also know where it's going … because it may not be going the same way that he is'. This witticism encapsulates an eternal political truth: a politician cannot risk getting caught ahead of popular opinion, otherwise he will be rapidly discarded by electors who've decided that their 'leader' isn't taking them where they want to go.

When he initially announced his vision of a big Australia on

The 7.30 Report, Rudd was only expressing his honest thoughts. In doing so he was, however, guilty of moving far ahead of one section of popular opinion. Although very happy to be presented as a 'conviction politician', Rudd couldn't allow any of his beliefs to become obstacles on the path of political success. That's why a subtle, but concrete and measurable, change had taken place with his population-policy message by the time of his next appearance on the programme in early 2010.

An important consequence of the about-turn on population policy was that it significantly harmed Rudd's personal credibility. A fortnight after he'd changed his rhetorical stance about the number of people that Australia could 'carry', *The Australian*'s excellent 'Cut & Paste' column was making fun of the way the PM regularly refused to answer questions about other controversial issues, using Rudd's own words to display a number of inconsistencies in the persona he projected to the public.

Before the election, for example, Rudd had claimed that his staff was 'out of bed at 4.30 in the morning. So when I wake up, it's a telephone call to say, "What's happening in the world, guys?"' But times had obviously changed, because now he was more likely to use phrases such as, 'I haven't seen those comments' or 'I haven't seen the text' to explain why he would refuse to comment on a particular issue. It was becoming apparent that the two images couldn't coexist in the same person.

Qualitative polling began to suggest that fewer people were willing to brand the prime minister as 'trustworthy'. Unfortunately for Rudd, this increasing cynicism provided a window through which a number of other perceptions about him were generated: in other words, it provided a way of interpreting his actions and comments. As increasing doubt began to eat away at his entitlement to be seen as an upholder of this key virtue, there was always the risk that voters might extend such misgivings to other things the PM said. Distrust acts like a cancer. After the disease has lodged in the body, it becomes difficult to remove. Although it may remain quiescent for a long period, if it's roused it can have a devastating effect.

Instead of simply losing his 'trustworthiness', the danger for Rudd was that people would suddenly flip to see him as deceitful. Similarly, 'intelligence' was perceived as one of Rudd's attributes — which was, at face value, a positive. But once he'd been credited as being 'smart' by voters, he couldn't lose that personality trait; instead, it almost always morphed into perceptions that he was 'devious and cunning'. Although he was riding high in the polls, there was the danger that when the collapse came, it would be spectacular.

After more than two years in government, it was inevitable that some mistakes would be made and that some policies would need fine-tuning. But Rudd's entire method of working had been to begin with an inquiry, which would then develop 'world-class' policy for implementation by a minister. As problems began to show up, they cast doubt on the entire policy-formulation process.

The trouble was, problems couldn't just be blamed on the staff responsible for implementation; at some point, it would become necessary to admit that others were at fault. If blame was to be traced back to the original investigation or idea, there was a danger that voters and the media might question other inquiries and practices; and yet it was vital that the ministers involved not be directly blamed for the stuff-ups.

When, in early 2010, Rudd handed Tony Burke the population ministry, he knew exactly what he was doing. Burke had been very effective in the agriculture portfolio. This was a particularly difficult ministry for a Labor minister to deal with, and yet he'd performed well in it. He'd been out and about in the countryside, diffusing concerns in a constituency that was traditionally negative towards the workers' party.

Burke understood the vast open plains of regional Australia, yet retained the political smarts that would enable him to find a workable compromise to rectify Rudd's initial verbal blunder and make the issue disappear from the political agenda. The people in the bush often wanted growth, and a majority of people throughout the country supported increasing population in both major centres and smaller regional towns. It was the people living in the major metropolitan capitals who didn't want an increase that was likely to further gum-up the limited transport or social infrastructure that was already failing to cope with the current number of inhabitants.

The difficulty for government was to find a way to manage a 'desirable' population increase. The idea of finding a way of restricting immigrants to living in rural centres was always going to be difficult, as it would involve the introduction of some kind of politically unacceptable 'pass laws'. Inevitably, a halt would have to be legislated to prevent the continuing urban sprawl. Burke would have to find a new compromise between the need for extra development and legitimate environmental concerns. This required a massive rethink about the future of Australia.

There was no way that the desires of everyone could be accommodated. Fortunately, those who wanted to have their say in this debate recognised that they had more chance of being heard outside the constraints of an election campaign, and by the middle of 2010 that's exactly what public discourse had become. Burke was left in peace to try to sort his own way out of the deep political morass into which he'd been thrown.

Both sides of politics had decided to keep away from the issue. They accepted that many people's minds had already been made up, and that there was no need to complicate their lives by presenting the facts.

***

In April 1976, less than a year after the end of the Vietnam War, a vessel carrying five Vietnamese men washed up in Darwin. Malcolm Fraser welcomed the new boat people who were fleeing the communist country, and a further 2,059 arrived over the next five years. Then there was a gap. The second wave of arrivals from Indochina began in November 1989 with a boat carrying 27 asylum-seekers. For most of the next decade, about 300 people continued to turn up each year.

But from 1999, there was a sudden and significant change in both the number of 'unauthorised arrivals' and where they were coming from. By the first year of the new century, the numbers arriving by boat had multiplied tenfold to around 3,000. Australia has always accepted a quota of people (around 13,000) whose status as refugees has been determined by the United Nations High Commissioner for Refugees; but, as an increasing number of boats turned up, concern rapidly shuddered through the community.

The arrivals were portrayed as queue-jumpers. This was correct, because most of the asylum-seekers had left their region of origin fearing that they'd never even make it onto a UNHCR list that determined their status as refugees, let alone be accepted for resettlement. In 2008, the year that Australia accepted 8,742 people from the UN organisation (making Australia the third-most-generous country in the world), nearly 2 million Afghans had fled their country for neighbouring states. Any chances of getting a new start in another country were virtually negligible. A rough estimate suggested that there were 10.5 million displaced people who could qualify as refugees, dotted in different places around the world.

Public opinion demonstrated an increasing concern about the arrival of the boats until, in September 2001, the Howard government introduced draconian new policies to deter refugees. Only one boat arrived for each of the next three years. A total of 1,637 asylum-seekers were detained in Papua New Guinea or Nauru, and lost the right to any judicial review if their claim was rejected. In fact, though, more than 70 per cent were accepted for resettlement, the majority in Australia. In the last year of the Howard government, 148 asylum-seekers arrived by boat. But the policy of keeping people in detention centres remained controversial, and was condemned by many on the left. Within three months of its election, the Rudd government had moved quickly to scrap the so-called 'Pacific solution'.

The coalition claimed this had sent a 'green light' to the people-smugglers. By the beginning of April 2010, 101 boats packed with thousands of asylum-seekers had arrived in Australian waters, and further records were being broken every month. In a reprise of Howard's line in the 2001 election campaign, Tony Abbott declared that 'we do not decide who comes to our country [or] the circumstances in which they come'. He'd identified Rudd's biggest policy failure yet.

Something needed to be done urgently to address the growing political perception that the government had lost control of the borders. Unsurprisingly, the bulk of the asylum-seekers were coming from two countries beset by continuing conflict: Afghanistan and Sri Lanka. The government needed to find a way to staunch this flow while not appearing to be backtracking on its commitment to deal with refugees in a humane way.

Rudd's own approach to asylum-seekers appeared to lack genuine compassion as he floundered around, searching for an answer that people increasingly believed he'd been partially responsible for creating. He had no doubt about people-smugglers. They were lumped together as 'the vilest form of human life', and Rudd hoped they'd 'rot in hell' — a surprisingly Old Testament view for a Christian to express.

The statement also appeared surprising for the erstwhile follower of Dietrich Bonhoeffer, who'd been involved in assisting German Jews to escape to Switzerland during World War II. Indeed, it was a Gestapo investigation into this that led to Bonheoffer's subsequent arrest and execution in the final days of the war. Although current asylum-seekers pay for their passage, many are subsequently assessed as having quite genuine fears for their safety in the countries from which they've fled.

Rudd appeared to have chosen his words carefully in an attempt to position himself as standing (metaphorically) right next to Howard. By vilifying the 'smugglers', the PM successfully managed to prevent the fragile public consensus from completely shattering, although it was weakening by the day. Everyone quickly agreed that such people were deserving of opprobrium, and it allowed Labor to still be on the side of the 'genuine refugees' (without specifying who these were or how they could manage to reach the country without hopping on boats). But, as the boats kept arriving, it was becoming increasingly obvious that a new policy would be required if the government was to continue appearing to be in control of Australia's borders.

By early 2010, that aspiration had well and truly broken down. January and February are the months of the monsoon in the Indian Ocean. Indeed, the previous year had only seen one boat (holding just 20 people) attempt the perilous passage during this period. The next year, even before the end of February, a new record of fourteen boats, carrying in excess of 700 people, had been apprehended — an average of two boats a week. Tents were erected on Christmas Island to accommodate the additional human cargos of the boats, and by the beginning of March more than 130 people were being forced to camp under canvas.

It was irrelevant for refugee advocates to claim that the number of boat people was tiny by comparison to the numbers of asylum-seekers arriving by plane, or the numbers of legal migrants. The single, vital question was who controlled the borders, and Australia's swinging voters were rapidly making up their minds. The massive influx appeared to be evidence enough that the government's changes weren't working.

The problem for the government was that the issue was most likely to weigh significantly with a critical group of swinging voters — the 'middle'. Peter Brent, a Parliamentary Library Fellow, provided a snapshot on his *Mumble* blog of these 'young couples with children … unengaged, conservative, reasonably affluent, self-interested, materialistic and prone to see themselves as victims'.

As the election date edged nearer, both parties suddenly became intently engaged with the need to mobilise this vital demographic and to turn them into foot soldiers for their own side. The preferential voting system meant that Labor could be relatively confident that the vast majority of Greens' votes would eventually return to the main left-wing party, so it assumed that this group could be ignored. They'd understand the need to allow their own principles to be trampled on, in the hope that the Labor government would still implement better policies than a Liberal one. Although it was unlikely that the 'middle' would swing against the government after just one election, harsh new policies were required to show that Rudd was serious about managing this issue.

The government abandoned the pretence that 'pull' factors hadn't made Australia a more desirable destination, and slammed a temporary ban on the processing of asylum-seekers from Afghanistan and Sri Lanka. Labor justified this discriminatory policy by asserting that conditions had changed in these two countries of origin; however, more importantly, the new restrictions addressed an urgent political and practical need. The detention centres were overflowing, and swinging voters in the outer-suburban seats no longer believed assurances that the government's policy was harsh enough to deter people from attempting to reach Australia by boat.

However, nothing could disguise the collapse of idealism and the sudden retreat to policies similar to Howard's. These had worked electorally before, and stopped the mass of human misery washing up on the shore. The message was supposedly directed at the asylum-seekers in an effort to stop them hopping on unseaworthy vessels to begin with, but there was another audience as well. The electorate needed to be convinced that Labor was doing something to halt the unrelenting flow of increasingly desperate people.

This wasn't the sort of policy backflip that Rudd wanted to be intimately associated with. As the three ministers — Immigration's Chris Evans, Home Affairs' Brendan O'Connor, and Foreign Affairs' Stephen Smith — were announcing the new hard-line policy in Canberra, Rudd was in Queensland visiting hospitals. 'Great to be working in this part of Oz,' he tweeted.

At exactly that same moment, the crew of HMAS Wollongong were pulling another 16 passengers from the water after their vessel had foundered in the Indian Ocean. The patrol boat then transferred its new passengers to Christmas Island, which was already overflowing with the flotsam of humanity.

***

Rudd was also noticeably absent when another issue, which pointed to deep and vicious undercurrents ripping beneath the outwardly calm surface of Australian society, erupted. The country has always had a schizophrenic attitude to multiculturalism, accompanied with anxiety about change and the 'evil demons' that lurked just below the surface.

In the year leading up to 30 June 2008, nearly 1,500 violent attacks, both robberies and assaults, had been reported by people of Indian ethnicity to Victorian police. That same April, a mass protest had followed a stabbing attack of an Indian student who was working as a taxi driver in Melbourne. Similar protests were also called in other states before the issue faded from the front pages of the newspapers. Authorities seemingly noted what had happened, but apparently didn't feel inspired to take action on the issue.

Further attacks continued. Anger festered within the Indian community, and at the end of May another protest was held in Melbourne, this time consisting of thousands of people. Anger spread, both in Australia and back in India, where India's prime minister, Manmohan Singh, felt so concerned about the situation that he phoned Rudd to discuss it. At this stage, although he was already one of Australia's best-travelled prime ministers, Rudd still hadn't bothered to touch down in New Delhi. People in Foreign Affairs noted that the subcontinent seemed to be a blind spot for the PM, who'd already delayed one trip to the area.

Although Rudd did finally travel to Delhi in November 2009, the visit was marred by a diplomatic dispute, as well as by perceptions that the PM had attempted to cuddle up to China (a traditional rival of India). The problem had begun when Rudd unilaterally dumped a commitment to sell uranium, citing India's failure to sign the Nuclear Non-Proliferation Treaty as a reason for preventing the sale. Ironically, Canada, also a signatory to the same agreement, happily signed a deal to provide uranium for nuclear energy just days after Rudd departed from the subcontinent. But the violence against Indian students in Australia gave the anger a hard edge. Capping it off was Rudd's continued refusal to accept that racism might be part of the problem. 'I don't accept your premise that there is a growing racism in Australian society', he told reporters. He later commented, 'Frankly, I don't think these debates about an apology take you anywhere, one way or the other.' It's uncertain whether Rudd recognised the obvious irony inherent in his statement.

Although there were more than 100,000 Indian students in Australia, with the education sector contributing more than $15 billion a year to the economy, things continued much as before.

As 2010 began, a young accounting graduate, Nitin Garg, was brutally stabbed, and died trying to staunch the blood that was flowing from his body as he staggered into the fast-food shop he'd been managing in Melbourne. The Victorian police — stupidly — insisted that they did not believe the attack was racially motivated, refusing to speculate further. Gillard, who was adamant she found a cartoon in the Indian media comparing Australians to members of the Ku Klux Klan 'deeply offensive', nevertheless insisted that 'We all know, tragically, in the world that we live in, whether you're in Melbourne or whether you're in New Delhi, you can come to grief through violent incidents'. She, like the police, had badly misread the politics of the situation.

On that Australia Day, while Rudd was launching his children's book about the family pets managing to rescue the Australia Day party at the Lodge, his nephew Van Thanh Rudd was arrested outside the Australian Open tennis championship wearing the wide-hooded outfit of the Klan with a sign 'Racism — made in Australia'. Victorian police swooped quickly to arrest the artist, who was charged with inciting a riot.

Rudd and his nephew didn't appear to share a particularly close relationship. The number of Indian students studying in Australia fell significantly in 2010.

INTERLUDE

Election 2010

John Howard's losing battle to retain his seat of Bennelong in 2007 marked a watershed in Australian politics. At the time, attention understandably focused on the remarkable spectacle of a prime minister being ignominiously unseated. The relevance of the changing demographics of an electorate that the Liberal Party had held since it was first established in 1949 was only noted in passing.

Yet this was critical in the unseating of the prime minister. Howard's margin of 4.2 per cent meant it was his seat that lay at the exact point where the swing would determine which party formed the next government. If the prime minister could manage to hold onto his seat, his party would (supposedly) continue to hang onto the Treasury benches; if he lost, the conservatives would be consigned to electoral oblivion. And so it went. The immutable law of the swing of the pendulum crushed anyone standing in its way without regard to seniority, and without any respect for their position.

Or so it seemed at the time. The broader Australian electorate was tired of Howard; voters knew that if the Liberals lost government (as was being predicted), their leader would resign anyway, and the inhabitants wanted to avoid a consequent by-election; and the PM was being challenged by a younger, popular media personality

(Maxine McKew), who worked the electorate very hard in the lead-up to the poll. These factors all played their vital part in Howard's discomfiture, but there was another key that offered a deeper key to understanding the result: demographics.

This was, in fact, supposedly one of the reasons that McKew originally proposed her candidature for the seat. With the backing of her partner (former Labor national secretary Bob Hogg), she'd identified this particular seat in Sydney's inner north-west as one that was ripe for the picking. Her challenge represented a considerable distraction for Howard, and she also represented exactly what the people of the electorate wanted: an intelligent (*tick*), mature woman (*tick*), who had been successful (*tick*), and had lived and worked overseas (*tick*), who always had a smile on her face (*tick*), but nevertheless worked hard and was well-known (*tick*). Her candidacy would have worked anywhere; but here, given the large number of people from a non-traditional Australian background, it was brilliant.

It's obvious that different electorates have different characteristics. Similar people tend to live together and, possibly as a result, tend to have similar needs. Since Federation, electorates with a large proportion of people who consider themselves to be working class have tended to vote Labor, whereas more affluent suburbs have tended to send Liberals to Canberra. The percentage of the electorate born in non-English-speaking countries had long proved a remarkably strong indicator of its likelihood of returning a Labor parliamentarian to Canberra. Bennelong had the 11th-greatest proportion of these immigrants within its boundaries. After the 2007 vote, all the 24 electorates with the largest proportion of non-English-background immigrants returned Labor members, without exception.

Appealing to the middle out in the suburban seats of the big cities had provided Howard with the solid majorities that ensured a decade of coalition government, but it didn't manage to safeguard his own political career. The changing demographics of the cities, and the influx of new Australians from different racial backgrounds, were leaving the coalition increasingly representing an Australia of the past.

Labor's electoral strategists were well aware that Abbott had done nothing to combat the perception that the coalition was a party that represented, culturally, an earlier vision of what the country should be. Migrants swelled Australia's population by more than half a million (550,000) in the Rudd government's first two years. This was the largest number of immigrants ever accepted within such a short timeframe. It roughly represented four electorates' worth of voters.

***

As a Queenslander, Rudd had provided a massive boost to Labor's chances of winning the 2007 election. The party had desperately needed to win a swag of seats north of the Tweed River, and it did: the ALP won a critical nine seats from the coalition (including Flynn, which was notionally a National Party seat). The state had swung by a massive 8.1 per cent, and it was vital to stop these from returning to the conservatives if Labor was to stay in office.

Yet the opposition presented a disunited front in that state. The merger of the state National Party with the Liberals into the Liberal National Party caused a great deal of infighting. Instead of being resolved early in the term, it wasn't until May 2010, not long before the election, that the new organisation finally began clearing the decks and establishing who the party's candidates would be. The Cambridge-educated part ethnic-Chinese Liberal MP Michael Johnson was expelled from the party, following allegations relating to his campaign account and other travel-sponsorship activities that were felt to be questionable. Although his seat of Ryan was notionally safe, the headlines generated by the story weren't favourable for the coalition. His political execution had been long and drawn out, resulting in more rumours swirling around the party at the time it needed clean air to get its message out.

Just days earlier, four other party members, including two state MPs, had resigned their membership of the party. Bitterness and contempt was on show just beneath the surface between the federal Liberals and the state Nationals. Without the discipline that comes with elected office, the internecine warfare continued. The Liberals sent former federal deputy director James McGrath to take control of the campaign, but this decision came too late to have any significant effect on the election. A 19-year-old, Wyatt Roy, was the opposition's candidate in the seat of Longman — a seat the Liberals needed to win in order to form government.

Another problematic seat was Dickson, the seat of Peter Dutton, a former policeman and coalition health spokesperson. A redistribution had made his seat notionally Labor; but, instead of fighting to retain it, he'd frantically attempted to find a safer electorate. He'd failed in his attempt, and was then forced to insist he'd fight on in an attempt to hold it. The unedifying scramble for another seat hadn't assisted his chances, particularly as he needed every vote to hang on. It was a number of self-inflicted blunders such as these, together with a more general lack of discipline, that militated against the ability of the coalition to capitalise on voter disillusionment with Labor. People may have been ready to look elsewhere, but this relied on a widespread anti-Rudd sentiment alienating people from the government. Ironically, the conservative nature of the Australian electorate was still predisposing it to giving the government another chance, rather than booting it out too soon.

Dickson was just one of a number of seats where the conservatives were severely outclassed on the ground. As the election neared, this factor began to gain increasing relevance. Candidates had not even been chosen in a number of seats that the party would have to win if it was to form government.

The seat of Eden-Monaro was a classic example. This large electorate is a key bellwether seat. Stretching from Canberra, south to the Victorian border, and across to the Pacific Ocean, the MP it has chosen to represent its interests has, from 1972 onwards, always sat on the government benches. Although the seat was held for Labor by a well-known former army colonel, Mike Kelly, by a slim majority of 3 per cent (he had required Greens' preferences to deliver his 2007 victory), the Liberals didn't select their candidate, Costello's former adviser David Gazzard, until the May before the election. If the government was to fall, this was a seat that the coalition should have been confident of winning. But Gazzard had been given an extremely tough job. The sheer size of the electorate meant that it was very difficult for him to get around and campaign effectively in such a short period of time, whereas Kelly had both the profile that comes with being a parliamentary secretary and the advantage of incumbency. Similar factors were at work in many of the marginals that the coalition desperately needed to win if it was to achieve power.

Abbott had two significant difficulties to overcome before he could be successful. The first was strategic: he needed to be able to appeal at a personal level to swinging voters, and to market policies that didn't appear too extreme to them. And, tactically, the Liberals had to quickly start getting their act together; otherwise, it was hard to see how they'd be able to win the vital marginal seats.

Having Rudd as leader offered a significant benefit to Labor north of the Tweed River. Apart from having a home-ground advantage, he spent a considerable period of time travelling in the marginal electorates of his state, talking to local newspaper owners and reinforcing the Labor 'brand'. The party hoped that this would result in a number of government MPs (who were sitting in seats that had previously voted for conservative members) managing to hold on in the coming election. Labor was very well aware that there was a significant danger of this swag of seats returning to the coalition if it messed with its leadership team.

***

After the 2007 election, party apparatchiks from both sides dissected the vote in an attempt to find out exactly why Labor had won. The unions emphatically asserted that it was the Howard government's radical reform of workplace laws that had destroyed a key element of the Liberal base. These were the so-called 'Howard battlers' who'd finally swung back at last — the supposedly natural Labor voters who'd been won over by the previous PM's particular version of 'Australian conservativism'. But this easy theory failed to explain the detail of the swing.

Labor only received 43.3 per cent of the first-preference vote. Only once before, in 1990, had the party managed to win office despite gaining such a small share of primary preferences. A strong flow of Greens' preferences turned out to be vital in delivering the 2007 result; they providing the party with the buffer of extra seats it required to dominate the lower house. Four out of every five people placing a Greens candidate first ensured that their votes would eventually flow back to Labor. Rudd's rhetoric had triumphed, convincing Greens supporters that he could be trusted on environmental issues. The Greens voters felt that the coalition didn't offer their votes a congenial resting place.

But there was a sting in the tail — Labor couldn't always rely on the Greens' votes returning 'home'. As the Greens' vote increased, so did the flow of preferences to the Liberals. Rudd needed to demonstrate that he had better environmental policies than the coalition.

This offers a clue to the real reason for Labor's triumph in 2007 — leadership. At the time, people trusted Rudd. Particularly as the year had worn on, the contrast between the younger opposition leader and the older Howard had reinforced an instinctive belief the electorate had developed that the ageing prime minister would never be able to voluntarily hand over to anyone. Attempts to dispel this notion in the final days of campaigning, when Howard staged an uncomfortable joint television interview with Peter Costello, failed to convince anyone. It was obvious he wasn't ready to hand over the reins of power. This popular feeling had been obvious to those who crunched the polling numbers.

Two factors were isolated as being significant. One of the major election-winning factors was Rudd himself. In the ten Newspolls preceding Rudd's accession to the leadership, Labor had averaged a first-preference vote of 40.1 per cent (which converted to 51.2 per cent of the two-party-preferred vote). Over the next ten polls, the party leapt over seven points to 47.9 per cent (57.0 per cent). Rudd's error-free, year-long campaign ensured that he retained most of these voters. He effectively promised Australia a change, without the need to alter anything much. The rhetoric was new and inclusive, but (and this was particularly important for a contented, prosperous people) there'd be no real need for 'transformation'. Except, of course, when it came to campaign rhetoric, where the old shibboleths were dusted off. Hence the need for an 'education revolution' to help Australia in the future, although this apparitional objective became somewhat vague whenever it came to the specifics of how it would work. There were assurances that the poor and destitute would be better cared for, and that society would become more 'inclusive'. Voters loved the oratory, with its implicit promises that, in some vague way, the future would be happier and more confident; again, no one troubled too much about the detail. That was all going to be revealed later, after intensive study. At the time, Australians had taken a good, solid look at Rudd, felt they knew him, and decided to trust him. They rewarded him with a solid parliamentary majority.

Rudd's critical position in achieving victory was emphasised by two further points. He was a Queenslander and, although this state had traditionally proved a hard slog for Labor, Rudd played happily with his identity as a banana bender with his first words to the party's national conference in 2007: 'My name is Kevin, I'm from Queensland, and I'm here to help'. The party's vote in that state jumped by a massive 8.1 per cent, providing Labor with its biggest share of the turnout in twenty years — the state returned more of the party's MPs to Canberra than it had since 1990. Rudd's presence on the ticket was vital. How the emerging disenchantment with the PM would manifest itself in 2010 remained uncertain, and presented a quandary for Labor as the election approached.

The last campaign had been based almost entirely around Rudd. Three years later, the same person has become damaged goods. His earnestly delivered words were not believed. Qualitative polling suggested that the more people saw of the PM, the less they liked him. Based on advice that was coming from party strategists, Rudd didn't give a Canberra press conference for more than a month around May 2010, until his absence had itself become a news story. The problem was the government had already become centred on the cult of his personality.

Labor's focus groups had reported that two words were becoming irrevocably associated with Rudd in the public mind. The first was 'arrogant'. Voters increasingly (and correctly) believed that he was rejecting outside advice, and that one of the reasons the government was failing to accomplish its objectives was because decisions were being centralised in his office. The real problem was the other word that the focus groups kept throwing up: 'weak'. This meant that the PM was in a double-bind: if he rejected compromise, and pushed ahead with his own preferred policies, he was conceited, egotistical, and arrogant; yet if he offered concessions, he was seen as vacillating, indecisive, and lacking conviction. UMR Research — closely aligned with the Labor Party — began to think that no matter what Rudd did, he couldn't win.

However, the focus on leaders wasn't entirely negative for Labor.

Abbott was a polarising figure. Many of those disillusioned with the government found that they were left with nowhere to go politically, because the conservative alternative appeared even worse. The Liberals seemed to be making no attempt to find any common ground with the Greens, because they still seemed to believe that there was no need to find a synthesis with those who had environmental concerns. In a two-party system, this left a huge constituency effectively untapped.

As the 2010 poll approached, informed analysts doubted that Abbott's bid to become PM would succeed. Australians had last failed to re-elect a first term government (Jim Scullin's Labor) way back in December 1931, in the middle of the Great Depression. The subsequent 33 elections demonstrated conclusively that a government could reasonably expect at least two terms. In June, this vital electoral history was pointed out to the caucus by Labor's former national secretary and long-time MP, Bob McMullan. He emphasised that the party was still in a winnable position. One day later, Gillard entered the PM's office and demanded his job.

In part, the ability of governments to hold on is due to what's been called the 'sophomore surge'. Although governments do gradually lose support as they get older, this tendency can be countered at the level of the individual electorate. There's a quite measurable trend for parliamentarians to increase their support the first time they face re-election. That's partly because they're better known around their constituency, and it might also be because they work much harder during their first term of office, filled with enthusiasm.

The other issue was the Liberal Party itself. Adopting four leaders in four years suggested a lack of stability: even more importantly, the resignations associated with the loss of government, and the subsequent culling of leadership aspirants, had denuded the party of much of its frontbench talent. When there are doubts about the leader — as qualitative polls suggested was the case with Abbott — the ability of the rest of the team comes into question, and it's here that the coalition had significant problems convincing voters that they had a stronger group of potential ministers than Labor.

It was inevitable that, with the loss of government, a number of former coalition ministers would have left. The complication is that this represented much of the party's so-called 'talent' walking out, for all sorts of good reasons. The divisions over the party's policy directions sent one set of tensions rippling through the elected parliamentarians. Another reason for the jostling was an attempt by different members to carve out a future for themselves in leadership roles. Until a new pecking order was established, it was inevitable that the party would have difficulty presenting a common front to the electorate.

***

I encountered the Greens senator Sarah Hansen-Young walking down the steps inside Parliament House. We exchanged pleasantries as she enquired about my book, her face friendly, open, and honest. The government had just put its climate-change bill to the house a second time. She was dismayed by it. As far as she was concerned, it was inadequate. We talked further about the broader issues.

'Do you ever think you'd do a deal with the Liberals,' I asked, 'giving them your preferences in order to get action on climate?'

She was still engaging me, but it was as if a veil had suddenly been drawn across her face — as if what I'd suggested was anathema.

The senator had been fixing me with her eyes; now they wandered. She began talking through the issues. Greens voters come from diverse backgrounds and take voting seriously, she insisted. The party couldn't 'instruct' them how to vote; there were many considerations involved in choosing who was to get the coveted Greens preferences, so it couldn't simply be boiled down to a simple, tactical voting strategy. Shortly after we had this conversation, Abbott took over the Liberal Party and it became clear that, in its current incarnation, there would never be the possibility of a deal with the coalition. Unfortunately for the Greens, they were also being locked out by Labor.

Senator Steve Fielding controlled the balance of power, simply because Labor had chosen to give him their preferences in the 2004 election, rather than the Greens' candidate, barrister David Risstrom. This saw Fielding elected with just 2,519 first-preference votes. It appeared unlikely he would be re-elected in 2010, and there was a strong possibility that the Greens would hold the balance of power in the Senate. From early 2009 onwards, Rudd had deliberately refused to meet with the minor party's leader Bob Brown, despite numerous entreaties from the environmental party. It was difficult to understand why.

Many years before, when the Democrats held the balance of power in the Senate, Howard was able to do a deal with them that enabled him to implement the Goods and Services Tax. Hard work resulted in the brokering of a solution that achieved all the government's key demands, significantly reducing the hardship accompanying the new tax. Rudd, however, appeared unwilling to adopt such pragmatic attitudes to achieve his own objectives.

Although Brown insisted that his door was open, Labor refused to knock until the polls showed that the government would be ejected from office unless it could gain the Greens' preferences.

Labor was wedged between its old working-class right-wing voters and the middle-class, concerned left; nevertheless, the party was no stranger to doing deals. This time, the main obstacle appeared to be Rudd himself. For some reason, it took him a long time to accept the reality that he needed the Greens. It was only towards the end of June 2010 that Labor was finally prepared to begin talking to the third party. The ALP was lucky that the conservatives hadn't been faster on the uptake.

Brown's concerns about Rudd's ETS had always focused on its compensation mechanisms for industry. Once imposed, the system would have made it prohibitively expensive to cut carbon emissions any further. There would have been a cap on pollution, but no way to cut it back. This was unacceptable to the Greens, who had a counter-proposal — a simple tax on carbon. This was a perfectly workable system that could have been adjusted easily, depending on the economic effect of the tax. According to the Greens, Wong was impressed by the idea when they presented it at their first meeting with her; she took it back to Rudd, but returned with a rejection. Possibly, the fact that the solution wasn't 'his' had led him to reject it. Instead, Rudd pushed ahead with the ETS, regardless of the basic political reality that he didn't have the numbers to get it passed.

The Greens encompass many different constituencies, from the apocryphal 'doctors' wives' (wealthy professionals concerned about environmental issues in inner-city leafy suburbs) to alienated people who earnestly believe that the rules of society (and particularly the distribution of wealth) just stink; but these sort of simplistic generalisations rapidly fall down under investigation. If there is a need to find a division within the Greens, it is perhaps better explained along the lines of pragmatism: between those who will compromise to achieve their objectives, and those who are less willing to negotiate.

What Rudd consistently refused to accept during his term was that the Greens were prepared to do a deal — under Brown, they showed a willingness to accept political reality and not to push for unrealistic solutions. Refusal to incorporate them into the political process was likely to result in a further marginalisation of the party, adding strength to those within it who refused to compromise.

This is why the decision of the Greens in Tasmania to support state Labor didn't come as a surprise. The Liberals may need to woo this party far more seriously if they ever wish to return to power. Labor knows that, in any compulsory preferential system, the majority of these environmental votes are always going to return to the mass party of the centre-left. The coalition is ignoring a decisive constituency that at the moment can only turn to Labor.

A continuing refrain from the government (reaching its crescendo in 2010) was the idea that its legislative program had been consistently blocked in the Senate, and that this was preventing it implementing its agenda. This was correct — but only because the government refused to do a deal with the Greens, Family First's Steve Fielding, or Nick Xenophon.

In early March, Conroy claimed that Abbott had 'blocked 41 bills — four times as many bills as in the Senate in the last 30 years'. This was true, but not the whole story. It was correct that the coalition only required the support of one other senator to stop legislation going through, but many times the bills weren't passed because the minor parties didn't feel they went far enough. The obvious example of this was the government's parental-leave scheme.

Labor's scheme guaranteed paid leave for 18 weeks. The Greens, Fielding, and Xenophon wanted 26 weeks. The Productivity Commission estimated that the additional cost of this scheme would be an extra $400 million. Labor wasn't prepared to find the money to fund this more generous alternative, but that was its decision. Attempts to paint the Liberals as the only party obstructing the bill didn't mesh with the facts. The government — at the highest levels — appeared unwilling to do the sorts of deals that were required to get the other senators onside. Eventually, the scheme passed through the Senate (with Liberal support). With an election drawing near, the conservatives realised that it would have been political suicide to stand between voters and the benefits on offer.

CHAPTER EIGHT

'Co-operative' Federalism

'We will not accept a recipe for inaction ... In a nutshell, it seems to boil down to Mr Brumby and Mr Abbott saying the current system is good enough. We're saying the current system needs to be fundamentally changed and the Australian Government needs to fund the future growth of the system.'

Kevin Rudd, campaigning in John Howard's former electorate of Bennelong,
15 April 2010

During the first parliamentary session of 2010, Abbott landed a number of hits on the government. As a former pugilist, he'd shown real technique in continuing to drive home the assault on Labor's weak points. While he kept hammering the asylum-seekers, the disastrous implementation of the insulation scheme, and the continuing question marks over exactly where the money that was supposed to build the education revolution had gone, the Liberals were scoring. Keen to press home the advantage, he'd gone one step further and pressed Rudd to commit to debates during the election campaign.

When Rudd accepted and brought the debate on that very next week at the Press Club in Canberra, many in Labor shook their heads. The agreed theory was to 'never give a sucker an even break'.

By accepting Abbott's challenge, Rudd was admitting that there were questions to answer, and many thought he was elevating the opposition leader's status to the equal of his own. But, actually, Rudd had a blinder of a strategy — a high-risk one, but if it came off, the payoff would be terrific.

The downside was that if the debate went badly, speculation would have continued, weakening the government until the budget was released. Nevertheless, even if the debate turned out to be an utter disaster, Rudd was gambling that the budget would shift the momentum back his way before the middle of the year; in any case, he knew he had to do something urgently to restore the government's momentum. So, in truth, the downside wasn't really that bad. On the other hand, if things went well — if Abbott failed to land a knockout punch — the positives were enormous. When Rudd first flung his challenge for a health-policy debate across the dispatch box, Abbott had been shocked. Indeed, it took the entire opposition a few minutes to work out what had happened. They'd been playing under the old rules, and now the prime minister was throwing the rulebook away.

He was finally back playing the old Rudd, the one who had first inspired the Australian electorate to back him, who was seemingly engaged in a 'bipartisan' attempt to achieve something for the country. The two experienced men had both been debating since they were youths; both thought they knew the game, but the PM was careful to ensure that the dice were loaded in his favour. Not only was health an issue on which Labor had an advantage; it was also a dangerous area for Abbott, who'd been a former health minister. This meant that, although he knew where the bodies were buried, this was because he'd interred some of them himself. This was an area dotted with minefields for the opposition leader.

Aware of this, Abbott decided to go on the offensive. He had to clearly link Rudd's failure to act on health so far with the current crisis in the system, while still being able to dance away from the same allegation himself. Knowing that Rudd could become completely discombobulated when caught offguard, the opposition leader decided on an aggressive attack.

As far as the audience in the room were concerned, Abbott was the winner. On points, maybe he was. There was certainly no unanimity about the scoring; nevertheless, it was conceded that he had done okay. But, outside, a far-larger television audience had tuned in, and didn't like what they saw. Few people, of course, watched the entire debate. Others relied on excerpts re-broadcast by the television stations, which came across as being singularly unflattering for the opposition leader. Abbott had wanted the focus to be on his demolition of Rudd's policy, but his tactics didn't suit television.

The vast majority of people, who just saw the brief excerpts, witnessed a PM who seemed to be genuinely engaged in trying to obtain the best outcome for health. He stuck to his lines and emphasised the positive. Abbott, by contrast, came across as negative and carping, refusing to work for the good of Australians, and instead trying to score political points. This may have been exactly what both politicians were attempting to do, but the television audience didn't feel as if Rudd was playing that game.

Few remembered the detail of the case that the PM was making about hospitals, but everyone heard Abbott's forced laugh as he attempted to respond. They could see someone who was trying to talk about policy issues contrasted vividly with someone who didn't seem to be concerned about the fact that the health system wasn't working. It was a simple, style-based observation, but a devastating one.

One of the ironies about the debate was that Abbott's decision to meet Rudd in a head-to-head conflict meant that he was unable to use his own detailed health-reform policy, which he'd desperately attempted to get Howard to release prior to the 2007 election. During the 2007 campaign, Abbott had come up with a plan to spend an extra $18.1 billion on health — a massive transfusion that would have transformed the system. But Rudd pre-empted Howard and made a virtue of his own fiscal rectitude during the election campaign when he declared, 'This reckless spending must stop'. Abbott never got his plan through.

The weekend after the debate, Tony Abbott was in Port Macquarie, competing in the Ironman contest. Altogether, he swam 3.8 km, before riding another 180 km and finally running another 42 km. Labor decided to focus on his sporting activities, and began turning them into a negative by suggesting he should be spending the time 'formulating policy'. The assaults were always delivered by ministers, while Rudd simply passed on his congratulations, making the point that he couldn't do it. The message was subtly nuanced. He was saying he was an 'ordinary guy'. By implication, Abbott was a freak.

It didn't help the opposition leader that he appeared on television wearing revealing swimmers. The satirists had fun playing with his body image. Labor was successfully turning Abbott's health and fitness into a negative image. They knew there was no chance that Rudd would be seen completing a triathlon.

The trouble was, the prime minister now had to deliver a health policy that would depend on co-operation from the states and territories. Suddenly, Rudd seemed to forget the tactics that had worked so well for him. Realising that the premiers were highly unpopular, it looked very much as if he'd decided to bully them. He should have realised that no one likes a bully. His personal style hindered rather than helped find a solution, although this didn't come as a surprise to public servants in Canberra.

'Let's get on with some health reform', snapped Rudd. New South Wales Premier Kristina Keneally had just finished a polite, warm welcome for the prime minister while he'd been busy shuffling papers and refusing to look at his state Labor colleague. It was obvious there was no love lost between the two, although Keneally insisted immediately afterwards that they'd had a 'very productive discussion'. Nevertheless, rumours immediately surfaced of a fracas a fortnight earlier at an International Women's Day function, when apparently he'd alleged that she was 'running a campaign' against his hospital reforms. It was just a quick hop from there before others remembered that he'd publicly warned the state Labor machine not to install the female premier.

Rudd's rudeness represented tactical stupidity of the highest order. Keneally's pleasant, communicative manner had seen her regularly polling net-satisfaction ratings some four points ahead of Rudd's, and she was easily the most popular Labor leader in the country. Picking a fight before a major complex negotiation that was going to require goodwill on both sides didn't seem to make a lot of sense.

This was followed by a disastrous display of contempt for Victorian Premier John Brumby, who was insisting he wouldn't be 'bullied' by a prime minister who was escalating the rhetoric, threatening a referendum on his health-care proposals. Given the unwillingness of Australians to approve referenda, it wasn't clear if this was an attempt to intimidate the states or instead to prepare the ground for failure. This was part of the problem for anyone trying to deconstruct exactly what Rudd's health reforms were intended to achieve: it was difficult to work out if Rudd was trying to solve the system or simply pick a fight.

On Wednesday 3 March 2010, Rudd had released a blueprint for a complete shake-up of the health sector throughout Australia. 'We're now about nine months late from implementing that commitment. I accept that.' Rudd told ABC TV's *Insiders*, before adding somewhat surprisingly that 'We didn't anticipate how hard it was going to be to deliver things. We didn't properly estimate the complexity.'

Some Labor observers, who'd had experience of government previously, found this comment bizarre.

It was somewhat difficult to believe that the PM could possibly have underestimated the intricacies of reforming the health sector root and branch; nevertheless, that was the reason he gave for the delay in announcing his proposed reforms. This was supposedly structural reform that Rudd had been working on personally with Nicola Roxon for months. 'Perhaps', commented one MP from the party's left, 'they ended up spending too much time in the waiting-room waiting for a TV camera to turn up'.

The suspicious also noted that the health-care proposals were progressively divulged in the wake of numerous government crises. Instead, it looked suspiciously like a distraction, particularly as the full details weren't all unveiled at once. Nevertheless, public focus immediately turned to Rudd's new proposals. The issue overtook public interest in the government's other projects, such as the education revolution and the insulation-installation scheme, which had turned into debacles. Suddenly, it appeared as if Rudd had a plan that would transform the health system, which everyone agreed was cactus. That was all anyone wanted to hear about.

By engaging with this issue, Rudd ensured he would pick a fight with Labor's state premiers. This made a great deal of political sense. After more than a decade in power, most of the state governments were so unpopular that the more they kicked and screamed, the better Rudd would look. In New South Wales, in particular, polling consistently indicated that voters were only waiting for the polls to boot out Labor's team. In addition, the health system was so disastrously under resourced and ill-equipped that no one could possibly claim it was perfect — even Brumby, who, it was widely agreed, had the healthiest scheme in Australia.

The detail of the changes came dribbling out. The focus of the reforms was attempting to fix a hospital system in disrepair. Attention was directed increasingly at a bureaucratic solution to a far broader health crisis, largely because hospitals were seen as the institutions at the sharp end of the emergency. Hospitals produced measurable outcomes — operations and cases — and so, probably inevitably, this was where the government's attention became increasingly concentrated as the 'debate' continued.

In January 2010, Rudd had publicly noted two salient figures. Spending by the states on health care had leapt by nearly 11 per cent a year for each of the previous five years, but revenue increases had failed to keep pace with this, being capped at just 4 per cent. Something had to give and it was, as it turned out, the state governments. The difficulty was that it was hard to believe that the problem was being addressed, rather than dealt with in a palliative manner. Health experts increasingly noted that although the scheme was good, it could be improved.

When Rudd eventually sat down with the premiers to negotiate a deal, he knew that they'd have to fold in the end. The states simply didn't have the ability to levy taxes that could keep pace with the phenomenal growth of health-care charges. Their GST revenue wasn't expanding at anything like the rate necessary to even keep pace with the new medical procedures that were available, and the demands placed on the system by an ageing population. The only detail that needed to be worked out was the price of the deal.

In the lead-up to the Canberra meeting with the states, Rudd began an intense media blitz, pushing the need for reform. He was seen on television almost every day, striding past hospital beds with Health Minister Nicola Roxon at his side. He'd sympathetically put his arm on patients' shoulders while nodding sagely as he chatted. He'd share concerns with doctors before practising artificial resuscitation on dummies. No hospital anywhere in the country was safe as the caravan of media crews and reporters was dragged through corridor after corridor, one ward after another.

Many in the government wondered why Rudd was out selling the need for reform rather than working behind closed doors attempting to work out how the problems could be fixed. There seemed to be no problem with his work ethic — he wasn't slacking off — but that didn't mean all his effort was being expended in a worthwhile manner.

Rudd had been quite successful in convincing everyone that the current system wasn't working, but that wasn't hard. His tactics were far more reminiscent of an electoral campaign than an attempt to win the battle of ideas with proposals for real reform. They were, rather, a succession of vacuous 'grabs', designed to appeal over the heads of those opposing him to the broader electorate. What Rudd failed to do was to outline the importance or specifics of his program, or how it would assist in providing better health care. People had to assume that Rudd knew what he was doing.

To a large extent, this proved to be the case, because no one thought that the system was functioning properly at the moment. At least in some cases, this was because Rudd himself was engaged in pointing out the flaws as he walked through the hospitals. The way that Rudd's policy dribbled out, bit by bit, didn't assist in building confidence that his scheme had been either fully thought out or was necessarily the best. This became obvious as medical professionals considered the different elements of the so-called 'health takeover' that were not incorporated in the new plans. As the meetings between the states and the Commonwealth continued in the stuffy, wood-panelled meeting rooms of Parliament House, and new money (billions and billions of dollars) kept being thrown onto the table by Rudd as 'sweeteners' to bribe the states into accepting his scheme, the bureaucratic foundations of the plan became increasingly evident.

Right at the centre — the beating heart of reforms — was a case-mix model. This scrapped the so-called 'block funding' of hospitals, instituting instead an activity-based model, which meant that each hospital would be funded according to the number of procedures it performed. Theoretically, this meant that efficient hospitals would be rewarded because they'd be able to perform more procedures at a lower cost. This scheme had already driven the efficiencies that allowed Victorian hospitals to treat more patients than other states, despite having the lowest per-person spending in the country.

In order to work efficiently, such a system required medical procedures to be quantified, even though this might mean comparing a complex operation at Sydney's Royal North Shore Hospital with a simpler procedure in a more relaxed regional environment. The bureaucrats were insistent that a formula could be implemented, and the states desperately needed the money. All the ducks were lined up in a row; they were just waiting for someone to come along and knock them down.

Whatever was happening in the meetings seemed to be all about shuffling money between different parts of government. There were plans to get 'more beds' and 'more doctors', although most of the big-picture reforms would not occur for four years, meaning they were postponed until two governments hence. Funding commitments for mental and community-health facilities were similarly left vague and inadequate. Nevertheless, the government was on the record as being ready to shovel $5 billion extra towards the problem over the next four years. At a meeting on 20 April 2010, the premiers cracked. Rudd got his deal.

Initially, the reforms were welcomed. Unfortunately for the PM, though, health professionals are articulate and have access to the media. They quickly got the message out that this deal wasn't all it was cracked up to be. It was, in essence, a bureaucratic fix that would assist palliative care rather than deal with the nation's broader, underlying health problems. In particular, areas such as mental health and preventive medicine had not been touched.

Despite Rudd's talk of fundamental reform, nothing had been done to address such horrific realities as the fact that a person attempts suicide every eight minutes in Australia, and that mental illness accounts for more disability than any other cause. Patrick McGorry, the 2010 Australian of the Year, spoke out loudly about the need for more action in this area, while John Mendoza was so disgusted by the government's lack of action that he resigned as chair of the National Advisory Council on Mental Health. He pointed out that mental illness received only 6 per cent of health funding, while representing at least 13 per cent of the health-care burden. Rudd responded with his trademark confident assurance that this issue would be 'next cab off the rank'. Mendoza presumably pondered the likelihood that the taxi might look more like a rickshaw than a limousine.

The negotiations had left Rudd with a budgetary problem: the extra $5 billion required to get the states to sign up needed to be found from somewhere. The government had twice tried to pass legislation that would have imposed a means test on private health insurance. In turn, the opposition had rejected this, insisting that when Labor was in opposition the party had promised it wouldn't introduce such a financial hurdle on access to government money. This blocked legislation provided Rudd with what could have been a vital double-dissolution election trigger … yet, amazingly, he announced his intention to throw the weapon away.

This was a bizarre decision, because there were many other advantages that would have accrued from using the bill as a way of taking the country to the polls. The first issue was quite simple, although it revolved around complex constitutional intricacies. Although the elections for the House of Representatives and the Senate are (usually) held at the same time, members' terms are different. As a result, even if Labor were to gain additional senators in the coming election, they wouldn't have been able to take their seats until halfway through 2011 — nearly a year into Rudd's second term. Implementing any of his agenda would have been impossible until the new senators took their seats.

A double dissolution can be brought on when a bill (a piece of legislation that has passed through the House of Representatives) is rejected twice by the Senate. This had already happened with the health-insurance legislation; and, by the end of June, it would have been possible to have a second double-dissolution trigger — the ETS. This would have given the government a chance to fight a simple election on the twin issues of climate change and health.

Rudd had earlier asked the advice of his 'kitchen cabinet' about how this issue should be dealt with. Gillard and Swan were adamant that the move would be too risky. Tanner is reported to have disagreed, but he was overruled when Rudd came down on the side of Gillard. He did not want to be forced to do deals with the Greens.

The ministers' concerns had revolved around the possibility of the Greens increasing their representation in the Senate. As explained earlier, a double dissolution meant that all 12 senators would be elected from each state, instead of the usual six, reducing the quota for a Senate seat from 14.3 per cent by half, to just 7.7 per cent. This guaranteed that the government would not be able to control the upper house.

What made this decision surprising was that Labor didn't have any reasonable expectation of controlling the upper-house numbers anyway. Although the Greens insisted that their door was always open to negotiations with the government, Rudd had refused to meet Brown since early 2009. The PM appeared to be implacably opposed to dealing with the environmentalists, preferring to attempt to negotiate deals with the conservatives.

While the Greens were prepared to negotiate to bring in some sort of scheme to reduce greenhouse-gas production, this was the last thing that Rudd wanted, because they insisted on real measures that would significantly harm industry. This was harsher medicine than the industrial wing of the Labor Party was prepared to accept.

The rhetoric about climate change had already reached a crescendo, and yet nothing had actually happened. Now health had joined the queue as another reform that the government was going to be unable to implement.

Something had to give. In the end, it was Rudd's credibility that was thrown out. Despite his tough rhetoric and regular assertions that he was prepared for a fight, he baulked at taking a risk. Yet, by forgoing the chance to fight a real political battle on this issue, Rudd risked revealing himself as nothing more than a political blow-with-the-wind, an opportunist possessing few (or even no) political principles. Rudd's political stocks began to look weaker than ever. His once pristine image had been tarnished, perhaps irretrievably.

INTERLUDE

Leadership

'I've told you already, mate, I'm not going to tell you what I think about that fuckwit. You'll have to get that from someone else.' The Labor parliamentarian was both direct and disciplined. His anger seethed from every pore, but he wouldn't say anything that risked undermining Labor's prospects in the coming election. Rudd was the leader. There would be no spill while the party had a 50/50 chance of victory.

The only obvious heir apparent was Gillard, who hadn't even begun to trail her coat as a potential pretender to the throne. But Rudd's appearance of invulnerability had collapsed. Although the process had been going on since the beginning of 2010, what was concerning Labor strategists was that the trajectory downwards had increased as the year had gone on.

The fall began with little slips, like the press conference where Rudd appeared rattled and sounded unemotional as he uttered his usual bureaucratese, failing to connect with his audience of journalists. *The Age*'s Michelle Grattan is one of those rarely inclined to hyperbole; nevertheless, in February 2010 she drew an analogy to the period before the 2007 election when Rudd said he was messing with Howard's mind. 'Now,' she commented, referring to Abbott's rise in the polls, 'the tables are turned. The psychological warfare at the moment seems to be going the other way.'

Shortly after that moment came Rudd's stream of apologies to *The 7.30 Report*, Laurie Oakes, the *Insiders* programme, and anyone who would listen. 'You've been disappointed?' Rudd seemed to be suggesting. Well, he'd been disappointed, too, in both himself and (more particularly) in his ministers. 'Well, look, let's just call a spade a spade,' Rudd said. There had been mistakes, he admitted, but now was the time for a new start. 'The key thing is for us to get on with the business of delivering to the Australian community ... we've got to lift our game,' he added.

Right through February, Rudd was into the full hairshirt and self-flagellation routine. 'Let's not try and sugar-coat this, Kerry', he said, as if the host of *The 7.30 Report* had somehow been wanting to let him off easily. 'There's no point beating around the bush about it. Accept responsibility for it and get on and fix it', he added.

What had Rudd learned? 'I think ... I'm disappointed in myself for not asking more questions', said the PM. He still didn't appear to realise that he couldn't manage everything himself or that he needed to learn to delegate and trust other people. But in this interview, only a few questions later, his conception of himself inexorably at the centre of everything resurfaced.

'Well, in our system of government, I am responsible for the lot of it', Rudd insisted, dismissing in a few brief words a long tradition of cabinet government, and attempting to replace it with a presidential model. 'In terms of the accountability of that to the Australian people, they will make that plain when we go to the next election ... that is as it should be'.

Here, stripped of flotsam and unadorned by decoration, was Rudd's conception of government. His role was central, and he wasn't going to change that in the slightest. For anyone. It was a demand to either take it or leave it. He'd acknowledged the government's mistakes and accepted responsibility for them; now it was just time for everyone to move on. There was no indication in anything Rudd said, despite intense questioning in a number of interviews, that he accepted personal responsibility or saw any need to change his own method of operating.

Rudd conditioned everyone to expect that he'd be taking 'a whacking in the polls' and that 'The bottom line is, I think we deserve it.' But when the opinion-poll results came out, it was evident that, although Labor's support-levels had dropped significantly, they hadn't plunged off the anticipated cliff. Pretty soon, everything was back to normal.

But everything didn't quite return to the way it had been. The shallowness of Rudd's support-base within the party had been revealed — not publicly, but it was there nonetheless. There was no personal loyalty to support him, primarily because in his personal interactions with other MPs he didn't seem to have made any real attempt to build up a strong core of supporters.

Howard had his 'class of '98', a substantial group within the party who aligned themselves firmly behind the person whose victory first brought them to Canberra. Rudd had never been able to gather a similar base; he hadn't been able to get people to warm to his personality.

It was his personal decision to promote Wong and Garrett to their portfolios, yet both of these proved to be the two ministers who displayed the least capacity for selling their ideas to the public or, apparently, keeping on top of their portfolios. Conroy had been allowed to spend enormous amounts of government money on a dubious enterprise, seemingly because he could still guarantee the numbers in caucus. Instead of guarding Rudd's back, his supporters have been busy protecting their own.

The alienation of the government's backbench was distinctly noticeable in February 2010 as the opposition pressed its attack on Garrett in parliament. While the inner coterie of government ministers laughed off the assault, an icy coolness could be detected by an observer looking at those in the outer limits of the ministerial line-up. The greater the physical distance from the PM in parliament, the more the detachment of MPs became apparent. Labor's caucus members sat observing the verbal cut and thrust around the dispatch box, but they weren't barracking for their team the way they once had.

Perhaps more critically, as the year wore on, Rudd was still failing to engage broadly and to encourage Labor parliamentarians to contribute to policy in other than a formulaic manner. They were keenly aware that they didn't have any real input into the decision-making process. Some parliamentarians might have only been suited to jobs as spear-carriers, but Labor had a plethora of people who were willing and able to help with policy. Rudd had done little to develop ways for these people to make valuable contributions. This situation was exacerbated by the feeling that a few ministers who had tried to contribute their own ideas had been ignored, while some were subjected to harsher scrutiny than others, depending on the portfolio and the degree of prime ministerial interest in policy details. The PM's predilection for centralised control remained his biggest vulnerability.

The internal result of all this was a caucus that didn't feel obligated to the PM in the way that Howard's backbenchers did. This further exacerbated the fragility of Rudd's leadership. When he became unable to deliver victory, there would be no firm bedrock of allies to whom he could turn for support.

'I don't think that anyone is deeply interested in the style applied to [my] decision-making', Rudd said to the *Daily Telegraph*'s Malcolm Farr. 'I think they are concerned about the substance of what we deliver.' But the electorate was beginning to realise that, despite the PR spin and a frenzy of activity around the PM himself, very little appeared to be happening.

The ripple of hubris and conceit was now spreading. All the pollsters agreed that Labor's vote had dropped as people became alienated from and angry with Rudd personally. Despite his supposed reputation as a great manager, Labor ministers regularly described the PM's office as a black hole. They kept submitting ideas and proposals for approval (or even rejection), but would hear nothing back. Nothing would happen until Rudd began tumbling in the polls for some other reason, but when that happened there would be absolutely no one to catch him. No one had become more disillusioned by the reality than Labor supporters themselves.

In response, Rudd offered another trademark feedback phrase: 'Get over it.'

***

In the latter part of Labor's long period in the political wasteland, Rudd burnished his Christianity. He used it as a talisman to symbolise the difference he'd bring to Labor if elected to the leadership. He proclaimed his faith loudly. Even the secular unbelievers in the party realised that Rudd was offering a method of outflanking Howard. Rudd re-introduced the idea that policy should be based on principle. There were admissions that, at times, this would be fraught with difficulty, but the promise was combined with the assurance that it was worth making an attempt to reconcile the tenets of a civil society with the practice of government — of marrying ideals with reality.

What increased the strength of his critique was that this was not some sudden conversion. A student who attended the ANU's Bergmann College at the same time as Rudd said he suspected that 'Kevin might have been one of those people who goes around the campus in the evening with a piece of chalk, scratching "Jesus saves", and drawing pictures of fish on the pavement'. Australians liked the idea that here was someone who wasn't afraid to be different. A politician who could use terms like 'morality' without blushing seemed to be a rare treat in the political scene.

Television requires what are called 'establishment shots' that allow the reporter to talk about what a person's been doing that day before using a 'grab' of the 'talent' saying something. These shots become integral to the story. Politicians know this, and happily provide the networks with opportunities to photograph them 'on location'—particularly if the background scenery adds to the implicit background narrative the politician is attempting to build around themselves.

That's why TV cameras began to appear on Sundays outside St John the Baptist's Anglican Church in Reid, just outside Canberra's parliamentary triangle. They'd get some vision of Rudd and his wife, Therese Rein, emerging from the church and chatting happily with parishioners. But there was one strict condition: Rudd was not to be asked any questions. This was the PM's own time. He was communing with God. The scene could not be tarnished with overtones of party politics.

Then, one Sunday—without any warning—Rudd stopped and delivered his own political sermon to the cameras in front of the church. The church had subtly been appropriated into supporting his message. As the ABC's Chris Uhlmann noted, 'Imagine what the reaction would have been if John Howard had done that', or even (he might have added) Tony Abbott, instead of the latter appearing at sporting events wearing budgie-smugglers. People on the left would have been incandescent with rage.

The author of essays for *The Monthly* who had authoritatively defined separate spheres for church and state now happily breached a fairly fundamental principle of the way he should have been behaving. By mid-2010, there was plenty of evidence from polls that Australians were rejecting the persona that Rudd was protecting to the public. Suspicions were growing that he acted one way in private, but completely differently in public. At press conferences, Rudd would coyly suggest that something was 'balderdash' or 'bunkum'; yet everyone knew that the minute he turned away to walk back to the office, his usual personality would re-emerge. His preferred swear words became 'rat-fuck' and 'fucker'; however, it was the way he treated other people that appeared to reveal Rudd's real concern.

The 'Rudd project' was about one person — himself. Everything else was expendable.

***

What had changed since the election of Rudd's government? Well, certainly the rhetoric was different. The people who are sometimes dismissively referred to as Australia's 'educated classes' — also those most involved in the country's public life — seemed far more contented with the nation's self-image. But beneath the stirring rhetoric, it was difficult to see that much was different.

In every media appearance, Rudd's verbal tic ('Let me just say') seemed to reappear. Yet, no matter how long the PM kept speaking, we never seemed to arrive at a satisfactory conclusion. The nation remained perpetually hanging on, waiting for the sentence that would suddenly bring everything together … but the string of words and images spun off quickly onto something else. No matter how long we listened, the grand plan was never quite revealed. There was always another issue that needed to be dealt with, something else that needed explaining … and there was never enough time. One of the results of this was that his audience stopped listening.

Rudd spoke enthusiastically about his vision for the future, but real questions had emerged about whether he was capable of leading Australia towards achieving these objectives. Did anyone still seriously believe in Rudd's vow to halve homelessness by 2020? And yet, who would dismiss this as a great objective that was well worth striving for? The difficulty lay in calling Rudd to account. The year 2020 was still 10 years in the future; the world would be very different by then, so who was to say that the goal wouldn't be accomplished?

***

At the beginning of 2010, when Rudd recognised that the party was wobbling in the polls, he took decisive action to attempt to arrest the slide: he blamed other ministers, and insisted he'd get more involved in making sure the derailments didn't continue. Instead, they got worse. It was quickly becoming apparent to the wider electorate that the prime minister was part of the problem. Many Labor voters had become severely disillusioned. It was those most concerned about climate change and related issues who were most angry with Rudd. Ironically, this was also the group least likely to park their votes with the Liberals. As the election approached, Abbott desperately needed to be able to appeal to these people — or at the very least ensure that they didn't give their preferences to Labor.

Twenty years before, in March 1990, Bob Hawke had faced his fourth electoral test as leader of the Labor Party since he'd first become prime minister in 1983. There was significant disillusionment with the government, but questions lingered about the capacity of the Liberals, then under Andrew Peacock, to form government. In the end, the coalition won 50.10 per cent of the two-party-preferred vote, but failed to win government. Although he received just 39.44 per cent of the first-preference vote, Hawke won the election. Preferences, particularly from the Australian Democrats, were vital in delivering the Treasury seats to Labor. It looked as if Labor was hoping for a similar outcome in 2010. Both sides were going to desperately need the Greens, although neither seemed aware of the fact.

As mentioned earlier, Treasury Secretary Ken Henry had been commissioned to conduct a massive review into the entire tax system, following a recommendation of the 2020 summit. At the end of 2009, Henry had duly provided what turned out to be a three-volume report (which had already been seen by Swan) to Rudd. Although sizeable, the report was neither too hard nor too intricate to be understood; it was simple but not simplistic. Henry's team had done a great deal of thinking and modelling of the different options contained in the tightly reasoned 1,284 pages. The report contained a total of 138 recommendations that covered every aspect of taxation.

Importantly, it emphasised the need to simplify the system and to use it to achieve positive economic and social outcomes. Proposals for change had been analysed to provide a clear picture of their potential social outcomes, and comparisons were made with other countries' practices. The report provided a clear, cogent, and urgent argument for reform right across the board. Rudd sat on the review over December and January. In previous years, the prime minister had used this time to churn out essays, such as the one explaining the origins and nature of the financial crisis. In the lead-up to Australia Day 2010, however, Rudd had decided instead to emphasise his credentials as a Renaissance man by focusing his energies working on a children's book about pets. In the story, a 'scruffy little dog' slinks into the Lodge and causes chaos, threatening to (gasp) destroy the prime minister's Australia Day party. At the last moment, the day is saved by the Rudd family pets, Jasper and Abby. The ethical implications of this tale were obvious, even to a casual reader. While the Rudd family remained undisturbed, everything was right with the world, but the intrusion of a scruffy dog (a metaphor, perhaps, for the opposition) could bring ruin. The important thing was that the PM's garden party should continue.

'It's delightful. It's actually very, very cute, even cuter than one might imagine,' gushed a spokeswoman, before she finally melted completely away, leaving just a little wet puddle as the only clue that she'd ever existed.

Rudd didn't mention the review during February. In March, he told an interviewer that, 'On the tax system, yep, we've got more work to do; but on the timetable for it, we're still working our way through it.' In truth, the review had been long completed; it was just the politics that was being 'worked through'. Rudd claimed to have only glanced at the executive summary — a bizarre suggestion that, if true, displayed his utter contempt for the work of a vital policy department engaging with the future. He pretended that he was prepared just to 'dump these issues' in the laps of Australians, but that wasn't the reality. Everything needed to be carefully massaged before it was released to the public.

Rudd sat on the report for months. This was an unusual sort of reaction for a self-confessed policy wonk who loved nothing more than grappling with ideas for the future. Nevertheless, there was no room in an already crowded media landscape for yet another document that was going to have a sensational effect as soon as it was released. Something had to be kept for the future to ensure that the government would look as if it had an agenda for reform to take to the next election.

It was only in May that the PM finally succumbed to intense pressure from his cabinet colleagues to release the report. Swan and others were confident that it would provide a clear agenda for the party to take to the coming election. And then, with the media hype and hoopla that normally accompanied the release of sensitive financial details such as the federal budget, the report was finally released.

It turned out that, of the 138 tightly argued, strong recommendations for change, Rudd had rejected 135. Swan used a press conference as the report was released to specifically rule out a number of the recommendations, including taxing the family home. It appeared extraordinary that so much effort and labour had been devoted towards studying reforms that were never going to be implemented because a small group of ministers — or Rudd alone — had decided that they were too dangerous politically.

Henry looked despairing at the media conference that delivered this news. The vast majority of his work had been reduced to a paperweight as Rudd focused on three ideas. One of the people on the committee that prepared the recommendations told me that they had worked hard on 125 of them, absolutely convinced that they were vital for the future of the country. None were implemented.

Of those that were, the first was a boost to superannuation. Naturally, this was welcomed by the finance industry, which stood to gain most from the changes. Social activists were less enamoured by the change. By enabling people to preserve more money in a concessional tax environment, it enabled those who could contribute most to super to save the largest amount of tax — in other words, the change would be regressive, unless other measures were adopted to assist low-income earners. This appeared to emphasise a trend that had continued over the past decade, one in which wealth was concentrated in the hands of fewer and fewer people. It was those in work and the wealthy who'd save the most. Labor appeared to be doing its bit to assist this shift of wealth while refusing to impose the review's other recommendations. Henry had noted the economic efficiency and social advantages of land taxes, yet these were immediately ruled out by the government. Small business had received a reduction in the tax rate; nevertheless, companies with significant labour costs immediately complained about the business impost of the extra superannuation for employees.

The Henry report had been cherry-picked to extract a couple of measures that were perceived to be popular, but Rudd now faced a problem of his own making: the major new revenue-raising measure at the heart of the reforms was a resources tax. Named, with a bow towards George Orwell, the 'Resource Super Profits Tax', it conveyed the idea that there was something almost gratuitously obscene about the money that mining magnates were extracting from the minerals beneath the soil. At the same time, Rudd and Swan glided over anticipated objections from the industry by emphasising that it had already been 'consulted' about the changes.

But a significant mistake had been the decision to announce which of Treasury's recommendations would be implemented at the same time as the report was released. This meant that, instead of being able to play the role of an impartial arbiter, Rudd had already committed himself to a particular course of action. A wiser approach might have been to allow the Henry review to be discussed in public first; this would have permitted parameters to be established before the government was forced to join the debate. But Rudd wanted to control everything and believed, unhesitatingly, in his own judgement. He'd decided to ignore the bulk of the report and to ram through the one tax change that was guaranteed to be opposed, poisonously, by the industry.

In the months after the report was released, this tactical blunder of picking on the minerals industry began to leave the government more and more exposed. Since he'd become PM, Rudd had been able to gather enough support to steamroll any opposition. Now he'd finally picked a fight with someone bigger than he was. What was worse, after his earlier abandonment of an ETS, any compromise was likely to be seen as another disreputable backflip.

Swan went around claiming that he had effectively been told by miners that they had always expected to pay more tax. This statement was remarkable enough in itself (Swan refused to give details to back it up); however, miners and economists both pointed out that the design of the tax, with its rebate for failed ventures, would lead to a number of problems. Analysts noted that, in the past, Rudd's credibility with the public had been at its highest when he was fighting an intransigent lobby. Cynics suggested that the government might have thought that the clash served its interests, because it allowed a fight over money with the exploitative miners (a small constituency) on grounds of Labor's own choosing.

But, as the fight went on, it became obvious that, although the party had received support for its tax plan from its traditional base, it was no longer significant enough to guarantee success at the coming election. And this reflected a continuing problem that Rudd was having in communicating his policies to the voters. The policies of the Howard years had apparently changed 'middle Australia'. Rudd's earlier embrace of a big Australia had demonstrated that his instinct wasn't necessarily a reliable guide to the public mood. Yet he had failed to enlarge his circle of policy advisers. Rudd remained convinced that he'd be able to persuade people that he was right, despite increasing evidence to the contrary.

In terms of its economic competence, the government was rated well, and for a long time this provided one of the reasons for Labor to be confident that it would be re-elected. But, by the middle of 2010, Rudd's options had become severely limited. The impending election was forcing the government to assert that its resource-tax policy was correct, simply because it couldn't afford to back down. At the same time, some MPs were angry that the party hadn't been given enough credit for the way it had managed to avert a local version of the global financial crisis.

Wayne Swan and Lindsay Tanner were the two ministers who'd achieved most during Rudd's term in office. Together, they'd devised methods that successfully ensured Australia escaped from the worst of the financial crisis. The implementation of some of the programs — such as 'building the education revolution' and the house-insulation scheme — had been disastrous, but that was the fault of the respective departments and their ministers, rather than an indication of weaknesses in the ideas behind the schemes. Simon Crean had also worked extremely hard to enable overseas trade to flourish during a difficult economic period. Rudd didn't interfere in the former leader's portfolio; however, he didn't treat the former leader with much respect, either. It would have been wiser to keep Crean close, but a distance grew between the two men.

Nevertheless, there were some very effective people in the ministry. Tony Burke and Chris Bowen, in particular, proved themselves able assistants to Swan, while Mark Arbib's competence ensured that the NSW right would continue to have a disproportionate influence in determining who would take over from Rudd. Although he was from the left and personally distant from Rudd, Greg Combet had effectively become the government's trouble-shooter, dropped into hot spots to clean up problems.

However, it was always Rudd who decided the policies of the government, and this led to a simple but major problem. The prime minister dictated the pace and nature of the whole process, from the instigation of policy through to its implementation. And when he was caught up working on other things — as he was most of the time — things ground to a complete halt.

But once he'd arrived at what he thought was the right solution, he insisted that everyone else should just accept his brilliance and his ideas, and bow to his judgement. The vital tasks of convincing and cajoling appeared to have been replaced in Rudd's world by an almost Chinese idea of discipline. There was no room for alternate approaches or differing views. The world was ordered from on high, and then the workers would clutch their 'little red books', waving them in the air and singing as they laboured to tackle the problems that had been defined by the leadership.

The problem was that this isn't the way that Australia — let alone a governing political party — works. People expect and demand the right to participate in the decision-making process. Rudd consistently failed to allow others to have any input into the process of framing policies. The prime minister was not simply the arbiter of disputes between ministers, as in previous Labor governments. He generated and defined the programs to be implemented, except for the strange times that he didn't interfere at all — as with the national broadband network, when there were real problems that required his intervention. Cabinet was reduced to a 'Gang of Four', and even this was dominated by Rudd.

On most issues, he insisted on being the one to decide both the course of action to be taken and the details of how the policy would be rolled out and unveiled — not just to the public, but also to stakeholders who might have otherwise felt the desire to assist in creating the right framework. Instead of accepting and encouraging contributions to the policy debate (as appeared to have been the original idea behind the 2020 summit), the reality was that Rudd, the 'Gang of One', had arrogated to himself the ability to decide every issue and to completely determine the direction of national development. This proved to be an impossible task, even for a great helmsman like prime minister Rudd.

This style of decision-making left the PM continually snowed under as issues piled up until he could address them. He failed, for example, to act immediately on Garrett's recommendation to terminate the insulation scheme. The leader continued to persist with his autocratic style, and failed to develop a more inclusive approach. It was not a politically astute way to behave. Rudd had forgotten that he would need friends to support him when things got tough.

Many Australians from both the left and right became disillusioned with the way that Rudd operated. The closer they were to the political process, the more dissatisfaction there seemed to be.

***

The lingering effects of the Global Financial Crisis were still being felt when, in an interview with Jon Faine on ABC Radio in Melbourne on 5 November 2009, Rudd insisted that his 'first priority' remained managing the aftershocks. As we've seen, Rudd's top priorities tended to change rapidly. A couple of weeks later, the primer minister announced that the Australian National University would host a National Security College. He noted in passing that national security 'is the government's first priority'. By 22 December 2009, when he was again launching a worthy institution (this time, the Chris O'Brien Cancer Centre), his main concern had changed again. By this time, public discontent was resurfacing about the lack of government action in tackling the enormous problems in the health system. Gazing earnestly into the cameras, Rudd informed Australia that health was 'priority number one'.

The PM's constant need to nominate urgent issues was understandable. Nick Minchin accused Rudd of an 'ever-changing feast of top priorities', arguing that the real number-one priority was 'saying anything in a bid to remain popular'. This appeared unfair.

It was understandable that Rudd could get carried away with the occasional rhetorical flourish. The opposition, however, became increasingly frustrated by what it believed was uncritical media acceptance of the PM's earnest assurances as time went on.

But the real question in this changing feast of vital issues still remained. What had changed? War had been declared successively on poverty, drink, and gambling, but nothing much had happened.

Earlier, at the 2008 Melbourne Cup, Rudd had been filmed proudly waving his winning ticket in the air, beaming and smiling while swigging from a Gold stubby of XXXX. It was an image to which any typical Aussie would relate, such is the dominance of the marketing of the race day and the way it has become accepted as part of life. Condemning Rudd's behaviour was to risk being accused of being a wowser; failing to endorse drinking and gambling on this 'national day' would be seen as unpatriotic. Certainly, the voting public didn't react negatively by contrasting this behaviour with the uncompromising message that the PM had sent with public attacks on teenage drinking. But it became difficult not to see Rudd's actions as performance art. It was difficult to know what he really stood for, because it seemed to change all the time.

The formula was the same. One idea after another was seized upon and dissected, and the problems bedevilling the issue were isolated and drawn like tumours plucked from the gaping wound. But then, instead of suturing the lesion and fixing the problem, Rudd would suddenly whirl off to immerse himself in the next big issue that required his personal intervention.

As the 2010 election approached, much of the intellectual left was utterly disillusioned with Rudd. Nevertheless, it was far from certain that enough of these people would park their votes with Tony Abbott in protest (although there was opinion-poll evidence that some of them were prepared to move over to the Greens, which threatened a number of Labor-held inner-city seats).

When Abbott was elected leader of the Liberal Party on

1 December 2009, the coalition had received an immediate transfusion. At first, this was of limited relevance, because it was on life support at the time and it appeared improbable that Abbott could engender wide appeal in the electorate. As 2010 wore on, however, opinion polling suggested that voters had finally begun to regard the coalition as a credible government, and the Liberals began to move within striking distance of victory in the polls. The Australian experience has been that it's not so much that the opposition wins power — it's the government that loses. The opposition had been trying to craft a plausible narrative that it would be able to take credibly to the electorate; however, Rudd's deepening unpopularity was starting to make this unnecessary.

The Liberal leader had managed to restore the coalition's base, and he had made the coalition competitive again. The key question was whether he could overcome the enormous support for Labor that Rudd had established during his initial years in office.

CHAPTER NINE

The Fall

'It's important I believe, in the interests of the party and the government, for these measures to be resolved as a matter of urgency.'

Kevin Rudd, announcing he would beat the leadership challenge, 23 June 2010

Most people have to wait until the morning to read Newspoll, but party strategists don't. While most people were sitting down to dinner on the night of 3 May 2010, a tight-knit and focused group of ALP insiders began to dissect the news that was quickly ricocheting around the party.

These people lived and breathed power, their lives consumed utterly by the subtle shifts and changes in public sentiment revealed in long columns of numbers, scattered across the page. It sometimes appeared, to the outsider, that their attempts to divine what was really happening out in the electorate were as worthless as the effort that Roman priests put into reading the steaming entrails of a goat. However, on that Monday night there was no doubt about what had occurred.

Over the previous fortnight, more than a million voters had walked away from the Labor Party. Its primary vote had crashed — down from 43 per cent to just 35 per cent. Barely one-third of the country's voters were prepared to endorse the government as their first choice; and, after preferences were allocated, the Liberals were ahead. The apparatchiks tried to reassure themselves: the poll had to be an 'outlier' (that is, wrong).

The shift in public sentiment was just too great to be believed. Over a period of 20 years of Newspoll's existence, there had only been four previous occasions when Labor's vote had shifted so seismically. On all of those occasions, it was the poll that was wrong. It didn't appear possible that the party could have lost so many votes so quickly. It was having a hard time in the media, but the only thing that could explain this sudden plunge off the edge of a cliff was the recent revelation that the government was postponing taking action on climate change.

Two days later, the Morgan poll showed there was no doubt about what was happening: Labor's primary vote had collapsed to such an extent that, even with Greens preferences, the parties were now evenly balanced. The insiders knew that this sort of thing had happened before — not with Rudd, of course, but governments traditionally suffered a malaise in winter, and Howard had regularly been behind in the polls at this stage in the electoral cycle before surging back to seize victory just a few months later. And the results didn't make logical sense: Labor was losing votes at double the rate that the coalition was picking them up, so voters obviously remained uninspired by the alternative. Some better, more qualitative information was needed to feed into the analysis.

That was provided within a week by AC Nielsen. The dramatic change in the party's fortunes had been accompanied (or caused) by an even more spectacular destruction of the prime minister's own personal-satisfaction rating. For the first time since his election two-and-a-half years before, more people disapproved of Kevin Rudd than approved of him. Nearly 40 per cent of people polled said they believed that the PM was untrustworthy, and almost half of those who identified themselves as Labor voters said that they opposed any delay in implementing the emissions trading scheme.

The machine men didn't spin the results this way, of course. They reminded analysts that the government had also slugged cigarettes over this period by hiking tax on them. They suggested that Rudd was being punished for acting nobly and trying to reduce the cancer rate. He was supposedly being punished for being courageous. But if this theory was correct, the decline in Labor's vote would soon stop. It didn't.

A month later, on 7 June, the unthinkable happened. Nielsen's pollster, John Stirton, reported Rudd's worst poll results since he'd taken over as leader. Labor's primary-vote percentage remained in the low 30s, while the Greens' had soared. But even the allocation of preferences now wasn't enough to help the government; the coalition was ahead, 53 per cent to 47 per cent.

There was no need for anyone to waste any more time attempting to interpret the polls. People would rationalise it in their own different ways; however, the message the insiders had received was, as far as they were concerned, quite clear. Rudd had to go.

***

There was only one candidate that the party could plausibly switch to, this late in the electoral cycle. Julia Gillard had been a loyal deputy for long enough. Now she had to act. The timing was simple: it was merely necessary to work backwards from 24 June.

This was the last sitting day of parliament before the long winter break. Any challenge before then would throw Gillard into the hot seat, expose the government to relentless questioning from the opposition, and risk destroying her political honeymoon. But a confrontation after that date wasn't possible either. MPs would return to their electorates and the caucus would disperse, eliminating any possibility of a change. As well as that, the government's polling traditionally picked up with the arrival of spring, and a new PM was expected to bring a further boost. The window of opportunity was tight. The challenge would need to be very carefully managed.

The first requirement was to keep the plot hidden, and that was simple. Everyone knew that Gillard was the only potential challenger. Others were ambitious, but nobody else had the media profile that would have enabled them to unite the party in the wake of the challenge. As well as that, she was most popular amongst Labor's 'base', the very voters who would be most likely to feel alienated and angry if Rudd was dumped. The two factors would cancel each other out, while it was assumed she'd also appeal to the groups that had become disaffected and were no longer listening to the PM.

Gillard had marched in lockstep with Rudd on all the major policy decisions that had caused chaos in the polls. Indeed, back at the beginning of the year, she'd been united with treasurer Wayne Swan in urging the abandonment of the ETS. This was the very issue that had destroyed Rudd's popular support. Now, however, things were different.

The move began without Gillard's knowledge or encouragement. Senator Mark Arbib had a well-deserved reputation as the numbers man for the New South Wales right. He had delivered the numbers for Rudd's assault on Kim Beazley, and now he was taking them away. His Victorian counterpart was Senator David Feeney, who was just slightly older than Arbib. Feeney had copped a huge blast from Rudd the previous September when he had protested against the decision to hack MPs' printing allowances by 25 per cent. (Printing allowances are one of the many little perks that benefit an incumbent government, helping it to get its message out.) Rudd had dismissively told Feeney he could 'get fucked' when he tried to oppose the move. Rudd had casually trodden on a lot of toes throughout the party: it was as if, now he was prime minister, he never imagined he'd need anyone's help, ever again. South Australian Senator Don Farrell was another tough powerbroker who'd been sworn at contemptuously by the PM. There was no shortage of people with personal grievances, although they'd swallowed their pride for the party's sake while Rudd rode high in the polls.

Quietly and with some sensitivity, Arbib and Feeney began exploring how committed others were to Rudd. It only took a moment to realise that Rudd had no support whatsoever; certainly not enough to prevent a successful coup. The only requirement was securing a pretender to the throne, but this was proving difficult because Gillard rejected the subtle approaches urging her to participate in the coup. Nevertheless, Senator Kim Carr had marshalled support for Gillard before, and went to work again. Very quietly, the information spread. In Queensland, elderly union boss Bill Ludwig (the father of Senator Joe) was informed. He controlled the numbers in the state and had never been a friend of Rudd's. Meanwhile another Victorian, Bill Shorten, had independently come to his own conclusions about the need for a coup. His concerns had predated those of the other plotters. Shorten had the opportunity to speak to Gillard, but she rebuffed his advances. He was, however, able to ensure that his articulate and media-savvy successor as head of the Australian Workers Union, Paul Howes, was also on board to stress that the opposition to Rudd's ways stretched across the party.

As the final parliamentary sitting week approached, Rudd realised he was in trouble, but he had no one he could turn to. The people he relied on most — Gillard and Swan — were the very people from whom he had most to fear. When he was soaring with stratospheric levels of support in the polls, Rudd hadn't needed to bother cultivating relationships in the way he had previously when he'd been seeking power. He'd dispensed with those contacts — it wasn't really possible to describe them as friendships — when he entered the Lodge. It wasn't simply that he lacked factional support; he lacked any support at all.

Time and time again, Gillard had vowed her loyalty to the leader. In mid-May, she'd laughed away the prospect of a challenge. 'It's not within cooee of my day-to-day reality', she said. But the question wouldn't go away, and thus she began giving a playful sense of what she saw as the extreme improbability of such a change taking place.

'There's more chance', the deputy leader volunteered, 'of me becoming the full-forward for the dogs [Western Bulldogs] than there is any change in the Labor Party'.

'There's more chance,' Gillard insisted, 'of me going round the world sailing solo a dozen times'.

'You may as well ask', Gillard suggested, 'am I anticipating a trip to Mars?'

'If Steven Spielberg rang me from Hollywood and asked me to star opposite Brad Pitt in a movie', Gillard fantasised, 'would I do it? Well, I'd be a little bit tempted. But you know what, I don't reckon Stephen Spielberg's going to give me a call.'

Gillard might not have been close to replacing Angelina Jolie; but, as every day passed, she was coming closer and closer to being the leading lady in her own movie. The question wouldn't go away.

Rudd had seen the private party polling and he knew he had to find an answer to the bleeding sore that was draining his credibility. The dramatic fall in the polls had given increased urgency to the need for Labor to find a policy to combat climate change. There was no chance of doing a deal with the coalition. The ETS that had been so laboriously negotiated with Malcolm Turnbull was dead, and there was no chance that Tony Abbott would enter into negotiations to let the government off the hook.

The only alternative appeared to be doing a deal with the Greens to impose a carbon tax. Their leader, Bob Brown, had been begging to meet Rudd for the past year-and-a-half, but the PM had been adamant in his refusal to talk. Rudd asked Gillard what to do. She strenuously urged him to hold fast. The blood continued to leach away as the last fortnightly sitting began.

After the sombre mood that had been set by the previous week's dire Nielsen survey, the Queen's Birthday weekend meant that Newspoll was postponed for a week. By the time parliament rose for the following weekend, *The Australian*'s Dennis Shanahan was confident enough to assert that Labor MPs were poised to get rid of their leader. He reported on the anger consuming the caucus, but the key requirement for a challenge was still lacking: the only possible contender had not unveiled her standard, even to the plotters.

By now, it was the government's dispute with the miners over the super-profits tax that was leaching support away: the PM claimed he was happy for the negotiations to go on for months, but MPs asserted that it had to be fixed much more quickly.

Saturday, 19 June also saw a New South Wales by-election in the seat of Penrith. The national implications of state by-elections are usually ignored; but, with a prime minister on the ropes, and because the seat contained a large number of 'Howard's battlers' who'd swung to the coalition in 1996, analysts were keen to see the result. It was devastating: the swing against the party was the largest ever recorded in New South Wales. The ALP's primary vote plunged more than 24 per cent, with a two-party-preferred anti-Labor swing of more than 25 per cent. It hadn't been able to win a single booth in any of the 19 booths in what had been a solid Labor electorate.

As far as the anti-Rudd faction was concerned, the prime minister was already dead; he just hadn't been cut down.

The PM believed he'd be safe if he could get through that week's scheduled caucus meeting on the Tuesday. But the mood was restive. The Penrith by-election had been considered a litmus test, and the headline news was terrible. The state seat was divided between two federal electorates: Lindsay (with new housing estates on the plains) and Macquarie (stretching up into the Blue Mountains). David Bradbury had won Lindsay back for Labor in 2007, after Jackie Kelly, one of John Howard's favourites, had held it since 1996. The electorate had been the scene of the infamous letter-boxing incident in the last days of the election campaign, when the (bogus) 'Islamic Australia Federation' had thanked Labor for supporting the Bali bombers. Ordinary voters were outraged when they found members of the Liberal Party had been distributing the pamphlets, and the seat had recorded a 9.7 per cent swing to Labor.

Bradbury, from the right, was worried. At the caucus meeting, he told his colleagues that voters in Lindsay were worried about asylum-seekers as well as a number of other issues, and he stressed that an answer had to be found to address their concerns. It was not a plea to swing to the right: he was urging the need to communicate better with the voters. Then Debus spoke. His electorate, which stretched up to the Blue Mountains, had also been seized by the Liberals in the anti-Keating landslide of 1996, but a significant redistribution had helped it return to Labor in 2007. Debus made the point that, up in the tree-covered foothills where his voters lived, people were also concerned about asylum-seekers, but they had no wish to see any return of the repressive policies of the Howard era. He emphasised the need for the government to find a new way of selling its message, making his point with a reference to the mining super-profits tax. He emphasised that caving in to the industry might gain some voters on the plain but lose others in the foothills. Debus suggested subtle changes that might make government policies — particularly on the hot-button issue of refugees — easier to promote.

His enthusiasm spread through many in the caucus. Perhaps there was a way, they thought, to use the winter break to get out and sell their policies properly. The party just had to keep its nerve, refine its policies, and turn the electorate around. Others were less sanguine. They believed that there was a far more simple way of bolstering the party's fortunes: all they needed to do was get rid of Rudd.

After the caucus meeting, the PM's chief-of-staff, Alister Jordan, sent Debus a text message to organise a meeting to further discuss his ideas. But it was too late for any well-meaning actions, because the plotters had already begun their final move. There was no need to count numbers; the only necessity was to manufacture a reason to justify executing the leader. Jordan's innocuous text was quickly redefined by the plotters as nothing more than an 'impersonal and bizarre message' thanking Debus for supporting Rudd. They informed journalists that the message revealed how beleaguered the PM had become. They suggested that he no longer trusted anyone, hinting that the PM's office resembled the Führer's bunker in 1945. The implication was that no deals could be made with a paranoid man. Jordan was about to become an unwitting player as the coup moved towards a climax.

It was well known that Rudd only really trusted his personal staff — people some twenty years his junior. With no friends to guard his back, he sent Jordan out to test his support amongst the caucus. One of those who had a discussion remembers the bizarre nature of the exchange. 'I wasn't in on the plot, but what would I have said if I was?', the MP told me. 'Was I supposed to volunteer the fact that Rudd was highly unpopular and that he'd brought it all on himself? If I'd said that and he'd survived, I would've been finished anyway. I told Jordan what he wanted to hear. I washed my hands of it.'

The irony was that many MPs were telling the truth. They didn't know about the plan to finish Rudd off. The assassins hadn't bothered to work the numbers, because they knew that no one was going to defend him.

On Wednesday, the day before parliament was to go into recess, a critical story appeared in the *Sydney Morning Herald*. Written by Peter Hartcher, it revealed that Jordan had been taking soundings of the feeling towards Rudd in the caucus. The story revealed the PM was 'deeply concerned' about his grip on the prime ministership. Nor, the story claimed, did he 'fully trust the public assurances of his deputy, Julia Gillard, that she is not interested in the leadership'. This particular source was then quoted as having asserted to Hartcher that Rudd did 'still enjoy solid support in the caucus'.

Because Hartcher was known to have a good relationship with

the PM, Gillard immediately drew the conclusion that the story had been leaked by his office in an attempt to prevent her moving against the leader. Regardless of how the leak had been obtained, it demonstrated that Rudd didn't trust her assurances. She was outraged.

Four tightly written paragraphs were all that was needed to destroy Gillard's resolution not to challenge. At the very least, it was the excuse she required.

Hartcher later insisted that the story had not come from Rudd, but by then it was too late.

At 9.30 that morning, Abib and Feeney went to Gillard's office and urged her to bring on a challenge for the leadership. Both believed that the crisis had taken on a momentum of its own and that Rudd's leadership was now irretrievable. She still refused to challenge, but requested a meeting with Rudd. Those who were urging her to act left the office, refusing to take her 'no' for an answer.

Senator John Faulkner, a NSW left-winger who made a point of always supporting the leader, attended the late-morning meeting between Gillard and Rudd. The confrontation resolved nothing.

It had become apparent that Rudd would not go quietly, so the right began organising in readiness for a challenge. They kept urging Gillard to change her mind, promising her that they could deliver the numbers, even though no one had yet begun to count her votes. Independently of her, they began working through the timing and preparing a coup. They insisted that the party could not go to an election under Rudd. The influential Australian Workers Union was contacted to bring Howes and Ludwig onside.

Eventually, Gillard began to shift. The earlier meeting with Rudd had increased her concerns, rather than mollifying them. Both Rudd and his deputy appeared tense in the chamber during question time that afternoon. It appeared to others that she was still attempting to find another way out. She was proving a reluctant assassin.

At around four in the afternoon, Wayne Swan was informed of

the widening breach, and was urged to join the coup as Gillard's deputy. He quickly realised that, if news of the dissatisfaction within Labor's ranks leaked out, the party would have no chance of winning the impending election. He agreed to come on board.

A deal could still have allowed Rudd to hand over to Gillard voluntarily, and thereby to establish himself as a self-abnegating Labor hero. She gave him time to do so, but Rudd couldn't bear to tear himself away from the prize he had coveted for so long.

Extraordinarily, a plot to cut down the PM was approaching a crescendo, yet few in the building knew about it. Despite the political requirement to get the story out so as to prepare the ground for the change of leaders, a genuine desire not to hurt Rudd ensured that no one breathed a word about that morning's meeting. The news had not escaped. That evening, Gillard went into Rudd's office for another meeting. She had finally resolved to act in the party's best interests. Gillard announced she wanted the PM's job.

Late that afternoon, the ABC's Chris Uhlmann became the only journalist in the entire building to get a glimmer of what was really going on. Just five words in a 'chance encounter over a casual coffee' with a Labor powerbroker were enough to reveal to the experienced journalist that something big was happening. His contact had asked, with surprising intensity, 'Could we win with Julia?'

With that question, the conversation ended abruptly. Even more frustratingly, Uhlmann was unable to report what he knew. He was now working for the ABC's news channel, which would not be on air for weeks, but he compared notes with the regular television news correspondent, Mark Simkin, who'd also been following developments closely. It was the combination of the two journalists' information, and their discovery of the meeting in the PM's office, that finally dragged the story over the line. The story broke on that evening's 7.00 pm News. A minister later told Simkin, 'I didn't know about it [the challenge], but the fact that the ABC was running it meant it had credibility.'

The plotters couldn't have organised it better if they'd tried, although the leak was certainly not deliberate. It's possible they were still hoping that Rudd would accept reality and resign honourably, without news of the coup becoming public. But the PM hadn't budged and, as soon as news of the meeting leaked, any attempt to preserve the PM's dignity was lost as events quickly spiralled out of control.

While the ABC was preparing its exclusive report, many caucus members were apparently oblivious to what was taking place. Wednesday night of the last sitting week is traditionally a time to relax, and there were a couple of large parties being attended by parliamentarians, staffers, and journalists. But as soon as the News went to air, a cacophony of ring-tones started pealing. Within minutes, the parties were deserted.

Gillard was talking to Rudd as the report was broadcast. The executive wing of parliament, where the ministerial offices are located, suddenly swarmed with politicians and journalists. The attempt to allow Rudd a graceful exit was doomed. Even now he lingered, attempting to hold on. The conversation went on for hours, but it could only end one way.

At 10.30 that night, Rudd walked into the 'blue room' opposite his office and announced to the media that he would be fighting Gillard's challenge the next morning. The reporters at the packed news conference already knew he was effectively gone. A person counting the numbers later insisted that if Rudd were to receive more than 20 votes in the party room, it would have been simply out of sympathy — although there were still 15 undecided.

Rudd spoke to his staff and became very emotional. He began to cry. But then he sat, apparently shell-shocked, and did nothing. Instead of hitting the phones and desperately lobbying for support in those last, vital hours, he waited, like a DVD on pause.

Finally, after an age, he began making calls to his MPs. It is probable that around this time, in the early hours of the morning,

Rudd finally came to the realisation that he had no support. He decided not to stand, although unfortunately he didn't tell his remaining loyal band of supporters. Craig Emerson, in particular — although a former partner of Gillard's — had valiantly attempted to talk up Rudd's prospect of retaining power on the radio. But it was too late.

At the caucus meeting at nine that morning, Rudd declared the leadership vacant, and withdrew his name from contention. Gillard was elected unopposed.

The Rudd experiment was over.

EPILOGUE

The Verdict

'I believe that when we look back at this, these reforms will endure into the future and make Australia, I believe, a fairer and better place than it would otherwise have been ... What I am less proud of is the fact that I have now blubbed.'

Kevin Rudd farewell speech, 24 June 2010

It was bleak and wintry as Rudd walked, for the last time, into the roped-off prime minister's courtyard. His police security detail was already packing up; they were about to move around the corner to Gillard's office. The journalists had stood in front of the bare wooden lectern, waiting and gossiping, until the doors to the office had swung open. A cacophony of clicking cameras began as photographers searched for the revealing detail—the trembling lower lip, the vacant eyes, the shaking hand.

His wife, Therese, stood immediately to his right, her hand supportively touching his back. Rudd's children—Nick, Jessica, and Marcus—flanked the deposed prime minister. His staff had already assembled down the far end of the barren space before marching across the stone to listen to his farewell. One or two had tears on their cheeks. All of them were young.

The blood appeared to have drained away from Rudd's face.

'I was elected by the people of this country to bring back a fair go for all Australians, and I have given my absolute best to do that … I've given it my absolute all,' he began. Then he recited a long litany of his hopes and desires, transformed into achievements. The list was long — too long — and then spaces began to creep in between the sentences … almost as they'd crept in between his undertakings and his government's actual accomplishments. The words embodying hope seemed to cause him the most difficulty and, slowly, the silences became extended gaps; the ideas, more and more disjointed. Occasionally, suddenly and strangely, he'd pick up, force a smile, and try using humour to engage casually with those around him: 'Hi, folks! How are you?'

But there was no communication in return. The journalists extended their understanding, but that was all — there was no sympathy or regard floating in the air. Those journalists who'd offended him had often been on the receiving end of his sharp tongue. The cold air rushed across the granite pavement.

Rudd had grown accustomed to treating others as if he was the emperor in a Manchu court. Everyone else — ministers, MPs, staffers, and journalists — was reduced to playing roles as subjects, and jockeying for favour. There were favoured courtiers, but no friends. He alone had been the one to make the arbitrary decisions, and had then insisted on unquestioning obedience. For nearly three years, Rudd had positioned himself in the centre of the universe, but now its axis had shifted. As he spoke, it became evident that he hadn't quite adjusted to the new realities of Australia.

The minutes dragged by as Rudd continued attempting to redefine his prime ministership; he provided a solid list of his achievements and of people whose lives he'd changed. But the words didn't mesh with reality, and certainly not with the bitter truth that his colleagues had discovered when they'd been spending time back in their electorates. Listening became painful. Rudd attempted to suggest that the cabinet had 'blessed and aided him'. And then came silences, growing more prolonged as he fought to hold back the emotions wracking his being. The pretence that there would be any questions vanished. Those watching his slow, 20-minute speech simply wanted him to stop.

'Having said all that, folks, we've got to zip.'

And, having said that, Rudd turned on his heel and withdrew, for the last time, back to his office — the soulless, empty room that had been his, but now belonged to the highest elected official in the land.

***

It didn't take long before a plethora of verdicts were offered to explain what had occurred. A couple of hours after Gillard had come to deliver her challenge, Rudd attempted to frame the conflict by suggesting that his actions had run afoul of sinister factional bosses. He hinted at policy differences and the risk that the party would 'lurch to the right'. The only thing that the PM couldn't explain away was his lack of support in the caucus and why so few were prepared to stand with him.

In fact, both Rudd's rise and his subsequent fall could be explained with reference to just three factors. Like him, they were all technical and dispassionate.

The Rudd project had always been defined by the polls. He'd been able to seize power from Beazley because he could wield an armoury of weapons that included terms like 'net-approval ratings' and 'two-party preferred vote'. The core promise that Rudd made was that he alone possessed the ability to articulate what the electorate desired, and that he could harness their support for his own venture. He'd insisted he'd lead the party to victory, rather than merely limp across the line, because he could communicate with the electorate — but not because of any policy differences with the former leader. Polling had provided Rudd with the key he'd needed to unlock the support of the factions.

This was the second key ingredient in his path to the prime ministership. During the time when he was foreign affairs spokesman, Rudd spent long periods lobbying the unelected faction leaders. He paid obeisance to the powerbrokers, enlisting their support and urging them to throw their weight behind him. He dangled the promise of power in front of them, if only they would back him for leader.

But there was one final obstacle in his path to the Lodge. Gillard was also ambitious, but she was, more particularly, admired. There was some uncertainty about her policy judgement; nevertheless, she commanded the votes and, more importantly, the friendship of many in the caucus, because they could warm to her as a person. Even in 2006, Rudd knew she was ambitious. He also knew she was from the left and would fall just short of the numbers she'd need to challenge for the leadership herself. In the winter of that year, the two met for Rudd to deliver his ultimatum. If she backed him, he'd make her deputy. Although he had far less support than she did, Rudd made it perfectly clear that there was no chance of him helping her. He was only offering her the chance to get on board his bandwagon. There was nothing reciprocal about it.

She accepted and, a few months later, Rudd had all the ducks lined up in a row. He had planned Beazley's downfall carefully. The leader didn't stand a chance.

Between the assassination and the election, all of Rudd's strengths were revealed. He communicated much more than a message: he offered hope and optimism; a vision of the future that ignited and excited previously jaded Labor voters. He spoke to the young. He didn't pretend to be hip, but instead embraced his gawky image, gently sending himself up on popular television and radio programmes, yet at the same time encouraging people to see him as someone who wanted — desperately wanted — a world infused with the ideals he articulated so clearly.

Rudd's lustre grew when he was invested with the power of

office. His oratory continued to inspire. The delivery was deadpan, but Rudd wasn't a performance artist. The desires he expressed resonated deeply within the electorate. Nothing much seemed to be changing, but everyone knew that a transformation couldn't be expected overnight. By early 2010 there were questions over Labor's competence, but Rudd personally remained relatively untarnished.

And then Rudd abandoned the one solid commitment he had given — to deal urgently with climate change. His support plunged over the edge of a cliff, and it would never recover. Rudd himself had clearly laid out the standard by which he expected to be judged on this issue. It was the gold standard. He was the one who'd first introduced concepts such as morality and integrity into the political debate, and now he wanted to escape from the consequences of having used them. The electorate insisted it would hold him accountable. It wasn't just that he couldn't guarantee victory: the polls insisted that *he* was the problem. Rudd had broken his contract with the voters.

The polls had given Rudd the keys to the Lodge, but once inside the door he hadn't welcomed other people to contribute to policy formulation. He had contacts — many contacts — but Rudd appeared to be too focused on work to develop proper friendships. It was as if, as soon as he'd become leader, he'd forgotten that he still needed the support of caucus, and assumed that he could rely on other people to assist him. As problems began to emerge and things began to fall apart, he repeated the mantra of Crean, another former leader. Both men had promised to 'work harder', but their capacity for hard work wasn't the problem. In Rudd's case, it had been a failure to delegate and a misunderstanding of his job that had originally landed him in his dire predicament.

As leader, Rudd was very successful in articulating the direction in which he wanted the government to go. Unfortunately, he was unable to drive there. He insisted on plotting every detail of the route that was to be taken, until he reached into every corner of the bureaucracy. The prime minister's department swelled as Rudd demanded complete oversight and control of everything. Eventually, many public servants — even quite senior ones — felt that their own input was considered worthless.

Rudd also needlessly ignored his political colleagues and prevented them from contributing — and this was the factor that ended up eroding his support so badly. Backbenchers asked themselves what was the point of being in government if they were simply warm bodies lining up to vote on the floor of parliament. So many decisions appeared to have been made before they came to the cabinet table that ministers began to wonder what they were doing there, too. The flaws in the government's process were apparent, but Rudd seemingly couldn't see them. He didn't bother doing anything to build up his own factional support base. He had no friends he could ask to sound out feeling in the party, and instead had relied on Jordan, his chief-of-staff, to canvass the mood of caucus. Many parliamentarians had been insulted. In the end, the only faction that existed was the anti-Rudd one.

The person who had been most affronted by the question that Jordan was posing had been Gillard. It was obvious that Rudd no longer trusted her, yet he was demanding her unconditional support for his project — even as it began to fall apart. The government was headed for oblivion. Gillard had been loyal in the past, while Rudd had reciprocated with dishonesty and mistrust. The deputy decided that her time had come.

Once again, all the ducks had lined up in a row. Rudd could hardly complain now that it was Gillard who finally felt compelled to pull the trigger.

The timing suited Gillard perfectly. It enabled her to make a transition in time for the subsequent election, and also meant that the failure to achieve productive outcomes in the many portfolio areas that Rudd has so ineffectively skated across did not have to dog Labor during the election campaign. It was true that she'd made a couple of significant missteps as education minister. 'Building the education revolution' endeared her to developers (a significant advantage when it comes to lining the party's coffers through donations), but not necessarily to Parents & Citizens committees at schools. Teachers were angry about the national testing regime, and not all parents were as committed to it as she would have liked them to be. But, after the Rudd experience, Labor and the nation were entitled to feel hopeful about being led by someone who was prepared to compromise and listen in order to broker acceptable agreements, rather than just push until he had what they wanted.

***

It's difficult to make a convincing case that the country became very different as a result of the 2007–2010 Rudd-led Labor government. In the middle of the Global Financial Crisis, for instance, Rudd promised to 'go after the remuneration of risk-taking financial executives' before the year was out, and yet it was difficult to reconcile this with actual government policies. More significantly, the government abandoned pledges to practically assist the lot of 'working families'. Promises to increase childcare facilities by building 260 extra centres (thereby enabling a single drop-off for families), were jettisoned in mid-2010. The government did manage to pass the nation's first-ever paid parental leave scheme; however, government modelling showed that, in the same year, other measures would cut childcare payments to more than 26,000 families, rising to more than 70,000 families in 2013.

Despite receiving expert recommendations to take on obesity, the government rejected suggestions that it should take action to penalise the food industry. Relationships counselling intended to help avoid messy divorces was cut. And although it commissioned studies about water use in the agricultural food bowl of the Murray-Darling basin, the government did not introduce any significant measures to reform the struggling system.

Even when it came to symbolic issues, Rudd had difficulty in delivering what he promised. In October 2007, he promised that a referendum on four-year, fixed-term governments for Australia would be held in conjunction with the 2010 election. This, like the move towards a republic, was dispensed with, and without any fanfare.

The list is not all negative, of course. Australia's phenomenally successful escape from the Global Financial Crisis may have been partly due to China's demand for resources, but Rudd helped maintain consumer confidence, and his policies enabled the nation to escape from a crisis that engulfed most of the developed world. Australians believe that they should be looking out to the world, and Rudd should be credited with having inspired this engagement. Perhaps it's ironic, particularly given that Rudd is a former diplomat, but it should be noted that most — no, all — of his own forays into foreign affairs appear to have ended disastrously.

With other issues — in particular, those relating to indigenous Australians, climate change, implementing policies, and establishing a vision for the future — Labor was far less effective. Slipshod strategy was accompanied by a casual approach to communicating ideas, which resulted in a spectacular failure to effectively establish an environment in which guiding principles could be properly implemented.

Rudd undoubtedly intended to do all the things he'd promised — it's just that those promises were fixed for dates so far out in the future that it was impossible to measure his accomplishments or the lack of them. It takes years to accurately establish whether there's been any change in the way society operates; but, from the perspective of the present, it appears to have continued more or less as before.

This leads directly to a second, and far more important, question: was there a nexus between this failure to achieve results and the way that the Rudd government worked? Was there something about the government itself — and Rudd's place in it — which made it unlikely that, while he was prime minister, he would ever achieve his goals? Were Rudd's promises just an endless cycle of spin?

The Italian philosopher Antonio Gramsci insisted that political developments must be intertwined with a comprehension of society and broader cultural trends in order for citizens to make sense of them. This insight is the only way to begin to understand the creeping changes to modern Australian politics, and its manufacturing of a culture of celebrity around the prime minister. Rudd played up to this. His instinctive mastery of different mediums and forums was unsurpassed.

There's a natural tendency to view the current period — events happening now — as being somehow exceptional. Particularly since the ignominious dismissal of Whitlam, first by the governor-general and then by the electorate, Labor has sought to harness the idea that it has been led by a succession of 'great men': Hawke, Keating, and then Rudd. This idea has provided succour in opposition and nourishment in government. It's offered a pattern that Rudd enthusiastically embraced. This placed him at the centre of the Labor firmament.

His carefully crafted image emphasised that, as prime minister, the buck stopped with him. This open and honest approach engaged our understanding; and, while Rudd continued to ride high in the polls, we trusted him to fix things. Unfortunately, it also turned an otherwise fertile field of political debate into a barren wilderness. We were expected to abandon our critical faculties as we put our faith in him to achieve the best results possible.

The funny thing is that, before being elected, Rudd seemed to offer us the prospect of breaking down this binary division and leading the country in a new direction. This didn't happen. Instead of charting a new way forward, Rudd appeared as trapped as anyone by the frameworks of the past. Despite his promises, he was unable to break through the tight networks of scaffolding binding our society.

Rudd led a government of managers and bureaucrats, noting down relevant factors on PowerPoint presentations, and developing action plans that appeared never to intersect with the real world. But, most importantly, everything was poised, perpetually waiting, because nothing could be done without Rudd's approval. In the meantime, the promises lingered in the air.

Rudd blamed factions and opinion polls for his demise, but this was only half-right. His approval rating had collapsed because the Rudd project had already failed. No Labor leader had ever been given more latitude by the party to do things their own way; for two years, the factions had stood by him, even though he treated them with contempt.

Cabinet was not consulted, and Rudd felt he didn't need the input of his colleagues. The PM had laid out a vision of exactly where he wanted to go. He sincerely believed he was the most brilliant man in the room, and so he was the best suited to take decisions to ensure that the country arrived at the desired destination.

It was, however, Rudd's own methods that prevented him from achieving his goals. In the wake of his downfall, some blame was focused on the chaotic workings of his office. But there was much more to it than that. The prime minister was the problem. Personality flaws that would normally be hidden were exposed in glaring detail under the spotlight of government.

This book has demonstrated how Rudd failed to achieve many of his objectives. Even though it was an important thing to do, simply saying 'sorry' was never going to be enough to redress Aboriginal disadvantage; instead, Rudd kept persevering with failed policies, and the condition of Australia's original inhabitants worsened. The government successfully escaped the financial crisis by literally giving money away, but the once-in-a-lifetime opportunity to make significant structural change to the economy was squandered. The government's decision to abandon the ETS left it with no policy to address climate change. Rudd similarly failed to achieve any lasting agreement on the Murray-Darling, or to find any other answer to preserve the viability of rural Australia. Australia's relationship with Asia (and the world) also deteriorated significantly, despite the PM's background in foreign affairs. This was nowhere more apparent than in the relationships with China and India, the two superpowers that will increasingly shape Australia's future.

A succession of problems, many of which could be traced back to the PM's office, bedevilled the detailed implementation of Labor's agenda. Ministers and their departments were not allowed to get on with the job; and instead of providing broader oversight, Rudd attempted to involve himself in the detailed implementation of government programs. Cabinet government was reduced to a process of rubber-stamping. More significantly, society began to fray as questions about the future size of the population, and its ethnic composition, agitated the community. In this critical area, Rudd proved unable to convey a picture of the country he wanted Australia to come.

By the beginning of 2010, the problems lay dormant, resting just below the surface of public consciousness. Turmoil within the opposition would normally have consigned the coalition to electoral irrelevance, but voters had begun to mark the government down for its incompetence. As the year continued, it gradually became clear that all the crises shared a similar point of origin.

Instead of achieving health reform with minimal fuss, Rudd entered into a bitter, knock-down fight, erupting into a major (and unnecessary) conflict with the Labor states. Even then, medical professionals emphasised that the agreed reforms failed to address real problems in many areas, but particularly in the vital area of mental health. Then came the long-awaited Henry tax review and, with it, Rudd's decision to ignore more than 130 of the recommendations so he could, without consultation, introduce a new tax (or, if you prefer, a 'great big new tax') on the mining industry. But, most critically and damagingly, the electorate realised that Rudd had no answer to the great moral issue upon which he had put the basis for his original electoral triumph. The emptiness at the centre was revealed.

Labor had never before so ruthlessly cut down a leader. Rudd's destruction was predicated by the opinion polls and performed by the faction leaders. But he had no one other than himself to blame.

One insider commented that, strangely enough, Rudd almost appeared to have suddenly had a massive weight lifted off his shoulders when the end came. He almost looked relaxed.

Acknowledgements

I'd like firstly to thank Scribe's founder and publisher, Henry Rosenbloom, for embracing this project. He's an amazing editor, particularly under the pressures of a tight deadline, and he worked very hard and forgivingly to ensure that my arguments were developed and articulated as well as was possible. Without him, almost impossible time constraints would have prevented this book ever being placed in the public domain. He continually challenged my assertions, and the book gained through this Socratic process. More than that — and far more importantly for political discourse in Australia — was his original willingness to publish this book. I know he doesn't necessarily agree with all the conclusions contained within these pages; however, he was receptive to my proposal at a time when Rudd was still flying high in the polls and there was no (public) hint that the executioners had already begun to sharpen the axe. It's the growing independent publishing houses such as Scribe which ensure that this country has a vibrant industry. Thank you, Henry.

I also thank all those who have shared their time, thoughts, and insights. A book about politics is never a one-person creation; I've attempted to acknowledge those I spoke to at some point in the text unless they requested anonymity. Unfortunately, as events rushed towards a crescendo, that became impossible. Towards the end, one of the participants told me, 'It was important [I] get it right, because this will be a record of an important time in Australian politics'. I hope they are satisfied with the result.

As always — and most importantly — I need to thank my family. They have offered me so much, and more than simply the time and space to write. My life's partner, Catherine, and my children, Anastasia, Eugenia, and Maximilian, have provided me with real insights into the meaning of a marvellous life, and the daring to hope that an even better future may yet lie ahead.

This book belongs — with hope, optimism, and all my love — to them.